D0872255

YELLOWTAIL

YELLOWTAIL
CROW MEDICINE MAN AND SUN DANCE CHIEF

An Autobiography

as told to Michael Oren Fitzgerald
Introduction by Fred Voget

University of Oklahoma Press : Norman and London

Library of Congress Cataloging-in-Publication Data

Yellowtail, Thomas.
    Yellowtail, Crow medicine man and Sun Dance chief : an
autobiography / as told to Michael Oren Fitzgerald : introduction by
Fred Voget.
        p.   cm.
    Includes bibliographic references.
    ISBN 0-8061-2333-8
    1. Yellowtail, Thomas. 2. Crow Indians—Biography. 3. Shamans—
Montana—Biography. 4. Crow Indians—Religion and mythology.
5. Crow Indians—Rites and ceremonies. 6. Sun-dance.
I. Fitzgerald, Michael Oren, 1949– . II. Title.
E99.C92Y45   1991
978.6'00497502—dc20
    [B]   90-50702
                                                                        CIP

This book is dedicated to all American Indian people

All royalties from this book will be used to support the Sun Dance religion or to purchase copies of this book for distribution to American Indian readers.

CONTENTS

ILLUSTRATIONS

PLATES

FIGURES

MAP

PREFACE

THIS book is intended to give us insights into the religious center of the Crow Indians through the eyes of Thomas Yellowtail, a Crow medicine man and Sun Dance chief. As a youth, Thomas Yellowtail lived in the presence of the old warriors, war chiefs, and medicine men who had known the freedom of the plains before reservation life. Those "old-timers" knew that nomadic life had passed away in their lifetimes, and they were saddened by the threatening changes they saw taking place in the world and on the reservation. Yellowtail in his turn has seen changes that would have been unimaginable to those old chiefs. These changes have accentuated the differences in societal values that existed from the first but that are even clearer now. Modern society, with its materialistic outlook, has orientations completely opposite the concepts of the old-time Indians and of those present-day Indians faithful to their heritage. While there are now precious few left who lived in the early reservation period in the presence of the old-timers, there are even fewer who have adhered strictly to the sacred traditions. Yellowtail, one of these invaluable and in a certain way irreplaceable bridges to the sacred values, is one of the last of the generation raised by elders who had fully experienced the nomadic life in virgin Nature that is central to the Indian way. His role in supporting the traditions is confirmed by the name Medicine Rock Chief, which he was given while a young boy by Chief Medicine Crow, for he has the qualities of patience and strength associated with the rock and the functions of Sun Dance chief and medicine man.

This book is also intended to provide a view into living American Indian religion. In this book, we see how the leader

of the Crow Sun Dance believes the religion should be practiced. We also learn about the process of the choice and training of a medicine man and Sun Dance chief. The tradition
which Yellowtail represents will continue through Yellowtail's
selection of John Pretty on Top as his successor. The announcement was officially made at the Sun Dance at Lodge
Grass, Montana, in 1984, and Pretty on Top was the main Sun
Dance chief at the Sun Dance at Wyola, Montana, in 1985. The
complete support of the tribe and success of that dance show
that the strength of the Crow Sun Dance religion will remain
unbroken.

Yellowtail is in a unique position to compare two ways of
life. As he and some of his great contemporaries (such as Fools
Crow of the Teton Sioux) pass on, there will be no more living
bridges to the elders of the "olden days," as Yellowtail calls
them. It is my hope and Yellowtail's that the words contained
in this book will help to keep the bridge open and the path
clear.

In any field of study, books and articles written on the
subject vary widely in scope and orientation. Anyone attempting to examine the values and religious beliefs of Indians
should be aware of the differences among the many books and
articles which have been written about Indians. For example,
there are books which have come from leading traditional
Indian sources such as the Sioux holy man Black Elk, with
John Neihardt's recording of *Black Elk Speaks* and Joseph Epes
Brown's recording of *The Sacred Pipe*. A second category of
written works about the Indian is from white writers who
have based their research largely on accounts and opinions
of many Indians who were not central figures in the tribe.
Whatever time was spent with central figures was invariably
limited in scope and breadth.

Because of the more limited factual foundation of these
white writers, most tend to view the religion in terms of its
political or economic implications rather than on its own
terms. The central nature of Indian religion is therefore not
adequately considered, even if the historical data and research
effort are substantial. There are inevitably different degrees

of understanding that emerge from such projects, creating a spectrum of conclusions regarding the role of religion in traditional Indian life. On one end of the spectrum are statements such as "the Sun dance religion of the Shoshones . . . was born of misery and oppression in the early reservation period."[1] This book may be considered to represent the other end of the spectrum, in which religion is the central part of Indian life because of its transcendent foundation.

Regardless of their orientation, many books have also been produced as a result of time-consuming and diligent work on historical matters by the writers. Fred Voget's *The Shoshoni-Crow Sun Dance* is such a work; it contains a complete summary of available historical information on the Crow Sun Dance. Since such exhaustive works of scholarship exist, I have not spent more time on redundant historical information but rather have allowed Yellowtail's own words to provide the sufficient historical background necessary for this work. Anyone wishing to understand something of the history of the Crow tribe may read the appendix, "Historical Overview of the Absaroke," which provides a brief review of the history of the tribe and information on the background of their current standing among Plains Indian tribes.

With a clear view of the different possible orientations, we can now discuss this book and start to meet and understand one of the great men of the Indian culture, one of a handful of the most prominent living Indian spiritual leaders. It is obvious that he incarnates the very essence of his ethnic background. This means that the Sun Dance religion and the Indian culture will be viewed and understood from his perspective, that is, in religious terms. This book in fact specifically excludes any personal observations Yellowtail expressed regarding tribal politics and other prominent tribal leaders. I regret the conscious omission of his views on the politics and economic forces on the reservation, but a prerequisite of his spiritual function and his access to the power from his "Medicine Fathers" is that he not become involved in tribal politics. He also did not want to print any negative opinion of another tribal member in order not to offend anyone.

In organizing this book I have created three distinct parts. The first is an introduction to traditional Indian ways through the story of part of Thomas Yellowtail's life. This story includes a great deal of information on major influences that helped form his values. A critical determinant of his views, however—namely, details of his personal visionary experiences—is conspicuously absent from this book. At Yellowtail's request, none of this information is conveyed. It would be inappropriate to speak of such intimate graces in a book, particularly because his visions are not specifically tribal in orientation. Having heard his major visionary experiences, I can state that they confirm the nature of his spiritual function not only for the Crow tribe but for all American Indians as well.

The second part of this book focuses on the heart of the Crow Indian religion: the Sun Dance. The Sun Dance religion includes the purification of the sweat lodge, the spiritual retreat or vision quest, the reinforcement of daily prayer with the smoking of the Indian pipe, and the Sun Dance ceremony itself. By the end of part two it should have become clear that the traditional Indian ways constitute a sacred tradition of unique beauty and depth and that even though many of the sacred ways have been lost, what remains still constitutes a valid religion and sacred path.

In part three, Yellowtail provides his conclusions, and they are applicable to Indians and non-Indians alike. A picture of Yellowtail's own method of daily prayer is apparent to the reader after finishing the book. This method in itself will, we hope, be a unique contribution to American Indian literature.

Throughout each of the three parts of the book I hope that the reader will develop a picture of the qualitative features and tendencies which were present and determinative in traditional Plains Indians life. These qualities were certainly present in the traditional cultures of other Indians as well. If the objection is raised that this picture does not represent fairly the Indian culture of prereservation days, I can only respond that it does accurately portray the qualitative norms that the olden-day Indians possessed, even though it is evident that not all Indians realized that ideal, just as not all the members of any culture realize the ideal.

If the proposition is raised that Yellowtail universalizes the Crow Sun Dance religion in an exaggerated way, one must remember that the use of the essential elements—the sweat lodge, vision quest, pipe, and Sun Dance—were in fact present among most Plains Indian tribes, including the Sioux, Cheyenne, Arapaho, Blackfeet, Crow, Shoshone, Bannock, Ute, Blood, Piegan, and Mandan. Other tribes shared many of these rites. Differences in outward forms and accentuations of various aspects of rites occur, but these variations do not undermine the general similarity of the underlying sacred values held by these tribes. The footnotes and quotations at the end of each chapter highlight certain of these tribal similarities. These quotations and notes tend to support Yellowtail's belief that the underlying spiritual realities of the different religious manifestations are one, even though the outward forms may differ in modality and accentuation. It is necessary to consult other works for a complete comparison of outer forms of other tribal rites or to determine the precise limits of the basic similarities of Plains Indians collectively. The works listed in the "Suggested Readings" provide sources for additional material on the customs or historical cultural developments mentioned by Yellowtail.

This book focuses on Crow Indian religion from the eyes of a venerable medicine man and Sun Dance chief. His concerns naturally center on all aspects of the religion, including the philosophical and "apocalyptic" theme. Without this transcendent conception of the sacred, the Indian way would not constitute a true religion but only reflect a primitive preoccupation with terrifying and mysterious natural forces that must be placated. Yellowtail is a medicine man, and as such the natural exponent of those themes, which demonstrate, precisely, the sacred nature of the Indian religion.

Some might say that some of Yellowtail's views are "idealizations." The Indians feel their traditional world is an idealization compared with the industrial world, and Indians themselves feel a nostalgia for it, despite its known rigors. From another angle, every tradition inculcates an ideal, and it is wrong to suppose it is never realizable. There are Tecumsehs, Red Clouds, Sitting Bulls, and Rolling Thunders (Chief Josephs) just as there are great men elsewhere, and they incarnate incontestably what Charles Eastman (Ohiyesa) called "the soul of the Indian."

One criticism made is that the Indians' conception of one god was later borrowed from Christianity and that they had no distinct picture of God. This criticism is based in large part on the fact that historical records indicate that different Indians, the Crow included, had used different names to refer to God, as if the critic forgot that all religions have different names for Our Heavenly Father. While this question is dealt with both by Yellowtail and in the footnotes, it is evident that the beliefs of all present-day Indians, Yellowtail's included, have to some degree been influenced by Christianity. It does not, however, logically follow that anything positive in the Indian religion is based on Christianity or that the essential rites are invalid. Many Indians focus on similarities between their traditional religion and Christianity as a proof of the validity of Christianity. The meanings behind the forms of Indian rites which predate the coming of the white man are explained by Yellowtail. It is beyond the scope of this book to examine whether and to what extent there may be influences of Christianity on the Crow rites.

I have known Thomas and Susie Yellowtail since 1971, and in 1972, I was ceremonially adopted into the Crow tribe and the Yellow Tail family by Yellowtail, having been given the name "Two Eagles." Since then I have had the benefit of spending extended periods with them at their home in Wyola, Montana. The first summer I lived there, the Shoshone medicine man John Trehero was also living with them. It was he (who passed away in January, 1985, at over one hundred years old) who instructed Yellowtail and passed on to him the function of Sun Dance chief. Trehero personally recounted to me all of the information provided by Yellowtail on Trehero's visions and the process by which Yellowtail was selected as the Sun Dance chief. The time I spent with both of these men, but Yellowtail in particular, has made a lasting impression on me. I have had the opportunity to work with Yellowtail on almost a daily basis as he carried out his tasks in keeping up his modest ranch, but also, and more importantly, as he fulfilled his responsibilities as Sun Dance chief of the Crow.

My understanding of Yellowtail's life and beliefs has been gained over years of visits with him and also by observing fifteen Crow Sun Dances as well as one Sioux Sun Dance near the house of Fools Crow. It was only after years of conversations that we both decided that a book should be written about "Grandfather," as he is called by many. After the decision to produce the book was made in 1980, the time we spent together to record this effort covered uncountable hours of concentrated work over four years in Wyola, Montana and Bloomington, Indiana, and for periods of a week at a time in camps in the Big Horn Mountains of Wyoming.

Our first discussions centered around what material would be included in the book. Then we began the recording process whereby Yellowtail spoke on the subjects that he felt should be preserved. Many of our conversations were recorded on cassette tapes. When we did not have tapes available, I tried to keep notes during the conversations. There were also instances when I was not able to make contemporaneous notes. In these cases I made notes the evening after we discussed a subject. I asked many questions about his life and the sacred rites of the Crow, including historical origins known to him and the exact performance of the present-day rites. When all of this work was complete, I reviewed all the tapes and notes and then made a list in the form of a table of contents of all the subjects on each tape or in each notebook. After preparing an overall outline for the presentation of the material, I could see what informational gaps were present in the recordings and notes. Yellowtail and I then reviewed the outline and added the necessary subjects to complete the material. I then prepared the text for the book, pulling from both tapes and notes. For example, the material on the sweat lodge ceremony came from numerous conversations, both on tape and in my notes. The resulting first draft of the book was already a simplification of the tremendously detailed stories and the many repetitions. It was not an easy task to edit the material so that all of the essentials be retained without including unnecessary details or repetitions of secondary importance that would have made a multivolume work. The current book is less than 80 percent of the text of the first draft, all the deletions being made to allow greater reader comprehension and interest.

Even though we would start each session with a specific subject or question, the recording process inevitably wandered over many subjects. Yellowtail can sit and talk for hours, absorbed in the details of a story, and he will repeat certain points over and over, stringing image upon image, to be certain he has correctly conveyed his message to his listener. Some of the detail he adds is in the form of stories that amount to a digression from the original subject because they do not add significant detail. This is one type of lengthy amplification that has been deleted from the final text. Nevertheless, the style and vocabulary are all Yellowtail's, and I trust the result will be of greater interest to most readers because of the concentration on the essentials.

My only regret is that the text fails to convey the flavor of Yellowtail's manner of speaking. As he speaks, he is completely concentrated, and he will gesture in Indian sign language and thus add a visual element to his flow of endless detail. All his stories are interspersed with a mild laughter in a manner that reinforces his natural dignity. One can immediately see that this is a man outside of time as we know it, centered in the spiritual world. He possesses an element of holy childlikeness extremely rare in these times, and there is no pettiness in him.

My problems with translating from Absaroke (the word for "Crow" in their own language) to English were minor because Yellowtail was his own translator. In other efforts with great Indian leaders it was necessary to rely on intermediary translators, a system that undoubtedly raised certain problems. The Crow language is Yellowtail's native tongue, and he thinks in Crow as he translates into English. On some occasions, such

as when he was explaining a method of prayer, he would
forget to translate and would speak in Crow. At these times
I always waited until he was finished before asking for the
translation. On many occasions during the recording we discussed the different possible translations for a word or statements before agreeing on the best choice. Then during the
editing process Yellowtail was able to review and reformulate
different statements to add to the clarity. The final product
is more complete than could otherwise have been possible
without the benefit of his direct participation in the translation
and editing. Yellowtail read the manuscript on several occasions, each time refining it and making additions.

Thomas Yellowtail's life found a perfect complement with
his wife, Susie, for if he is the priest, she was certainly the
general. Mrs. Yellowtail died on December 25, 1981. She was
very outspoken in her traditional beliefs, to which she dedicated her entire life in every way so that her family and her
tribe might live. The efforts of both Thomas and Susie Yellowtail on behalf of their tribe and all Indian traditions were
recognized in 1970, when they were jointly awarded the honor
of Outstanding American Indian of the Year at the All-Ameri-
can Indian Days in Sheridan, Wyoming. In 1987, Susie Yellowtail joined such notables as Gary Cooper, Chet Huntley,
Mike Mansfield, and Charlie Russell when she was posthu-
mously inducted into the Montana "hall of fame" in the state
capitol building in Helena. I have not included more about
her in this book because her life will be the subject of a book
already in preparation by Joseph Epes Brown and Marina
Brown Weatherly. She remains in the hearts of everyone who
knew her. Without her encouragement and support, this book
would not have been possible. *Aho, Grandma Susie, aho!*

On June 22, 1989, while traveling in Yellowstone National
Park with Yellowtail, we were discussing his authorization of
men to become either medicine men or Sun Dance chiefs. He
informed me that he had been wrongly criticized for giving
away his medicine power to multiple individuals. He asked
me to correctly set forth the information regarding his authorization of medicine men and Sun Dance chiefs. He emphati-

cally stated that the only person he has ever authorized for either function is John Pretty On Top (see n.5, p. 215; nn.5 and 8, pp. 221–22). In the past, he has requested other medicine men to help him doctor patients in the Sun Dance lodge. Except for Pretty On Top, these men have not received authority to doctor from Yellowtail. Yellowtail has no knowledge of any authority for anyone other than Pretty On Top to be a Sun Dance chief for the Crow.

On special occasions Yellowtail has authorized certain men to doctor on themselves and their immediate family, but not anyone else. Anyone other than Pretty On Top claiming that Yellowtail has authorized them to doctor patients or run a Sun Dance is incorrect.

MICHAEL FITZGERALD
Bloomington, Indiana

Introduction
BY FRED VOGET

THOMAS Yellowtail, a Crow Indian and respected Sun Dance medicine man, with the assistance of Michael Fitzgerald, presents his philosophy of life and describes the place of the Sun Dance, and of the sacred, in the life and future of his people and in the future of all the world's peoples. Yellowtail's philosophy is a product of a lifelong search for meaning which took place in a world which first pitted Christianity against traditional Crow worship and then a secular and "modern" way against the way of prayer.

Yellowtail is an especially important and authentic spokesman for the Crow Indian way. The personal experiences and spiritual outlook narrated by those who lived the life of buffalo hunters and warriors made a lasting impression which led him to emulate their harsh regimen. His youthful years also were imprinted by the restrictive and coercive policies of federal and state government's efforts to force the Crow to give up their customs and religious ceremonies. However, during the 1930s Commissioner John Collier reversed the harsh policy and encouraged Indians to revitalize their communities by applying traditional values to contemporary problems. The new policy stimulated Yellowtail and other Crow to reinstate traditional dances and ceremonies which had lapsed during the coercive period and in part as interest among the Crow diminished.

Thomas Yellowtail is the hands-on successor to the Shoshoni medicine man John Trehero, who introduced the Shoshone Sun Dance to the Crow in 1941 at the invitation of William Big Day. The Crow had their own Sun Dance, but performed it for the last time about 1875. Following the command of Seven Arrows, the dwarf spirit-being who owned the Sun Dance, Trehero in 1969 instructed Yellowtail in the ways of the ceremony and transferred his spike-elk power by blowing it into Yellowtail. Trehero periodically assisted Yellowtail in Sun Dance performances until Trehero's death in 1985. When Seven Arrows intimated that Yellowtail should select a successor, he taught John Pretty on Top and transferred medicines. In 1984 during a Sun Dance at Lodge Grass, Yellowtail formally surrendered his stewardship.

Yellowtail's life is panoramic in sweep, since it touches base with the past through living memories, with the past as it became modified and organized into a reservation culture about 1910, and with the decline of tradition following World War II. His contemporary interpretations raise intriguing questions about changes between past and present beliefs and practices as well as continuities.

Changing historic contexts alter cultures, and inevitably such changes influence religion. The reservation context for the Sun Dance today is striking in its contrast with the buffalo-hunting and warrior life of yesterday. Reservation life also brought the Crow and representatives of American culture into confrontation over hair styles, dress, education, work habits, economic objectives, marriage, descent, inheritance, political authority, and religion. These confrontations spread through Crow society as missionaries forced a choice between Christianity and "superstition." This pressure led Crow to reflect and exchange views on the preservation or abandonment of their language, customs, and religion. The choice involved their very existence as a people.

During this time missionary teaching, schooling, reading, army service, farming and ranching instruction, wage work, urban living, some professionalization, social and political service, nursing, hospitalization, interrogation by friends and ethnographers, and travel broadened the knowledge base and experience of the Crow. Yellowtail himself traveled in Europe with an Indian dance troupe. He also read *Black Elk Speaks* and met with medicine men concerned with preservation of the Indian sacred traditions.

Yellowtail's philosophy and procedures in the Sun Dance reveal many continuities with the past despite changes in form, emphasis, and meaning. He stresses the importance of a Creator as the starter of life and the importance of the prayerful path to the Creator for Crow ethnic identity and for all world peoples. In metaphor each worship is like the spoke of a wheel, all of which meet at the hub, the Creator. Tradition in this pluralistic view adds strength to the sacred and contributes to the well-being and future of mankind.

From the very beginning of contact with Europeans, the sacred was central to the regulation of life among the Crow and Hidatsa, from whom the Crow in all probability separated during the seventeenth century. In all their primary activities they reached back to the very creation of the universe to obtain mystic power (*maxpeh*) to find buffalo, raid for horses, overcome enemies, control weather, heal sickness, move camp, direct ceremonies, and seal agreements. In some ways the creation had never come to an end, for individual Crow throughout historic times in visions and in dreams received special gifts of mystic power which benefited themselves and which at times could be used for the public welfare. At a sacred lake in North Dakota, No Vitals received a gift of Holy Tobacco by whose care, guidance, and protection the Crow were destined to be victorious over their enemies and to endure as a great people. However, they were obligated to treat Holy Tobacco with respect, to cultivate it ceremoniously annually as instructed, and to make sure that they always possessed seed and white blossoms.

The annual planting and harvesting of Holy Tobacco and the Sun Dance were important ceremonials governed by private medicine bundles. Tobacco worshippers, at any one time, were divided into some five or six chapters, each founded on a medicine bundle, and new members were adopted in the spring with a substantial exchange of wealth between a candidate and his adoptive "father" and "mother." The adoptee was given a body painting, four medicine songs, and a choice of four medicines. Owners of Sun Dance bundles were not organized into chapters, for their function was to guide a mourner through a ceremony designed for vengeance against the enemy. The contents of Sun Dance bundles were very much alike and included an image of a man, skunk skin necklaces, and a deerskin kilt. At any one time there might be four or five owners, but one usually held a more powerful bundle.

Sun Dances required cooperation among bands, and frequently the tribe gathered for a ceremony which might take place every three or four years. As in other ceremonies, the initiative was taken by an individual according to need and spiritual direction. A man in deep mourning in dream or vision received a sign that his mourning would be avenged and he would be made happy again were he to seek help through the Sun Dance. The camp during the Sun Dance was under the direction of the bundle owner selected to direct the ceremony. Everything was done to assure success. They solicited the assistance of Sun, the most powerful of spiritual beings, by building a "little lodge" in imitation of the Sun's own tipi. While moving to the dance location, the mourner and his dress were consecrated at four stops along the way. The twenty poles of the lodge were scouted by warriors in search of the enemy, and twenty young men noted for their bravery were selected to draw the poles to camp. Before cutting a main pole, a woman gave an oath as to her virtue and prayed for the success of the venture. In building the lodge, young warriors engaged in sham battles and outstanding leaders recited their coups and reported dreams foretelling the death of an enemy.

The mourner-pledger danced in place on a bed of white clay and blew his prayers through an eagle bone whistle with his eyes riveted on an effigy of a little man in a hoop ringed with eagle feathers and set in a cedar tree cut for the ceremony. If the pledger saw the figure turn black, a sign of victory, or if he were struck down and in vision saw a dead enemy, his desire for vengeance had been granted.

During the dance young men in search of medicine were

skewered and suspended with thongs from the lodge poles. Outside, suppliants, skewered and tethered to posts, ran back and forth straining to break the attachment. Others had leather thongs attached to their backs and dragged seven buffalo skulls behind them, beseeching the seven buffalo bulls of the Great Dipper to give them plenty of horses or to aid them in wresting a gun from the enemy. In nearby foothills mourners wailed for vengeance, and some, presumably close relatives and clanmates of the deceased, cut off finger joints as offerings.

The Sun Dance mobilized *maxpeh* against the enemy, and the victory sign given the pledger marked the end of the ceremony. On leaving the lodge, the feathered hoop, new blackened in victory, was attached to a pole and left leaning against one of the lodge poles. Fine cougar, silver fox, and albino buffalo hides, and the collected finger joints, were left as offerings to Sun. Now all that remained was the revenge party, setting out at a time intimated in the vision or as later dreams might direct.

Healing was not part of the traditional Sun Dance. Curing was carried out privately on invitation to attend a sick person. Today, curing is public and an important function of the Sun Dance medicine man. Yet, as during World War II, the Sun Dance can become a primary instrument for victory over the enemy.

Leaving aside formal differences between the borrowed Shoshone and the traditional Crow sun dances, continuities with the past are striking despite alterations in objectives, procedures, and meanings. Today's camp is largely the responsibility of the pledger in conjunction with the district recreational committee and Crow police. A medicine bundle is essential to a leadership role, and medicine men and bundles are ranked according to their successes and close relations with the founder, John Trehero. An ability to interpret dreams and foretell the future and a good character enhance the reputation of a Sun Dance medicine man.

An individual commonly waits for a dream sign before sponsoring a Sun Dance today. As of old, he must give wealth to the medicine man who takes him through the ceremony without harmful accidents. A sponsor shares his Sun Dance with many individual participants, as in the past, and these commonly use family medicines and paintings or borrow from paternal uncles and aunts (formerly clan fathers and mothers). Motives for participation range widely and may include health, easy childbirth, changing one's luck, and getting power to cure.

The present Sun Dance stresses physical suffering to gain some good, but as Yellowtail observes, the medicine fathers informed the Crow in visions and in dreams that it was no longer necessary to skewer themselves. Now sincerity of purpose is expressed through abstention from food and water during the ceremony and the sending of prayers by steady dancing interspersed with cigarette smoke prayers. As of old, the preparatory sweat bath and prayers are vital to the sincerity with which a suppliant approaches the suffering in the Sun Dance. A steady and sincere dancer who "charges the buffalo" attached to the center pole at some time may be run over and in his unconscious mystic state may receive something good, perhaps a power to cure. Helping to build the lodge, furnishing pennants and tobacco offerings for the centerpole, bringing cattails for the weary dancers, giving cigarettes to the dancers for smoke prayers, and building support poles for the dancers are all prayerful actions which may return some good to the volunteer.

A medicine man no longer is described as a worker of supernatural things. He is simply the one who performs ceremonies and doctors patients. In former times straight tubular pipes were used to offer smoke prayers in the Sun Dance and also to draw the evil matter from a patient. Today medicine feathers are used to transmit power from the consecrated centerpole to the patient to draw out the bad stuff. Diagnosis and doctoring appear to be based as much on popular medical diagnoses as on Crow concepts of illness involving ghosts and sorcery. Medicine men attend patients at home or in hospitals, or doctor them at a distance. Yellowtail sends his medicine father, Seven Arrows, as far as California to cure patients. The monthly prayer meeting associated with the Sun Dance serves patients on a scheduled basis.

Medicine men today, as formerly, may instruct those who wish to change their luck by fasting and praying in solitude or in the Sun Dance. Such instruction in the past accented procedures rather than philosophical discourses on the nature of the world and the place of worship in the human destiny. This pragmatic approach is basically true today. Philosophic discourse for the Crow is generated largely in academic situations and by challenges raised by friendly churchmen, ethnographers, lay researchers, and publications.

The contemporary religious tradition of the Crow cannot be viewed as a changeless reflection of a distant mirror. Today the Sun Dance has emerged in reinterpretation as a traditional "church" equivalent to Christian churches. The Center Pole as the collector of mystic power also has focused attention on the Creator as the ultimate giver of power and blessings and diminished the importance of medicine fathers. Throughout, the traditional Crow's emphasis on a personal relationship in worship has remained constant.

A view of the Sun Dance as an Indian church gives the ceremony a special legitimacy and place in the future of Crow identity. Its position rivals peyotism in expressing Indian ethnicity, and it is superseding the Tobacco Society, which now appears to be in decline. The recent introduction of the Sioux cutting Sun Dance has aroused opposition because of fears it will bring competition to the established Crow-Shoshone Sun Dance.

Yellowtail's narrative addresses a wide range of issues which take the reader further along the way to a better understanding of how the past becomes a useful part of the present, preserving ethnic identity with integrative linkages to American society and culture and to the world at large.

PART ONE

EXPOSURE TO A
TRADITIONAL LIFE

YELLOWTAIL BEGINS IN PRAYER

ACBADADEA,[1] Maker of All Things Above, hear my prayer. Now we have filled our pipe and offered our smoke to the Heavens Above, to Mother Earth, and to the directions of the Four Winds.[2] Before we start our work, we must send this prayer. Medicine Fathers from all the four directions of the world, hear my prayer. Acbadadea, I send this prayer to You as I am going to speak about our sacred ways, so that the knowledge of our sacred ways can be given in a more complete form to many people. Help me! Guide my thoughts and words, and give me wisdom to present Your religion, so that our people may know it and follow it, so that our people may live!

I think it is necessary that the younger ones know something about their religion. Their minds are confused, not knowing what they should do. They should know that there are religions, that their people have a religion that is different from other religions, and that our religion was given to us Indian people long before our time. They should know something about their heritage and traditional life, how it is different from other ways in which people live, especially in this modern world. Without this knowledge they do not have anything to fall back on, and I don't see how a person can live in this world without the center that is given by religion. They should know this, and respect the importance of prayer.

You have chosen me to help carry on the Sun Dance. The young people have heard my prayers at the Sun Dance—when they listen as spectators. I always say my prayers and speak in hopes that my words will penetrate the hearts of the listeners, so that they will know the truth of what I have said.

Once they know the truth and understand the greatness of
the gifts they have been given by You, Acbadadea, then they
will follow Your ways because of the love that they should
feel for You in their hearts. Even if they are not filled with the
love of You, those who understand Your greatness should
fear the consequences if they do not follow Your sacred paths.
So help us reach out and touch the hearts of our people, of all
people. I pray that my words and prayers will penetrate into
their thinking and that they will come and join a religion later
on. It makes me happy when I see young boys and girls
praying and membership in our religion increasing. Yet there
are others that take to the white man's modern ways because
of bad teachings and because of what they see around them
that misleads them; they think something is wrong with their
Indian beliefs and ways of living. They should think first about
their Indian heritage and the Indian religion to which they
belong. They should join and try to straighten themselves out
before they get too far with these bad things.

I know it is important to explain the Indian religion to our
youngsters, so they can know something about their heritage.
For then they can have a basis upon which to decide whether
to follow a path that You, the Maker of All Things Above,
have set forth or whether to wait for the consequences. It is
my prayer that all Indians will realize that You have given us
the Sun Dance religion because it provides the knowledge and
the way that is needed to follow Your ways and to know You.
This understanding is also important for non-Indians, for even
though they have different religions, they can see that all
religions are the same in their true meaning and that they all
lead to You.

Maker of All Things Above, I am thankful for what You
have given me. As my life comes to a close, I realize that You
have given me strength to stay with my prayers and even to
be a leader of my religion. I would like You to give me strength
to go on for a few more years, as long as I am able to conduct
what You have given me to take care of. Just as You have
given me the strength and words that will be put in this book,

so, too, should You give understanding to those who read these words. This is my prayer.

Hey-a-a-hey! Hey-a-a-hey! Hey-a-a-hey!
Grandfather, the Great Spirit, behold me on earth. It is said that you lived first. You are older than all the prayers that are sent to you. All things on earth, the four leggeds, the wings of the air, belong to you. It is said that you have made all things. Also, you have set the powers of the four quarters to cross each other. . . . I thus will send up a voice in behalf of everything that you have made.[3]

—Black Elk, Oglala Sioux

2

EARLY YEARS AND
TRADITIONAL VALUES

I was born on March 7, 1903, just south of Lodge Grass, Montana. My father's name was Yellowtail, which was the shortened white man's name given to him that has become our family name. The full meaning of his Indian name was "Hawk with the Yellow Tail Feathers."

In my younger days, the old, great warriors who participated in the Plains wars were still living, and many of the traditional ways still lived, even though we were already on the reservation. I still remember seeing the old warriors around the camp fires and at all the traditional ceremonies. When they danced in the warrior's way and then gave their war whoops and shot their rifles into the air, we children were certain that we had seen the end of our days, and—whoosh—did we run for cover! We would hide under the blankets or behind something and just peek out to see these tremendous leaders, until another shot came out—and we dove for cover again!

The Lodge Grass Valley was called the "Valley of the Chiefs" because of all the great war chiefs who were living there in my early years. I only wish I remembered more about all of their stories. I never participated in any of the traditional life of the Indians who roamed over the plains, but when I was a youngster all of my teachers had lived that life, before Indians were forced onto the reservations. These elders took great care to explain and show to us by their example the values by which all men should live. It is their spiritual values and attitudes toward which we must center our lives.

So in my time, I did learn about our traditional ways, and Grandma and I have tried to practice those ways during all

our years up to this day.[1] Grandma and I were married on
April 27, 1929, and the changes that we have seen on the
reservation and in this world have been greater than I could
have imagined. The world we see now is very different from
the one our ancestors knew, and even the one we knew as
children. Almost all of the changes I have seen take place
make me sad, and I will speak about them. My hope is to tell
about our traditional ways, and how those values and the
sacred rites that remain with us are even more important to
our people today, because without them we cannot live. You
have also asked many questions about my own life and I will
answer them, not because my life has been important, but
because young people nowadays should see the differences
between their lives and those of us older folks.

I hear people today talk about "traditional Indians" and
"modern Indians." They say, "Get rid of those old, traditional
ideas and start to think like a modern Indian; it is the only
way you can get ahead." Many people seem to think that we
have to make progress away from the old values and beliefs,
toward some new types of ideas that are supposed to be better
for us. They are mistaken. It would be better for them if they
progressed from their new, modern ideas back to the old,
traditional beliefs. They do not understand anything about
the traditional ways.

When I hear someone speak of our traditional life or of
traditional Indians, I always think about the values of the
people who lived in the olden days—values which were established in order to walk a sacred path through life. It is hard to
speak about the attitudes that a person has toward the world
in which he lives, and most people today don't even consider
who they are in relation to the world around them, or in
relation to Acbadadea, the Maker of All Things Above. The
life of the traditional Indian was rooted in the sacred, he
saw the natural world around him as a miracle created by
Acbadadea.[2] The traditional ways allowed the Indian to reflect
on the mystery of life, and they were always aware of their
place in creation.

The traditional American Indian is an individual who has

self-esteem in his sacred way of life, a person who is trying to follow the straight path in everything. He tries to do things right and not be greedy. He doesn't try to invent things in order to possess them; he is not that way. He is a person who is willing to help others. He will want enough to live on, but that is all the Indian cares for. He shares whatever he has been given with his fellow man and does not try to get ahead of the others. He knows the meaning of poverty and of gratitude. He also knows about religion; he knew long before the white man came and brought all kinds of religions. Indians are ready to help others and do not require much of anything. In my case, when I make medicine and doctor people with my prayers, I don't ask for anything. It is up to the individual that I pray for. If he offers me something, I am ready to accept. It is that way among the people of all Indian nations. Anyone who follows the sacred ways can help others live. That is why the Indian is not rich in possessing wealth and money. We Indian people are rich in spiritual wealth, which is more important.

The Indian people have recreational doings such as dances. At our powwows we enjoy a little fun. Even during the dancing and celebrating, our traditional ways are present. At every powwow, the Indians will have a big giveaway. They will give away what they have on hand, even if they are not rich. Even being poor, the traditional Indian is ready to help and give what he has. He would take his shirt off and give it to one that needs it and he would go without.[3] That is the way of life of the Indian. I think it is a very good thing. We may be poor in one way, but we are rich in spiritual things, and it is great to have spiritual possessions that can help others. In the Indian way, whenever someone does something good, they have a giveaway. It is just the opposite for white people. The Indians show humility by giving something away. When someone has a giveaway, they give because they are thankful for what they have. If they have done something well, it is really God, Acbadadea, who has given them the ability to do it. Praising songs are sung for people who are being honored. I have my personal praising songs that I sing for such people.

I would gather them in front of me, if I were there, and sing my praise song, march around the floor, praising them up. Then I would say words for them. "These are my children now and they have done a great thing." Then I would pray for them. All the relatives would come forward and give the man who praises and prays for people a lot of gifts. That is separate from the main giveaway. I hardly ever use my praise song on anybody, because people might think I am expecting too much, too many free gifts. Of course, I pray for the people anyway.

When a traditional Indian possessed spiritual powers, he did not try to come out and make a show of what he had. Indians are always private in protecting holy things. It is very difficult to talk about some holy matters, and they are not advertised. Some spiritual matters that pertain to the tribe as a whole are of course public. But individual spiritual matters pertain only to that person, and no one should boast about the gifts he has been given.

The person who possesses spiritual powers must respect them; he must be afraid of them. Fear is a part of the respect of sacred things. Once you know about these things, you will also love them, because you will see that without a sense of the sacred you are less than a man. Man must realize that his importance is nothing compared to Nature and that the sacred realities are even much greater than Nature. A medicine man is required to refrain from many things; in my case, for instance, there are things that I am required not to do and to stay away from. There are general rules that must be observed by all people, and there are special rules that are given to some men as a condition for their medicine powers.

If a man violates these rules, it may bring harm to himself and also to other people. Many of these rules are secret things that each holy man knows about, and it is important for him to observe these rules so that the sacred things will not be lost. It is not just how you act, but how you are in your heart that is considered by the Medicine Fathers.[4] If you think that you deserve more than another man or that you are better than everyone else, you may not be given any help. But if you follow the sacred path, then you will probably be allowed to keep what you have been given.

When one of us has been entrusted with sacred things, we should try to pass them on so that the spiritual path will always be present for those who choose to follow it. At such time when a man is getting old, getting close to the time of retirement from the world, he can pass on what he has to a younger person who may carry on the work with the medicine things. He should select someone worthy so that his people may live. After this knowledge and the spiritual gifts have been received by the younger person, then the older man is ready to pass away. He has fulfilled his final responsibility, and the spiritual tradition will not be lost. This is good, and the next one can carry it down the line on to the next generation.

As I explain more about our traditional life, these things will become clearer. Spiritual matters are difficult to explain because you must live with them in order to fully understand them. I have lived with these all my life, and I am still learning. Now it is time for me to talk about things which apply to all people of the tribe. We have talked about many of these things over the last three years, and soon our work with this book will be finished. We have discussed private matters about my dreams and visions that do not concern our tribal, sacred way, and those will not be part of the book. When my stories are told, one part of my responsibility to pass on my sacred knowledge will be fulfilled; I will then only need to select and instruct my successor in the duties of the medicine man.[5] I have been blessed with medicine powers that I never expected, and, as chief medicine man of the Crow, my duties will only be done when my successor is ready to carry on. I may be around for many years yet, but we must always be ready to meet our Maker. In 1981, I suffered a heart attack after the Sun Dance, so this may be an indication that I am to carry on for only a few more years in my duties as Sun Dance chief.

After the dancers come out of the Sun Dance, many of them go to the river to bathe. This refreshes the dancers, and reminds them of the ordeal they have just completed. During those three days that you spend in the Sun Dance, your body is burning. When you come out you want to go to the river. Last year, I worked pretty hard in the Sun Dance; it was very hot working on people and doctoring. After we finished the dance and came out that afternoon, I wanted to go bathe and purify myself. My head was strange, I felt different, and I thought that maybe I had a sunstroke. I went swimming in the river; it was lukewarm to others, but to me it was like getting into ice water. This was in July, when even the water in the river would not feel cold, but it was like ice water for me, and something was wrong with me. I got out and back into my clothes and when I came back that evening, I was shivering. I was freezing. Then they took me in to the hospital and found out it was a heart attack. I was lucky that I recovered from that and came out of it, and now I am back again. I regained my strength, and I am back to work again and today I feel all right. We don't know how or what is going to take us. It is the same for every individual in this world, so everyone should be prepared each day to pass on and meet his Maker.

I intend to continue in the Sun Dance.

I will continue in my efforts to preserve our spiritual ways, and when I am called to leave this world and journey on, when Acbadadea, the Maker of All Things Above, calls me to Him, I will go, knowing in my heart that I have done everything I can to purify myself and help carry on our sacred traditions so that my people may live.

We should understand well that all things are the work of the Great Spirit. We should know that He is within all things: the trees, the grasses, the rivers, the mountains, and all the four-legged animals, and the winged peoples; and even more important, we should understand that He is also above all these things and peoples. When we do understand all this deeply in our hearts, then we will fear, and love, and know the Great Spirit, and then we will be and act and live as He intends.[6]
                                        —Black Elk, Oglala Sioux

MEDICINE ROCK CHIEF

WHEN I was just a small boy about the age of six, I was given my Indian name. The name was given to me by one of our most famous chiefs, Chief Medicine Crow, and he named me after his main medicine: the medicine rock. It is a great honor to receive a name related to a man's main medicine, and that is what Chief Medicine Crow did; he gave me the name Medicine Rock Chief. My namesake, you might say, is the medicine rock. That medicine is still among us today. It is being kept carefully in a sacred manner and it is living still.[1] It is kept only about three miles from our home. The medicine bundle in which the medicine rock is kept will be opened probably in May, or sometime this spring.[2] It is opened both in the spring and then in the fall. In May, after the first thunder, they wait for a day when there is good weather, when there are no clouds. First, they smudge it with incense and say prayers before opening it. There are three sacred incenses that can be used to purify anything before a cere-mony: sweet grass, sweet sage, and sweet cedar. If we have a fire with hot coals, then we can use sweet sage or sweet cedar. If we have to use matches, then we can light the braid of sweet grass and watch the smoke rise up toward the heavens. If I have my eagle feathers with me, I will hold them in the smoke so that all of the feathers are covered with the blessing of the sacred incense. The smoke represents the path of our prayers up to the heavens and to all directions of the wind. By holding anything in the sacred incense as it rises, we say that we are "smudging" the object to purify it. Before we begin any ceremony, we smudge the objects that we will use.

After the bundle is smudged, people sit around it and offer smoke and say prayers. We always offer tobacco smoke before we make our prayer to Acbadadea and to each of the Medicine Fathers who are represented in the medicine bundle. This smoke carries our prayer to Acbadadea. After the prayer, they view the rocks and medicine objects contained in the medicine bundle, praying inwardly during some time. Then the bundle is put away, and it is not opened again until fall, before winter sets in. Early in October, probably during what we call Indian summer, when the weather is good again and there is no rain, no clouds, during that time they open it again, and repeat the same ceremony. A few people are invited to view the medicine rock, to hold it up, then put the bundle away, and then that's it until the next year.

When we hold ceremonies in this sacred manner, we show our respect not only to the Medicine Father who has passed on the power to us, but also to all of creation. By observing our prayers and performing the ceremonies, the Crow maintain the sacred center that connects us to Acbadadea.

That rock was the main medicine of Chief Medicine Crow. It is a great medicine. He took it on his war parties and it helped him to accomplish all his war deeds without getting any injury. He would go out on successful raids and come back, bringing back horses, scalps and guns. All of these deeds allowed him to become a chief, and he did all these things two, three times. So that made him a great chief, put him way up there as a high-ranking chief among all of the Crow.

My name, Medicine Rock Chief, should be well known among the Crow, but it is not. Only Chief Medicine Crow's wife and his son, who just passed away a few years ago, called me by that Indian name. Because it was given to me by his father, his son knew it; he and his mother were probably the only two Crow who called me by that name until they were gone, and now no one calls me by that Indian name, for nobody knows it.

The rock was found at a place called Absarokee. Absarokee is up the Stillwater River near present-day Columbus, Montana. At one time there was a second agency that was established for the Crow at Absarokee. It was near this place that the medicine rock was found.

The rock was found by the wife of Sees the Living Bull. He was the father of the great chief and medicine man Chief Medicine Crow. Thus the rock was actually found by the mother of Chief Medicine Crow. Then Chief Medicine Crow became the owner. When Chief Medicine Crow received the rock from his father, it became his most important medicine. It was while Chief Medicine Crow had possession of the rock that he gave the name to me. After his death, the medicine rock was handed down within his family. That is how it happens; when the owner passes away, the medicine bundle goes down within the family, to the next one in line to be keeper of the sacred medicine rock bundle. It is owned at the present time by a grandson of Chief Medicine Crow with the Indian name of Shines Bright. If I can find time to attend the ceremony that they will have this spring, I would like to see it again. I saw it once, about fifteen years ago. That was the one and only time I have ever seen the medicine rock and its offspring.

The rock was pointed out to the mother of Chief Medicine Crow while she was on a vision quest. She was fasting, away from everyone in the hills near Absarokee. She went up toward those mountains, somewhere in the hills, by herself. In the morning when the sun was up and bright, from where she was, the sun pointed out something shining. Every day during her fast when the sun was up, she would see something glistening in the sun, from where she fasted. So she was wondering what that was. One day—they say on the third day of her fast—the sun was up and the object shone again. This time she went to see what that shining thing was; she walked over there and it was a rock. She took it and kept it, brought it back to where she was fasting. When she had finished her four days, she came back to the camp, and she brought this rock back with her. Later on, she had visions about the rock, and they told her that this was medicine that was given to her. Being a woman, she thought maybe her husband should be the one to have it, so she gave it to her

husband, Sees the Living Bull. They all had further dreams
about the rock; they were being told what to do with it, how
to take good care of this medicine that had been given to them.
They kept it according to the visions and had more dreams
about it. They always kept it as a sacred thing and took care
of it. Sees the Living Bull received many good things because
of that rock. He became a medicine man from the powers that
his rock had given the family and had successful raids when
he went on war parties. He became a chief himself.

Chief Medicine Crow's friend Chief Two Leggings was also
one of the greatest Crow chiefs. They would go on war parties
together, and they would be successful, bring back horses,
accomplishing great deeds. Of course Two Leggings had other
medicines, his own medicines. These two great men were
always together. Finally, Two Leggings asked Sees the Living
Bull to adopt him as a son or give him medicine and pray for
him. He kept asking the old medicine man, Sees the Living
Bull, to adopt him into the Tobacco Society. At last Sees the
Living Bull accepted this young man, Two Leggings, as his
adopted Tobacco Society son. After that, wherever he went,
Two Leggings would steal horses from the enemy on war
raids and would bring them back to give to his adopted father.
Two Leggings would give him horses and other things, for he
felt indebted to Sees the Living Bull, who made medicine for
Two Leggings as his adopted son. Medicine Crow and Two
Leggings were two of the greatest warriors among the Crow,
and they both received blessings that came through the medicine rock. After his father died, Medicine Crow became the
only owner of the rock and he started getting even greater
powers from the rock.

Of course, the real power comes from God, the Maker of All
Things Above, but it is passed on to us through our Medicine
Fathers. All of the Medicine Fathers live in Nature, come from
Nature. So the Indians are able to receive direct blessings and
gifts from beyond this world we see, from God, through our
Medicine Fathers. You might say that Nature reflects the quali-
ties of God that are present everywhere. Of course there are
rules that must be observed in order to receive any of these

gifts. Powers or knowledge are never given to anyone who does not live according to the rules that must be observed. If someone is given medicine and then does not live in a sacred manner, then he will either lose the medicine or he will be punished in some way depending on what he has done.

As I said, Shines Bright is the present owner of the medicine rock. Each spring he performs the prayer ceremony, which is similar to the prayer meetings held for the Sun Dance. For many years, each spring there was an additional rock in the bundle, just like the medicine rock, only smaller. Every time they opened it, they counted the number of rocks; there are lots of them. They would find one more each year. Nobody put it in there, but each spring, when the rocks were counted, there was one more: the offspring of the rock. I understand that for several years now there have been no new offspring, but the medicine is still strong and new offspring may come again soon.[3] So that is the story of the meaning of my name, Medicine Rock Chief, and of how that great medicine is still kept among the Crow today in a sacred medicine bundle.

In olden days almost every family had a medicine bundle in their tipi, and this sacred presence made the entire tribe strong. All members of the tribe knew the importance of the medicine bundles and what they represented.

It is necessary for everyone in a tribe to know about the spiritual matters that pertain to it as a whole. It is the responsibility of each generation to pass this knowledge on to the next. In olden days this was done as part of everyday life, and the children were taught great respect for the sacred ways and how to walk a straight path.

The individual medicine that a man might receive if he followed the sacred ways was often his own property and did not concern the tribe but only the individual and his family. This individual relationship between a person and his spiritual possessions, like his visions, his medicines, his Medicine Fathers, is private. You might say that the Indian religion had a public part and a private part. Both parts are very important, and they depend upon each other for support, but they are different.

The way in which medicine bundles are kept by their owners shows the way in which an individual must treat his
spiritual possessions. The medicine bundle contains the
things that a person has been directed to collect as a result of
his vision or dream. The medicine he has been given links
him to all of the medicine powers of the universe. He will
probably be told how he should prepare his medicine bundle
in order to protect his medicine. The instructions can come
directly from the Medicine Father, whether he be a bird, an
animal, or whatever, or the medicine man of the tribe can
explain to the person what he should do. After a man takes
these steps, he has new responsibilities, and he must follow
new, difficult rules to protect and keep his gift. These responsibilities are both outward and inward.

It is important to keep the medicine bundle away from
people. In the olden days, one would give a special place to
these bundles, and they were not bothered by anyone. It is
still that way today. In order to use them or open them, it
requires quite a ceremony. The bundle must be smudged with
either sweet cedar or sweet grass, and prayers must be said
before opening it. This is always done by offering the prayer
with smoke. The Medicine Fathers that gave these things to
the person must be called upon to be present. Only after these
procedures, and any special rules regarding that particular
medicine, are completed is one allowed to open the bundle.
This generally takes place with just a few people and it is not
public. In this way the power that is present in the medicines
is respected, and the medicine will be renewed through the
prayers.

In olden days, every family set aside a special place in the
tipi where they made a stand out of three poles, like a tripod,
on which the bundle was placed. In this area of the tipi no
one who was impure was allowed. No one could touch the
bundle without first undertaking the purification and prayers.
If it is kept in a house, there are times when it must be taken
out because of things that should not be allowed to be around
it. For example, when any women are about to enter a place
where medicine objects or medicine bundles—sacred things—

are being kept, they have to find out if any of them is having her menstrual period. If so, that one is not allowed to enter the house or the tipi.[4] In olden days there were special tipis where the women would go at their time of the month. Customs like this are very important in relation to spiritual medicine objects.

There are other general rules to be observed. For instance, if a ceremony is taking place, they keep people from crossing in front of the person performing the ceremony with the medicine bundle. The person performing the ceremony generally faces the east, and the bundle is in front of him. No one should cross this line. It is the same way in the Sun Dance, when we have our morning ceremony for the rising sun. Of course, some little child may not know this and might want to run around. Someone should watch the children if they are present, to be certain that they don't run around—especially in front of someone performing a ceremony—and don't make too much noise. These same general rules are followed in the Sun Dance. The purpose of all of these rules is to show great respect for spiritual things. Not just anybody can participate in these ceremonies, and not just anyone can follow a spiritual path or receive something. The longer and farther you follow your path, the more of yourself you may be asked to give. The sincere ones will learn all the rules, and they will lead their lives in accordance with the spirit of these requirements.

I should also say something about the misfortunes that can occur if a person disobeys the rules. If the powers or rules are violated, then the sacred power will leave the medicine bundle and the sacred presence among the tribe will be diminished, and the person who is responsible for this may undergo some great misfortune. It may happen to that person or to the family, and maybe a whole family will be wiped out. In these cases, all of the power leaves the medicine bundle, and there will be nothing left except the material thing that was in the bundle. When the power leaves the material object in the bundle, it will not do anyone any good. The entire tribe loses part of its sacred power as this happens. If everyone would correctly follow the traditional ways and all of the rules, the sacred presence within the tribe would increase, but if many people continue to violate the rules, not only those people, but the tribe as a whole, will suffer.

Sacred objects are living beings, and must be treated with special care. Sometimes, when an old man passes away and leaves behind his sacred possessions, his family does not know what to do. They may know that these sacred things must be treated with respect, but they may not know what to do to preserve them. They may be afraid to touch them, and so they just put them on a shelf somewhere. This will also cause the sacred power to leave after some amount of time. We must constantly show our thanks and respect to the medicine powers, through prayer and through the observance of all the rules in our daily life and in our special ceremonies. The presence of the bundles among our tribal members reminds us of this obligation. All of these things are important even if they may seem small.

For instance, I know a medicine man from another tribe who used to be a good medicine man. I understand that he has lost all of his powers because he was drinking. That man may still have the feathers and other objects that he used in his ceremonies to call forth his Medicine Fathers, but all the power is gone from the feathers and medicine bundles. The Medicine Fathers will take away the powers from a man who mistreats his medicine objects. It may start slowly, but they could take away the powers until the person has nothing left. That is the way we heard about this medicine man. They say he does not have the powers he once had. He is just a common man now. They say that he is not feeling very well, either. Maybe the Medicine Fathers are punishing him by making him feel sickly.

There are many things that are forbidden for me. For instance, I may not take part in any gambling games or anything in which you bet with money. I cannot drink alcohol or take drugs, and I must never use my powers for any evil purpose or in order to hurt anyone. Of course, I must observe all of the obligations to carry on the Sun Dance. Some things are forbidden and some things are required.

The Medicine Fathers are with you all of the time. They watch everyone, especially a medicine man, very closely. If he does the things that he is forbidden to do, they can punish him. Even if they don't take his powers away, they might punish him in some other way. If they just take his powers away, he is back to being a common man. If he tried, he would not be any good at all. Once they have been taken away, he cannot get them back.

In telling the story about my name, you can see how the name a person has relates to something of importance in his tribe or in his life. Today we give someone a first name because we like the sound or know someone else by that name. Our last name can't be changed and no longer carries any sacred meaning. In the traditional way, the names that were given had a sacred meaning, and even when you called someone by his name, you were reminded of the sacred events and sacred responsibilities of the title. A man could even be given a new name if something important happened in his life. You can see how everything in a traditional Indian's life related to the sacred.

Those who are healed do not talk about it among themselves and spread the news. That is not the Sioux way. If a thing is holy and sacred, if it is a miracle, it is not talked about. It is too special for that. Visions we receive are in the same category. They are something personal between Wakan-Tanka and the seeker that affects the whole of his life. Even the person's family will not discuss it or tell their friends.[5]

—Fools Crow, Teton Sioux

4

EARLY RESERVATION LIFE

WHEN I told you about my name, Medicine Rock Chief, you could see how each young child is introduced into the traditional ways when he is very young. There are thirteen clans among the Crow tribe, and my clan is the Whistling Waters. Each person has relatives through the clan also, so all the members of the tribe can learn a great deal from their relatives both through blood and through the clans.[1] The entire tribe worked together for the benefit of every person in the tribe, and the clan system helped to strengthen the cooperation of every person working toward the common welfare of the tribe.

In olden days, all of the Indians followed the sacred ways, and no one disagreed about the manner in which we should worship God. With the coming of the white men, this changed. When the missionaries came to the Indian reservations, they condemned everything that the Indians did. Not only the Crow, but also the other Indian tribes; the missionaries did the same thing everywhere. They would condemn all of our sacred things by saying, "It is all Satan's work."

The Indians found that half of the time they could not understand what the white preacher was talking about, and they weren't really interested. The white men would get an interpreter up there who didn't quite know how to translate some of these things, and it was amusing sometimes, to listen to these translators talk. Some of the words that the missionary used, the translators couldn't understand in the first place. They were trying to translate, but no one understood what the other was saying. I think that made everyone angry. The white men tried to take the real meaning of the Indian religion away from us because they condemned everything that the Indian did. They told us to get rid of our medicine; they suggested that those people who had medicine bundles should throw them away. Some did. They believed what the missionary said and advised them to do.

Those Indians who listened to the white man's preachers lost all of their real belief. The young people were confused because what they had believed in all of these years, since they were little fellows, was all lost. They ended up by not being able to use any of these Indian objects. Grandma tells the story of one Catholic priest who used to come to her school and give all of the girls rosaries to try to get everyone to come to the Catholic church. If you came you would go to heaven; if you didn't, you would go to hell. But many of the children never did go; they just made beautiful necklaces and bracelets out of the rosaries. This attitude of distrust towards the missionaries came up because we knew that what mattered was how you lived all of the time, not just whether you went somewhere on Sunday morning or not. It was clear that the missionaries didn't know that, because the Catholics were very mean to the Protestants. Each denomination was really mean to the other. To hear the white man talk, you would think that no one had a chance to go to heaven because no one could agree on how to pray on Sunday.

At school you were forced to belong to one white man's denomination or the other. Most of the people were Catholics, but we were Protestants, so we caught it from the right and left all the time. The traditional Indian form of religion never caused friction of any kind. One sacred society gave me a sacred pipe, and they did not have any friction with the other sacred societies. These new religions that the white man brought were the cause of a lot of friction. An old couple had a beautiful pair of horses, and the missionary told the old man that Jesus wanted his horses. The Indian went home from church and he unharnessed his team. He saddled his saddle horse and took the horses over to the missionary's house. The next weekend the missionary was driving them, and the old man was pretty upset about that. He wanted to know if the missionary was God. He couldn't figure that out, because the missionary was using his horses. "He told me that Jesus wanted my horses, but He didn't, because the missionary was using them."

The Indian couldn't quite figure out the white men or the contradiction in their churches. Grandma could tell many stories about her experiences. Some are really funny. They are sad, too, when you think of the damage all of this did to us Indians. The white men had everyone on the reservation hating each other because of religion and money. It was the white man who increased hatred among Indians.[2] Of course not all Indians followed the sacred ways in the olden days, and problems always arose. But the sacred center of the tribe gave us the right and authority to deal with our problems, and everyone could always remember our sacred values were above all to be protected.

In those early reservation days, traditional Indians used to gather on Sundays. There were no cars, just buggies, wagons, and horseback. Men would come on horseback, but also bring the family in a wagon. They would gather from all over the reservation. They would leave their homes in the morning in order to be there before noon. They would stop among the trees, in the shade, and eat their lunches. Then, after lunch, they would go up on the hill and have shinny games. That is what we called them; it is like hockey, only on land, not on ice. They used to play these games every Sunday. One had to choose sides, and a lot of people would play. They would set up goals over there, just like football goals. They meet in the center and throw the ball up in the air, and when it comes down, one team goes this way and the other side goes that way. The ball is being hit with shinny sticks. Finally, when one side gets the ball through the goal, it wins the game. They would play it again. They might play two, three games, till the late afternoon. After that, they would get over here and have horse races. Quite a few horses they would bring, all different types of horses. A bunch over there with their horses would challenge others. It might be a short distance, or long, whatever. They knew the horses that were distance runners.

This was great fun and enjoyed by everyone. You were able to see all your friends that you never saw at any other time. You could visit and play. The old men would discuss important problems, and everyone could announce times and places of important doings that might be coming up. Announcements of all events were made when everyone was together, because the Indians no longer lived in villages but were spread out.

During that time, the church Indians would be going down to their church. When they were about to go out, the missionary would say, "Now when you folks go home and go by where they are having the shinny game and racing, don't stop there. Go by and don't even look at the people. Look the other way as you go by." These were things that the missionary would tell his church members, and those were the things that would compel the Indians to hate each other, man against man. He would also tell them, "If you have any medicine bundles, get rid of them, don't keep them. Now you are in Jesus' Way; you do not need them, get rid of them." Of course, some Indians would agree and would throw their bundles away. Some burnt them, and that is the wrong thing to do anyway. You should never burn any medicines you want to get rid of. You can throw them in the river, but not burn them. You can't do just anything to get rid of something like that. If somebody has medicine that they don't want to keep, they ask me, "What do I do with these old medicine things that I can't keep? The owner has passed away now, and we do not want to keep them, what should I do?" I tell them, "Don't burn them, take them to the river, take a smoke and pray with it before you throw the sacred things in the water, but do not burn them. You may tie a heavy rock to it so it will sink; then throw it in a deep place so it will go down and not float up." Those are the things that I tell them. But then they will stop saying the prayers that they used to repeat when they kept these medicine bundles in a sacred manner. The Indians lose not only the medicines, but also their reminder of constant prayer and a sacred way of life when they relinquish the medicine bundles and stop living in the traditional manner.

Some missionaries also told everyone to burn their pipes and not to use them in offering prayers. As our people did this, we lost a great deal of the sacred presence in the tribe and also our constant reminder of our daily religious duties. This was the way that hatred and division among the Indians, because of religion, were started by the first missionaries. Today, however, most of the churches on the reservation do not forbid the Indians to practice their Indian religion. Some churches even encourage their members to go to the Sun Dance. It is good that we all work together with our prayers.[3]

There were many other changes that took place on the reservation when I was growing up, just after the turn of the century. Before the reservation days began, there were various sacred dance ceremonies practiced by all of the Plains tribes. As life for all of the Indians changed and the sacred center of the tribe became weaker, so too did we forget to maintain our old customs, especially the dance ceremonies. In place of our sacred dance ceremonies came powwow dancing. By 1910, powwow dancing was strong everywhere, and I can remember some of the old warriors that I saw as if it were yesterday. How I used to run and hide when they performed their war dances! Even in those days, people remembered the origins of the dances, and I remember the special pipe ceremonies and prayers that were always observed.

The powwow was an opportunity to come to see those who were now scattered all over the reservation, and to hear announcements of importance. As a young fellow I was able to hear the great chiefs speak and to learn from their presence. The powwow was an important way for all of the Indians to gather many times throughout the year and to honor the sacred ways that were still alive among us.

The powwows continued until about 1916, when the war broke out. That changed many things on the reservation, and people found it harder and harder to come together, and finally there was no more dancing. It was this way in about 1924, when several of us young men joined together to try to revive the Indian way of dancing.

There was a group of us who tried to reorganize those ritual dances as they had been done in the olden days. We were careful to try to reproduce the dances the correct way, according to what the old-timers told us. In olden days there was a Tail Feather Society among the Crow that had responsibility for many of the sacred dances. Each member of this society had a special set of eagle tail feathers that could only be worn by a society member. When the members danced, they imitated the movements of the bird through the dance motions. When the dancers wore all of the eagle feathers and performed, it was something to see! Because of our work in trying to reorganize the Indian way of dancing, eight of us young men were adopted into the Tail Feather Society back in 1924. Some of the original members were still living, and they wanted to show their appreciation for our efforts.

The traditional dancing died down again during the 1930s, and there was almost no Indian dancing around 1943. That is when a group of us started to revive Indian dancing. Some people called us the "crazy bunch" because they thought we were crazy to try to reestablish the Indian dancing. At that time there was no dancing at the Crow Fair that is celebrated by the entire tribe each summer. Once we rented a flat-bed truck and danced on top of it in the parade. We tried to do things so that people would be able to see the Indian dancing and would join us in our efforts. Many people did join, and the number of dancers grew. Today, there are powwows all over the country, and many, many people participate in the dances. I feel that our "crazy bunch" was in some ways responsible for this great increase in popularity of Indian dancing.

As in many things, powwow dancing, the way it is practiced today, is different from the way it was when I was a young man. There are more people enjoying the powwows, but the powwow has lost some of its meaning for some of the participants. In former days the clothing had meaning and was designed either according to established rules or according to a man's medicine or vision. Today, each person wants to be an individual, and so the ways they fix their dancing feathers are quite different. In my day, the pipe offering was an important part of the ceremony, and we performed certain dances that had special meanings. We enjoyed our dancing a great deal, and we always were aware that in performing our dances we were connected to our sacred center. Nowadays I don't see much of that awareness any more.

On the Crow reservation things may be changing. In the winter of 1981 several young men came to me and asked me to teach them the correct way of performing the Tail Feather Dance. There had been no adoptions into the Tail Feather Society, and there were only two of us still living among the eight who were adopted in 1924. As more and more people were interested in dancing over the years, new dances were created, and many of our traditional dances were lost. I was very happy with this new interest, and I helped with teaching these young men. We worked together several times, and in 1982 I adopted a young man who acquired my original eagle tail feathers. There are eight of these new owners of tail feathers, and in 1983 they performed their first complete ceremony by themselves. Now we have the dance each winter at Lodge Grass. I helped them the first few years, and now they are on their own. I was there this last winter to give them encouragement, and they did very well. They learned the special songs, the dances, and the procedures. First there is a special pipe ceremony and prayers are offered. Everyone in the dance hall is quiet, and all are participating silently with their prayers. After the pipe ceremony is completed, the owner of the drum will get up and hit the drum. That opens the way for the dancing to commence. They perform each of the ritual dances one after another, and it is very good to see! My heart was happy when they completed the evening, and now I know they can carry on this tradition.

The white men and their ways were responsible for many of the changes that came to the Indians. In reservation life problems occurred that we Indians could not manage. Our Indian dancing almost died out, but new efforts may help connect the dances with our sacred ways. There is hope for that situation, but otherwise, serious problems are noticeable and no change for the better appears to be in sight. Alcohol is one of the worst problems. It leads us into all kinds of mischief, and it causes the death of so many, many of our youngsters. They bring liquor into our reservation, and this causes these miseries.

Drugs are the same way now. The bad drugs are another thing that the white men have brought among us in just the last few years. They even use marijuana in school. I tell all young people to leave the white man's liquor and drugs alone and to come to take part in the traditional dances and come to prayer meetings. Join the prayers, stay with it.

I think what really works against the Indian is that he tries so hard to be like the white man; he will do anything that a white man does, thinking that he will be uplifted. Indians have many things that are so much better than anything the white man has. They can really be uplifted by their own sacred things, but they do not seem to realize it. We don't need modern progress, we need prayer. We don't have many traditional people left to teach them. I do not know what is going to happen to the traditional Indian way; it is disappearing so fast, it isn't the same anymore. We try to teach our children something, then they go to school and some of their friends will tell them something else, and then they are confused. Very few of the people today know why they should do this instead of that. They have no guidelines on which to judge their actions except what they see on television. Without a sacred center, no one knows right from wrong.

Their [the white men's] Wise Ones said we might have their religion, but when we tried to understand it we found that there were too many kinds of religion among white men for us to understand, and that scarcely two white men agreed which was the right one to learn. This bothered us a good deal until we saw that the white man did not take his religion any more seriously than he did his laws, and that he kept both of them just behind him, like Helpers, to use when they might do him good in his dealings with strangers. These were not our ways. We kept the laws we made and lived our religion. We have never been able to understand the white man, who fools nobody but himself.[4]
                                        —Plenty-Coups, Absaroke

5

WORKING DAYS

BOTH of my parents were born in 1863, so they were raised before the reservation days were fully upon us. My parents taught me the benefit of work, and right from the beginning I started a lifelong practice of waking before sunrise. I still have this habit although I don't work as hard during the day because of my age.

In the days when both of my parents were still living, I was always up before dawn. No one was up in the house at that time, and I was alone as I offered my morning prayer. After my prayer I dressed and went outside. I would leave my saddle horse staked outside the house on a long rope. At that time we didn't have machines, and all of our ranch work had to be accomplished with our work horses. We didn't have any pastures fenced, and so the horses would be out in the hills around our home. I would saddle up my horse and then roam the hills until I could find all of the work horses I needed for the day. It would take some time to find the scattered horses, and then I would wrangle them together and drive them down to the river for their drink of water. After they had had their fill, I would bring them in to the corral by the house, where I would harness them up and put them in the barn. I would feed them some oats so that they could have the strength to be able to work with me for the full day. By this time the sun would just be ready to come up over on the horizon.

By the time I came to the house from the barn, my mother would have breakfast ready for me. I would eat a good breakfast, and then the sun would just be up and I would be ready to go to work. I would hook the team up and go out into the fields. I enjoyed working and being outside surrounded by all the beauty of Nature. We would plow and plant in the spring, do our haying in the summer, and then harvest crops in the fall. In the winter we had to tend to the animals, and all year round we were working to keep up with this or that problem that needed attention. And so it was. I have been an early bird all my life, and that is the only way I know. My parents were responsible for my training, and for all of their help to me I felt obliged to help them in every way I could. My father passed away in 1927, and by that time I was ready to think about beginning my own family. With my two brothers and two sisters we continued to look after my mother until she passed away in 1969, when she was over one hundred years old. She remained active all through her life and even continued tanning deer hides by hand and helping around the house, up until her death.

This habit of hard work that I learned from my parents carried over to my working days for Grandma and our family. We started working for our own family after we acquired our own land together. All the Crow were given an allotment of land when we were children. Grandma's allotment was over on Pryor Creek. That is where she was born and raised, so her land was over there. After we were married in 1929, we traded the land in Pryor for the piece of land that joins mine on the east side of Wyola so that we would bring our lands together and have one large piece of land.

When we were working the land and fencing it, we spent all the spring and summer out there, and some parts of the winters also. When hard winter came, we would come back to our house, for we camped and lived in tents. Every year we usually camped up in the hills until almost Christmas. I remember the winter of 1948; that was a hard winter that people remember. We were out there until December 17. We moved just in time, for there came a storm that didn't quit until there was no getting around at all. That was the year that even trains were stalled on the railroads. In Wyola, there was no travel up the Little Horn Road. We were living up there and there was no travel with automobiles for a whole month. A lot of cattle died on account of the hard weather. It was starting to storm when we came back that day, traveling by team and wagon. The storm never quit, and we couldn't get to our haystacks, so we couldn't haul hay to feed our cattle. When the snow finally stopped, my brother Carson and I would use four horses hooked onto a bobsled to carry hay to the stock. The snow was getting so hard crusted that we would be sliding over it just like over solid ice. When we hit a soft spot, one side would go down, and over we would go. The whole load of hay would tip over. We just had the hardest time. That's probably one of the reasons why I remember the winter of 1948 so well.

All of the outside work, even in winter, was very good for us. Even today I remember all the wonderful times we had while we were young. We worked hard, but it was a good life. About the only problem that I have from those days is my snow blindness. We never had sunglasses, and we would have to spend all day out in the snow and bright sun. Sunglasses are one of the good things that the white man has brought to us.

During all those years, we tried to follow as many of the traditional ways as we knew how. I will explain many of the important ceremonies later, but all the young people should know that our outside lives kept us close to the beauty of Nature and made us physically and spiritually strong.

The traditional Indians like to take a plunge in the river to begin the morning. That is the first thing even before the offering of smoke and prayer. This purification wakes them up out of their sleep and prepares them to begin the day. It was a practice that they did in the old days even when it was winter. They were living in tipis and the camp crier would rouse the young warriors to get up. No one would refuse when the camp crier asked everyone to get up. "Get up all you young men. Get up and go take a plunge in the river." The river may have ice formed. If the river appears all frozen, there may be an opening somewhere in the ice and deep snow. They had no overshoes in those days. They put on a blanket and went down to the river, took a plunge, and came back to their tipis. After this purification the people would say their first prayer of the day with their smoke. They might stand by the river or return to the fire in the tipi, but after the plunge, the first duty of the day was prayer. This practice was taught in the olden days.

I practiced the river plunge for a while in my day. In the summer it is good; in the winter it can be difficult. I did it every summer almost until the present time. I only did it for one winter in my younger days. We camped while we were trying to get a house built. This was not long after I was married, and we still didn't have a house. It was a cold winter. The snow was deep. Our two tents were set up, and that was what we lived in. One was a cook tent, and the other we lived in and slept in. Of course we set up heating stoves in there. In the morning I was up early, put wood on the fire, and headed for the river. Grandma would get up, and while she was getting breakfast, I was at the river. The river was about twenty to twenty-five feet behind our tent. A deep swimming hole was back there, and I would get up and throw a blanket around myself. The snow was probably a foot deep outside, and I would run, and as I would get to the river bank my blanket would come off me and I would take a dive over the ice, which extended from the edge of the bank about four to five feet out toward the center. I would dive over that into this deep hole and swim around. Some of those mornings the temperature was maybe twenty or twenty-five degrees below, yet I went anyway. And that is the way the olden Indians lived. That life may seem hard, but it was good for them. It kept them healthy, in body and in spirit. I will talk more about purification when we discuss the sweat bath. The sweat bath ceremony is like a major purification, but the river plunge is a smaller purification that should be taken every day. This cleanses us physically and spiritually and prepares us to say our prayers and assume our other responsibilities.[1] We should think of the need for purification and use the sweat bath and river when we can. It may be impossible today for us to plunge into the river every day, but we should consider the type of person who could do such a thing and try to keep the same virtues that such men possessed. In those days they didn't know anything about wearing warm clothes. Yet they endured all that cold. They didn't know what an illness or a cold was.

I couldn't do that anymore, yet in the olden days even the old men followed this practice. We would go hunting way up into the mountains, and we didn't wear anything special, just ordinary clothes—of course warm clothes, woolen shirts, and so forth, but I stood a lot of cold without heavy jackets. I found out what it was like to live like the olden Indians. The warrior could endure almost anything.

We would travel as far as fifteen miles from our home to hunt for game. We would go all the way up to the mountains, leaving while it was still dark, around three to four o'clock in the morning. In the wintertime, daylight doesn't come until around six or seven o'clock. By that time we were way up in the mountains. Daybreak comes, and the trees start popping because it is so cold. That time of day is very sacred as you greet the sun.[2]

Now we are all pretty tender. We catch cold easily now, as we are living the life of the white man. We want to stay in the house where it is warm and not get out in the open where it is cold. We stick our heads out now and say, "It is cold," and we come back in and close the door and stay in. People today are missing something great—great for the body and the soul. It was good, but our ways of living are different nowadays, and we are susceptible to every illness that comes along. Nowadays no one thinks about prayer when they first rise. Up until I had my heart attack I would still jump into the river. Not every day and not through the winter, but I did go as much as I could. Even when I do not go to the river, I always put water on my face and hands and then say my prayer. I follow that custom to this day.

Now that I am older I can't work as hard as I used to work, but I still manage to occupy my time with things that need to be done. I have many responsibilities now as Sun Dance chief that I never had during my working days, but each year since I can remember I have taken the time to cultivate a good garden for my family. When the time comes, I will plow the garden and be ready to plant. I grow just about every type of food that can be planted. Last year my garden at home was about one and a half acres. It supplies us with much of our food all during the summer, and when harvest time comes, we put up as much as we can to last all through the winter. Many years ago we dug a root cellar by hand, and as you can see, it is still there. We can many of the vegetables and dry or store all of the rest. Our garden at home provides us with good home-grown produce the year round.

Out in the hills I plow and plant my potato garden. It is almost two acres in size, and each fall I can harvest several tons of potatoes. I irrigate it at least twice during the heat of the summer by diverting the stream that flows nearby onto the entire patch. The system must work well, because we almost always have a good crop.

All this is hard work, but the benefits for our family and friends are great. The exercise is good for me, and I also just love to be outside. I will be up and into the garden at the time of the sunrise, and in the cool of the morning I will work for a couple of hours before the sun is up and it gets hot. This is a sacred time of day, and I am surrounded by the sounds of Nature. To be able to greet the sun with the sounds from all of Nature is a great blessing, and it helps us to remember Who is the real provider of all of our benefits.

In my life, just as with the olden-day Indians, I have worked hard to support our family. I did not care to have more than I needed, but I did not want to wait for someone else like the BIA[3] to provide for us. We do not throw away the things that the government or the tribe gives to us, but we do not need them to provide for our needs. Today most people fall into two different types: those who want more than they need or those who expect someone else to look after them.

Because of money, many people want to accumulate more things than they really need. The machines and material wealth of this modern world allow people to be able to possess more things. Everyone wants the same thing that someone else has and everyone wants to possess something that he doesn't need. The children want toys that just make them idle their time away. None of the toys teach valuable lessons or skills to the children anymore, and some youngsters have so many toys that they do not respect the gifts that they have been given.

Too many people fall into another group that always expects something for nothing. Many of the Indian people wait for the government or the tribe to give them money so they will not have to work. Many of the Crow who want to sell our coal want all the coal money to be given to the tribal members. If this is done, then most of the money will be wasted within a week or a month. Many young men will buy a new car and drive fast and then wreck it. Others will buy alcohol or drugs. Very few will use the money wisely. After a short time, the resource will be gone, and the Crow people will have nothing to show for it.[4] Doing such things may create other problems also, like the need for more water on the part of the coal companies. The coal companies need our water to mix with the coal to make the slurry so that they can pump the coal through the pipelines to places thousands of miles away. Without the coal, they might not need our sacred water and we would not be fighting in courts over our water rights. When I see workers building something, I see that many of them just stand around and watch the few that actually work. I wonder what would happen if everyone just came and watched the other workers? Many of the things we buy are not made well, and I can see that no one cares if the thing he makes is well done. If your life depended on your weapons, and your own family used everything you made, you would do the best job you could. In our olden times, every warrior looked after those who were in need, whatever the reason for the need: illness, death, or old age. Everyone saw what was necessary and shared without asking; if someone was able to work, there was no question of not participating. Everyone wanted to do his part in the work, for himself, his family, and his tribe. Each person did his or her best, both because everyone's life depended upon it and also because each person knew this was a sacred duty and that no one else could meet Acbadadea in his or her place. To do less than the best was not possible. As the women made the clothes, shelter, and cooking items, as the men hunted or made the weapons, even to the feathers that must be put onto the arrows, all knew they had to do their best. You have tried to tan a deerskin by hand before, so you know how difficult it is to do this job well![5]

Just as the traditional Indians could not depend on someone else to do their work, they did not depend on someone else to say their prayers. Every day, in whatever they did, they lived in a sacred manner. Each of these things may seem small, but it is a series of small things that make up our lives.

In the life of the Indian there was only one inevitable duty,— the duty of prayer—the daily recognition of the Unseen and Eternal. His daily devotions were more necessary to him than daily food. He wakes at daybreak, puts on his moccasins and steps down to the water's edge. Here he throws handfuls of clear, cold water into his face, or plunges in bodily. After the bath, he stands erect before the advancing dawn, facing the sun as it dances upon the horizon, and offers his unspoken orison. His mate may precede or follow him in his devotions, but never accompanies him. Each soul must meet the morning sun, the new sweet earth and the Great Silence alone![6]

—Ohiyesa, Santee Sioux

6

HUNTING STORIES

IN my time I have had many hunting experiences: some have been successful, while others have been either empty-handed or full of laughter. Hunting was a main occupation in the traditional Indian's life, and the attitude with which each man hunted was as important as the weapons that he used. Each major hunt was started with the purification of a sweat bath and a prayer. In every case, the offering of a smoke and a prayer was always present. It should be the same way today. There is a reason to hunt, and if you just want to kill for fun, you should not hunt. We were given animals for a purpose, and through our knowledge of animals and Nature, we come closer to the Maker of All Things Above.[1] As we walk through Nature on a hunt, we should consider what we are doing. As I tell you the story of my last hunt, you can see how I understand my responsibility.

My years are up there now, where I can't stand a great deal of physical work, so I don't go hunting anymore. This last fall in October was my last hunt. I was called on to give a talk to one of the classes in Billings at Eastern Montana College, and I went to Billings for that purpose, and I wasn't thinking about hunting at all, but when we stopped for the night our host said, "I was preparing to go hunting deer tomorrow. How about you joining me and going hunting with me?"

At four o'clock in the morning we took off. We got out there into the game country just at daybreak and started our hunt at a nice place. It was hilly—mountainous, with pine trees. So we went to a point in the valley right below us, a kind of canyon. This is always good. I started out walking up that canyon. I looked to see if I could see one or the other of my hunting companions walking up that canyon or on the ridges, but I couldn't see anyone, so I kept going. To my right over here was a little creek. The creek bottom was green grass, and a little water was coming down that creek. Above me, as I walked along, were the highest cliffs. About halfway down the canyon there was another belt of rock where there were many caves. As I walked along, I saw does around but no bucks. All of the beauty around me made me think of some of the good caves. That is where the mountain little people live, in those caves.[2] These little people are spirit helpers in many ways to the Indians, as we will talk about later. Indians know about that, of course. White men may know by now that there are such little people, but they probably do not really believe it. So I stopped and I went up to one of the caves and sat down. Before proceeding in the hunt, it was necessary to stop, take a smoke, and offer a prayer to the Medicine Fathers. They will always hear the prayer of a sincere hunter and help the hunter to find success. It is not through the great skill of the hunter himself that success is achieved, but through the hunter's awareness of his place in Creation and his relationship to all things. I said, "Little people of the mountains, the caves in the mountainous areas are where you live. There must be some of you here. I am hunting. I am one of your adopted sons who works for you. You live here, and there, and not just one colony of you—there are many colonies of you along the mountains. I am hunting here today, and it has been quite a while since I did any hunting. We are looking for deer. Help me get something. If I get something I will leave part of it for you here. I will also leave some for the eagle flying up there. You will be looking down if I get something. You are my Medicine Fathers. Little people, Poor Eagle,[3] help me get something. I would like to get a little meat for my family back home. We are in need of meat." I said a prayer like that, smoking, and when I had rested a little, I started out again.

I came off the hillside and hit that path again and started going up. Pretty soon I heard a shot. Bang! It was on my left over there. So I ran a few feet and came to a log and little creek right here and a small growth of thick pines in front of me. A big cedar tree was standing here, and I got behind it, and I figured from that shot that a scared bunch of deer might be coming down my way. I was all ready, and pretty soon, sure enough, "boom, boom, boom," I could hear the thumping. He came in sight, horns like that, right across from me. The thickets were a little too thick, and you couldn't take a shot. I waited for him to come into an opening where I could shoot him. As soon as he got up on across the little creek, he turned and came towards me. I stood behind this little cedar tree in front of me, so he didn't see me. He was coming right towards me, then he turned sideways and stood still right in front of me. I fired and down he went.

The answer was immediate. About ten minutes after I took the smoke and offered the prayer, I got this. I shot him just behind the ear so there was no body shot to spoil any meat. I said a special prayer after that. I said, "Now, little people, just a few minutes ago I asked you to help me get a buck and now I have got him here. Here is the meat for you. Poor Eagle, here is some feed for you. You are my Medicine Father. You are the master of all the eagles and you will be flying up there and you will see this. I will leave this here for you. *Aho!*[4] And before we left there were two eagles flying around.

I believe I have told you that one of my main Medicine Fathers is the spikehorn elk. When Rainbow passed his power as a medicine man to me,[5] he placed the spikehorn elk inside my body. I will explain that ceremony to you later. As you know, for several years Rainbow came to our house in Wyola and spent several months at a time with us. During these visits he would mention things that I needed to know to continue fulfilling the responsibility as medicine man and Sun Dance chief. On one occasion he asked, "Do you know of any young artists that can draw an elk for you, a spikehorn elk?" I said, "Yes, one of my relatives over here is a good artist. I believe I can ask him to draw the elk for me." Rainbow said, "If he does, we can trace the drawing of the elk that he makes for you onto a piece of rawhide, and then take scissors and cut out the elk."

So, we came over to see this young artist about drawing the elk for me. He said, "All right, I know what a spikehorn elk looks like, but I've never seen one." There are not many of them, even in the mountains, for they are very rare. This animal has two long horns but no branches on his antlers, just two long slightly curved horns. The Crow call this animal *koshkisah,* which means, "the well known bugler," for this animal has the loudest call in all of Nature, and it is by this characteristic that he is named. The white man's name refers to his physical appearance, but the Indian name recognizes his position in regard to all the other animals in Nature. This animal could be considered the king of the elk, for it is the strongest and perhaps bravest of all the elk. This young man had never seen one before, but he knew what one looked like, and he agreed to help. We also told him that we needed the tips from the horns of the spikehorn elk for our ceremonies, so if he found one while he was out hunting, he should bring the horns for me to use in our Sun Dance ceremonies. This artist laughed, because he went hunting often, but he had never in his life even seen one. But he promised to help if he could.

We thanked him for his help and gave him some money and a blanket for his efforts and went home for the night. The next afternoon around three or four o'clock a pickup truck drove up our drive. I thought, "Somebody is coming; I wonder who it could be?" The young artist drove up and got out, and he was all smiles. He said, "Look what I have got for you!" We went up to him and looked into the back end of his pickup box; there was the head of a spikehorn elk, just fresh from the kill! He got one right away. We were all anxious to hear his story.

He told us about what had happened the morning after we had left. That morning, his wife was looking outside towards the river and saw some deer, right across the river from the house, so she ran and said, "Mickey, there are some deer running across over there, white-tailed deer." So the young man grabbed his rifle, grabbed some ammunition, and ran out of the house only to see the deer walk away into the woods. He decided, "I'll go across the river and try to find them." There were some fallen trees on which the deer had crossed like on a natural bridge across the creek, so he walked over these logs to get on the other side. He saw the tracks, but the deer had gone into the thick timber already, and he couldn't see them. On the other side of the woods is a meadow where he keeps some horses, so he decided to go through the woods and catch one of his horses that he would need later in the day. He walked up the little hill and saw his horses, but something was bothering them. And then he saw a spike-horn elk that had come from someplace and was chasing them around, herding them around. He said to himself, "Am I seeing things?" It was a spikehorn elk, no other. He rubbed his eyes with his hands several times to make sure; he thought he was seeing things. The elk went chasing the horses around and then stopped and stood still. My friend took a good aim and shot it; down it went. Sure enough, he had just what we needed.

We were surprised to see him so soon. Of course everyone realized that this was a miracle and that the elk had come to present itself to us to help us in our prayers. We were grateful to the elk and to the Medicine Fathers for helping us out so quickly. We still use the one antler tip in each of my monthly Sun Dance prayer ceremonies, and the other tip is used to doctor with. I hollowed out the tip so that I could blow through it onto the part of the patient that may need special attention. You have seen me use both of the antler tips, but you may not have heard me tell the story of how I received them. This hunting story was successful because of the Sun Dance Medicine Fathers.

I will tell a short story about a little fishing trip we took. We wanted to go up the river a short walk and fish our way back down to the house. I went with my niece's husband, who is a Cherokee boy from North Carolina who now lives in Montana. They had come up to visit us, and the sun was out when they arrived. There was a storm brewing up in the west; dark clouds were there, indicating that there was a rainstorm coming soon. We went anyhow ahead of that storm. We went up the river to where there are several good fishing holes, while the women were home cooking dinner. All we took was our fishing poles, fishhooks, and grasshoppers for our bait. We started fishing, and that storm was fast approaching. It was dark and we could see that when it came, there was going to be a downpour of rain. So we hurried and fished a little bit. We just hadn't caught anything yet. Finally, we had to pull up our lines and start running for home, because that storm was coming fast.

This was the month of June when the grass along the river banks was high, especially the timothy and clover that grow up tall. It was up to about our hips. We were taking a straight route towards the house, cutting across the fields. A fence runs between my house and the neighbor's land, and along that fence goes a power line. The electric poles go along this fence through the timber and on to the other side of the river. As we were approaching that fence the rain was just about on us and we were running fast. All of a sudden, about a couple of steps ahead of us, a pheasant flew up and scared us so that we stopped right there. This bird was thinking about us down below, and I guess it didn't think about what was ahead of it, because it was flying right straight up toward the power line. We didn't have a gun, but I acted like I was carrying a shotgun. I threw up my fishing pole, held it up, and aimed at the pheasant as if I had a shotgun in my hand. As I aimed at it, I said "Bang!" and pretended to shoot the bird. It hit the wires. It was a big rooster pheasant. The way it hit those wires must have caught it so that its neck was twisted around the wires. As I said "Bang," the pheasant fell just as if it were hit with a shotgun blast, and it dropped down to the ground right onto the path where we were going to cross the fence.

I turned to my nephew and said, "Pick it up, you will have the bird I caught for you." He picked it up and said, "Well, I didn't think anything like that would happen." We ran in the house with a bird instead of a fish. The women were getting their skillets ready for the fish that we were to bring in, but here we brought a bird. So that's the way I killed a pheasant with a fishing pole. I tell this and people don't believe it could happen, but it is a fact; that is the way the story went.

I know all sportsmen especially like to hear stories like the one I am going to tell now. I have had some funny experiences, and when I tell people, they hardly know whether to believe what I tell them. This time it was in the late winter, and we were still feeding cattle. It was almost early spring, but there was snow on the ground yet. My brother's cattle and mine were all running together. This one morning, as we fed the cattle, we noticed a fresh deer track in the snow. We saw that and we said, "This deer will be right up here somewhere; it will be in the timber very close to us." So we unloaded our hay and we hurried to begin our hunt. Soon I heard a shot, and I knew my nephew had found the deer. It was a young buck deer, and he had a good set of horns on him. The deer stopped and looked at my nephew, who didn't take time to get off from his horse but pulled out his rifle and shot at the deer. The deer went down from that one shot. I came away from the river and came to where my nephew was. He didn't get off his horse, and he was looking down at the deer. I said, "Did you get him?" He said, "Yes, he is there on the ground kicking around." So I said, "I'll cut his throat; here, hold my horse."

I gave him the reins of my horse, and he held them while I got off. The deer was lying on the ground kicking around, wanting to get up, but he couldn't. I figured he was hit pretty well. What I wanted to do was to get up to him and cut his throat and let it bleed, for that is the thing to do; it is quick and painless for the animal. So I went to him and got my knife out. I took hold of the horns and pulled his head, but at that moment he came to his senses and jumped up on his feet in front of me.

When he jumped up, I threw my knife and grabbed the other horn so I had him facing me, and I had him at the base of his horns. I saw that my nephew's shot was just a little nick on the base of the horn. It had stunned the deer when the bullet hit there, but it had not hurt him in any way. When I got hold of him, he had his senses back again and he was ready to go, but I wouldn't let him go. He would jump and try to jerk away from me, but I held on. Every time he jumped, we went round and round. When he came up off his feet, he would come up with his hind legs all the way up to my hands to try to kick my hands off from his horns and he would hit my hands. My hands were bare; I didn't have my gloves on, so when he hit my hands with both feet, he cut them badly. My nephew was just frozen there on his horse, watching the merry-go-round that I was having with the deer.

Finally, I figured that when he would come up with all four feet off the ground up into the air, there would be the time for me to flip him down to the ground. So when he jumped with all four feet up in the air, I gave him a sudden twist, and he missed the ground and went down. I quickly straddled my legs around his neck and locked my feet under him. He tried to get up, but I held him down with my weight.

After we were down on the ground, he still kicked, and when he did that he started tearing up my pants from my knees down with his hooves. His hooves were just like sharp knives. But I wouldn't let go. I hollered at my nephew to give me my knife. He got off the horse, found the knife, and handed it to me. Then I was able to cut the throat and the deer started to bleed. He soon was finished, and I was thankful that my fight was over. The deer put up a great fight, but on that day it was my turn to win. We ate well for several days, and I soon recovered from my wounds.

You have heard me tell many of my other adventures as a hunter. Everyone laughs when they hear the story of how I "roped" fish with just some copper wire, and almost no one believes that I shot thirty-three ducks with three shots from my shotgun. I still believe that might be a world record! I hid for several hours in the big straw pile by the edge of the wheat field that had just been harvested. Hundreds of ducks used the field as a roosting place for the night, and I used it as a hunting ground. Even I was surprised when I finished putting the ducks into my gunny sack and realized that there were thirty-three in all and that I had averaged eleven ducks a shot. I have never heard anyone top that record.

As a younger man, when we were out working our cattle we often came upon deer, and occasionally I was caught without a gun. At these times I still tried to catch the deer and once jumped from a cliff onto a deer. It was winter, and I saw the fresh tracks in the snow, so I knew that a deer was just over the hill. I quietly crawled over the rocks and found myself looking down on a big doe about fifteen feet below. I jumped and sailed through the air and came down on top of it. I straddled the deer as we fell to the ground and cut its windpipe with my knife. The deer was surprised, and so were the men I was working with when they realized what I had done.

On two occasions I had to rope a deer, and once I even roped an elk. The first time, we were up on Owl Creek in a grainfield. I saw the deer while I was on horseback and watched as my brother-in-law scared it and the deer started to run toward me. As I came toward the deer, it was looking back toward my brother-in-law. When the deer finally saw me, I had already taken my rope off the saddle and was ready for a deer roping. It happened just like you see a steer roping in the rodeo, and I made a lucky catch and looped the rope over my saddle horn to keep it from breaking loose. My brother-in-law finally came up and shot it. It was impossible to approach the deer while it was on the end of the rope.

All of these stories are fun to hear, and they bring back memories of wonderful times. As we consider the fun of hunting, we should also remember the importance of hunting to the Indians and the attitudes with which each hunter should approach his goal. Indians of olden days depended on hunting for their survival, and it was almost an everyday occupation. Without it they would quickly perish. Today, we still need meat, because it is difficult to afford the basic things we need to survive. Hunting is necessary to the Indian, and it can also be a source of great enjoyment to be in contact with the beauty of our natural surroundings, but we must not forget the proper attitudes toward the game we seek and our relationship with all things. These attitudes must be present not only when we hunt animals, but also as we try to find other types of objects. One example can be seen when you hear the story of how I seek and gather the sacred medicines that I use in my doctoring ceremonies.

Our Medicine Fathers have given us two main plant medicines to use in our healings. I use other medicine in my doctoring, the most important of which is probably the power that has been put directly into my body by the Medicine Fathers and which is transferred to any patient through my eagle feathers and my prayers. However, I have been told to use two types of plant medicines with my patients, and these also are important to insure success. One of the medicines is called "lightning root" and the other "deer weed." These plants only grow in one place in the world, and that is over at a certain place on the Shoshone reservation, close to where Rainbow, the great Shoshone medicine man, had his great vision. We will talk much more of Rainbow later, but you should know that these two medicines were shown to Rainbow after his great vision. They are given to us by our Medicine Fathers.

Rainbow first took me to this sacred place many years ago. Each time I go to this spot, I follow the same procedures that Rainbow taught me long ago, and I was always successful in my mission. First, you have to drive up the mountain until the dirt road ends, and then you have to take a little walk up into a certain valley. On my first trip with Rainbow, after we walked just a short way, he said, "Now stop. We must offer a smoke and prayer before we go on and start looking for our medicine." We both took off our hats and laid them aside and prepared our tobacco to be ready to offer smoke and prayer. When we were ready, he said, "Look up there at that big rock. Do you see anything?" Upon the hillside there was a big boulder about fifteen feet off of the ground, and on top of this rock, two eagles were sitting and watching us. All during our prayer those two eagles sat there and watched. One was a bald eagle and the other one was a golden eagle, two different kinds of eagles. They were working together and watching over the sacred medicine. In our prayer, we said a few words just for these two eagles. "Thank you, *Aho!* You are here to guard this sacred medicine and this is good. It is to be preserved for the benefit of those who are authorized by our Medicine Fathers to use it in their healing. We have been authorized to use it, and we are here to take just enough to help us heal the sick and needy. Your power is great, and you know what is in our hearts. Help us, show us the medicine. *Aho!*"

After our prayer, we took just a few steps and Rainbow said, "Look! That is lightning root. We will dig this one." I never knew what the plant looked like. It looks something like sage from above the ground, but it is different. Under the ground there is a root, and that is the part we need. We will dig it all up when we are on the hillside and we will peel off the covering later and keep the body of the little root. We need to prepare it into a fine powder for use in our medicine, but that is all done later. We dug for about an hour and found many of the plants, enough for our use. We were told by our Medicine Fathers that a person living close by could take no more than six at any one time. It is important to take only what is necessary and never too much. The sacred medicines are well protected just where they are. I am allowed to take more for my use because I have to drive over three hundred miles to come to this place, and it is difficult for me to make that journey.

After we dug the lightning root, we took out our sacks and cut the deer weed. It grows above the ground in bushes, and it is easier to find. We boil this plant and make a brew that looks like tea. You have tasted deer weed and you know how bitter it can be to drink. But the results of its use are great. It doesn't take much. Just a pinch of lightning root or a small glass of deer weed will be all that is needed. It doesn't need a large quantity because of its great power.

The total time necessary to collect both plants is usually no more than two hours. When we are finished, we always stop and thank the two eagles for their help. On several occasions, after I had collected the medicine, the two eagles soared high above in the sky, and that is a beautiful sight to see. These two eagles can be considered as the protectors of our sacred medicine, and when you hear me speak about the "two eagles," you will know the meaning: those who are sent from Above to protect our sacred treasures.

I have been to this spot many, many times over the years, and I have always seen the eagles there. I have taken my grandson with me before, and he knows now where to go. When he recently went on my behalf, he offered his smoke and prayer and the two eagles knew what was in his heart and allowed him to find the medicine. I have been asked the location of the medicine by many people, and I have never let it be known. Many years ago, when Rainbow was asked by different men about this sacred spot, he told two different people. Neither person had his authorization to use the medicine, and they probably desired to make their own medicine without proper instruction or authority. One man went to the spot and was driven away by the eagles, who immediately knew his intention and attacked him. About fourteen or fifteen years ago, another man came to the spot and searched for hours without finding the sacred plant. The eagles just sat and watched as this man spent the day looking for medicine with no success. A short time after that man's failure, Rainbow and I went to the spot and found all the medicine we needed.

You can see by this account how important it is to have the right intention in everything you undertake. You are always being watched from Above in whatever you do, and you will sooner or later receive the consequences of your actions. Acbadadea is beyond all things of this world, but He is also within all things, and His representatives are like the two eagles who protect all of his sacred treasures. So everyone should realize that a man's actions and intentions are observed and that even the way in which he fulfills his daily chores is important. A man's attitude toward the Nature around him and the animals in Nature is of special importance, because as we respect our created world, so also do we show respect for the real world that we cannot see.[6]

We did not think of the great open plains, the beautiful rolling hills, and winding streams with tangled growth, as "wild." Only to the white man was Nature a "wilderness" and only to him was the land "infested" with "wild" animals and "savage" people. To us it was tame. Earth was bountiful and we were surrounded with the blessings of the Great Mystery. Not until the hairy man from the east came and with brutal frenzy heaped injustices upon us and the families we loved, was it "wild" for us. When the very animals of the forest began fleeing from his approach, then it was that for us the "Wild West" began.[7]

—Chief Standing Bear, Oglala Sioux

7

TRAVELS NEAR AND FAR

IT seems as if I have been on the move for most of my life, yet Grandma traveled even more than I did. She is the famous one in the family, next to my brother, Bob, that is. During my life with Grandma we received more blessings than anyone can possibly imagine, and in turn we have always tried to live according to our traditional Indian way. We all hear of the travels of Indians before the reservation days, and I guess I have carried on that tradition also.

My travels started when I was a young man, before my family days, when I would participate in different horse races. The two events that I chose are no longer in use today, probably because they are too dangerous. The wild horse race was really something to see. They would bring a group of wild horses into an arena surrounded by grandstands so the horses couldn't get out. They were fierce horses, and watching them try to keep away from everyone was exciting. Trying to catch them with a lasso could also be very difficult. Each rider had two helpers to give him extra manpower. After we caught a horse we had to subdue it enough to put a hackamore over its head. It would have been impossible to put anything in the horse's mouth, so we just put on that type of halter so we would have reins to hold. When each man had a horse ready, the announcer would start the race. The two helpers were allowed to assist until the saddle was on and cinched up tight; then they would jump away, and you were on your own. It was a struggle just to mount the saddle with the horse all spooked and jumping up everywhere. If you were successful in climbing into the saddle you had to run the horse around the track and across the finish line. It may sound easy, but this was really unpredictable. I remember one race in which I was trying to convince my horse to go around the track and I thought I was making progress. All of a sudden another rider went past me going the other way! It took me a moment to realize that I was right and he was going in the wrong direction. That rider probably knew he had a problem but he may have been happy enough just to be on top of the horse and not on the ground. I never was able to win one of these races, but it was good practice and great fun to participate.

I also competed in the relay horse race. In this race each contestant had four horses, and he had to ride each one around a track one time. At the start of the race you were on your first horse, saddled and all ready to go. When the race commenced, you went around the track until you came back to the start, where your helper was waiting with your other three horses. Each of the fresh horses already had a bridle and reins, but no saddle. When the racer stopped, he had to unsaddle his horse and transfer the saddle to the next horse, cinch it up, mount, and be off. It didn't take much time to transfer, but the difficulty was that one man and one saddle had to ride four different horses.

I did well in these races until my relay race at the Sheridan Rodeo in Sheridan, Wyoming, ended my racing days. I was in the lead after the first horse, and I jumped off quickly and transferred the saddle and was off. I was still leading after the second horse as I came in for my second exchange. I was in too much of a hurry, and I must not have tightened the saddle very well. After I mounted the third horse, we were off at full speed and went flying down the straight part of the track. Everything went well until a curve, when the saddle kept going straight instead of turning with the horse. As I went over with the saddle, I realized that the seat of the saddle would end up under the horse's belly between its flying legs and that this was not the best position in which to ride the horse! I let go and went flying through the air and came down head first; it was a wonder I didn't break my neck. I hit the ground and was twisted over and over and over, I don't know how many times. When I stopped, I hit the outside fence of the track, and at least I was away from the path of the other horses that soon came charging by. It must have been quite a sight: both my fall and my horse crossing the finish line first with no rider and an upside-down saddle. Some of the spectators must have been very puzzled. I had to go to the doctor, but nothing was broken and I only had a sore back; but I also had a valuable lesson, and I never participated in those events again.

After my marriage we continued our travels. My farthest travel was with Grandma. As you know, I loved to dance in the Indian way, and with five other couples we went on a six-month goodwill dance tour of Europe, North Africa, and the Holy Lands sponsored by the State Department in 1952. We had many, many experiences during that time. We met some people during that trip who have remained close friends throughout our lives. Those friendships have been important, and in many ways that trip provided blessings I could not have imagined before we began our journey.

We started out in Sweden and then went to Norway, Finland, and Denmark. From Germany we proceeded to Belgium and from there we went to France. From Paris we flew to the Middle East and Israel before returning to Europe, where we played in Italy. We took a one-week vacation while we were in Italy, and Grandma and I went over the Swiss Alps to stay with friends in Switzerland.

After we returned to Italy, we flew to Morocco and then finished our tour in Spain, where we gave our farewell performances. The stories I can tell from our adventures would take too long to recount. We enjoyed bringing our Indian dances to many people from all over the world, and it made us feel good to know that so many people loved the Indian traditions. All during our performances we attempted to be as authentic as possible in every way. We showed the different dances and carried out parts of ceremonies in the correct way. Many people saw our performances, and all of the compliments we received made us feel good. The trip produced great benefits both for the performers and the audiences.

We have met interesting people, and our life has been full

of meaning and blessings. We have a great family, and the three children Grandma and I produced were just the start of the children we raised in one way or another in our home. Now our grandchildren and great-grandchildren are spread far and wide. My travels now are mostly limited to fulfilling my responsibilities. I have traveled to the four directions and now I wish to remain at the center.

What is life? It is a flash of a firefly in the night. It is a breath of a buffalo in the winter time. It is as the little shadow that runs across the grass and loses itself in the sunset.[1]
—Chief Crowfoot (Isapwo Muksika), Blackfoot

8

RAINBOW

JOHN Trehero, the Shoshone medicine man whose traditional name is Rainbow, has been one of the greatest medicine men of this century. He is still living today at almost one hundred years old.[1] He has been a medicine man ever since he had his great vision many years ago. After that vision he had the power and the right to run the Sun Dance for the Shoshone and the Crow. I do not know just what year it was when he went fasting on the mountain, over there on his reservation. He did not go alone; he went with two of his friends. The three of them went together up on the mountain above Din-woody Lake, about forty miles west of Fort Washakie. They found a cave, and they went into this cave. They went past the entrance, into an area that was like a room. The cave goes on way back into the mountain. How far it went they did not know. They knew it was the cave where the little people live, so they went there to fast on their vision quest. Upon their arrival it was getting dark, so they started right in. All at once a roar—thunder—came. There was lightning and thunder, but there was no storm coming. It was just to test them to see if they were sincere, to see if they would stay or whether they would get out and run. When the lightning and thunder roared all at once, the other two men ran out of there and beat it away from the mountain. They thought that John would come along. So they gave up right then and there. They went home and John stayed.

Rainbow spent three days there before he came out. On the third day he kept hearing a bell, drum beat, singing, way down deep in the cave. It was all dark, but he kept hearing this bell ringing, drumbeat, way back there, and he wondered what it was. Finally, he was visited by a little man. He came from the middle of the mountain, where it was dark. This little man, named Seven Arrows, had come to visit him. He said, "I see you have the nerve to stay. I see you are sincere. Your friends have gone home. I would like to take you back in here, show you some things." So John got up and the little man took him way back there into the mountain. They came to a place where some men were playing a game. This game was throwing a spear or lance at a rolling hoop, like throwing darts at rolling wheels. It was a gambling game. He stopped and after watching it a few minutes, the little man said, "All right, you saw that, now let's go on further." They came to another big cavern with people there, and another kind of gambling; it was horse racing. The little man had John watch that for a little while, then he said, "All right, let's go again." They went on. This time they came to a hand game, and they stopped and the little man had John watch that awhile. In a hand game, one side tries to trick the other opposing side, which will guess which man's hand is hiding an object. People still play it today. So, the little man said, "That's not good. Now you have seen that, let's go on further."

They went way on into the hill, and another drum was beating as they approached. As they drew closer to the drum, they saw a tipi, and the bottom of the tipi was rolled up halfway to let in air, for there was a sick person in there. There was suffering that they could hear as they approached. They could also hear that an Indian doctoring session was going on. A drum was used. One beats the drum and sings a song while the medicine man is working on the patient. They stopped to see this now. John stood out there and watched the medicine man working on the patients. John could see that this patient was a real skinny person, practically just skin and bones. The medicine man was working on that man with medicine songs being sung for him. After the medicine man had finished working on the sick person, he gathered up his things and left. So that was the fourth thing, the last thing, that the little man wanted to show John. The little man said, "This is what I am going to give you; this is what is good. I know you are sincere and will use your powers only for what is good. I want you to go back now; go back, take up your fasting. You should not use what I am going to give you to do any of the other gambling things that you saw back there. Go back home now, and I will tell you later what things I want you to work with. You will be able to help people to get well when they are sick. Now take up your fast and go from the mountain down to that lake and wash up, take a swim." So John said, "All right." Seven Arrows escorted him back to the entrance of the cave.[2]

Rainbow left the cave and got up on the ridge and looked down over the country and the lakes down there. There are two lakes, good-sized lakes, called Dinwoody Lakes. There is a narrow place in the middle of the two lakes. I have taken baths there when we camped along the lake with John. A few years ago, we went with John to this place on the upper lake. We saw where he had fasted and where he received his medicine, the skins of the animals, the little pipe and tail feathers, where he had been given powers. Ever since that first vision quest, he started to work on sick people, and he has followed the traditional Indian ways. Seven Arrows has always come to Rainbow to point out the path to him so that he would not fall away.

In trying to follow the different Indian ways, Rainbow started to go to peyote meetings. He went a few times, three or four times. In the summertime he also participated in a Sun Dance on another reservation. It was not the Shoshone way of the Sun Dance but the Sun Dance of a different tribe. He thought he might be able to go to both, and he just did not know which way he wanted to take up and stay with. He was being watched whatever he was doing, whatever religion he went to. So Seven Arrows came to him and he told John, "Now, John, you are trying to follow two religions. I have seen you going to two: the Sun Dance and the peyote. Now, it is up to you, John, you pick one."

And Seven Arrows went on, "Make your own decision. There are two trails there, look and see. You can see two trails leading away from where we are, way on over the hills. One

of them stops right over there." John could see the end of that
trail. The other one kept on going, over hills and into the
horizon, and John could not see the end of it. Seven Arrows
said, "So now you see those two trails. That one that ends
over there is the peyote way. That is how far it goes. The other
one goes on and on and there is no end to it. That is the Sun
Dance trail; it is straight and will take you as far as you can
travel. Now it is up to you; choose one of those, and drop the
other one. Peyote does not belong to you; it belongs to the
Mexicans. But this Sun Dance way is an Indian religion and
belongs to your people."

So John said, "I was young yet and I wanted to keep going
to the Sun Dance and to the peyote religion; but according to
what I was told, I had to choose one and drop the other. I
could see myself that the Sun Dance religion goes a long way
and this other one does not go very far." He said, "I decided
to drop the peyote religion and follow only the Sun Dance
religion."

Many young men now are trying to follow both ways. They
attend peyote meetings and then, when the Sun Dance comes,
they go in there also. In this manner they try to belong to both
religions, and this is not good for anyone. When someone
tries to follow both paths, he is asking for trouble.[3] Years ago
a father and his son both brought peyote items into the Sun
Dance lodge against my wishes. I told them it was not good,
but they brought them into the Sun Dance anyway. They did
not last long after the dance was over. Both the father and the
son died the next year. You can see how important it is not to
break any of the rules of the Sun Dance.

After dropping the peyote way, Rainbow said, "I was going
only to the Sun Dances, and I was given more power. I was
told what to do, given medicine things, and told how to use
them. Seven Arrows gave me all the things I needed to work
with. He also told me all the rules and how to run the Sun
Dance in the Shoshone way so that our traditional way was
restored. It was Seven Arrows and all of the Medicine Fathers
who gave me the authority to officiate the Sun Dances every
summer among my people.[4] I kept on gaining a little more

and more power and knowledge; then I started coming over
to the Crow reservation and ran Sun Dances there every year
in the summer. So I would lead dances over at Fort Washakie,
then over here at Crow, then, I would go the other way over
to Utah and run the Sun Dance over there for the Ute. I also
helped the Bannock Indians in Idaho. So every year I would
dance three or four times in one summer. As I was getting
older, the work was starting to get hard for me. Young men
saw that I was getting older, and they started coming to me
and asking me if they could have my medicine things and
powers, take my place and relieve me, so I could retire. I was
still going right along yet, getting old, but still going. Finally,
Seven Arrows said, 'Rainbow, there have been several men
who have come to ask you for your medicine things. Those
men are not worthy to replace you. They are not the kind of
men that could, that should, have your medicine things and
replace you. Do not give in to any of them; we will find a man
for you. We are looking for your successor.' "

So Rainbow told me, "I did what I was told; I would not
give in to those who asked for my powers.[5] Finally, we were
having a Sun Dance at Shoshone. I was leading it, and quite
a few Crow were there, dancing. The dance went on and the
weather was hot, very hot. On our second day, when I was
working on the sick who came in, there came a whisper, right
in my ear, while I was at the center tree. The whisper said,
'John, tomorrow, when you finish this dance, but before you
go out of here, you give your little feathers I gave you to the
fourth man from the left. Do this before you go out of the
lodge. He is the man who is to keep the feathers. I will tell
you later what else to do.'

"I came back to my place, and I looked to the fourth man
from my left. When I looked over there, I saw that it was you.
So I called you and I told you that you were to have my
feathers. I have loved them; they have done a lot of good
things for me and have helped my people. I continued using
this little feather fan, for there were more people who were
coming in to be doctored. The next day, around noon, I was
through with it and I turned it over to you. The next winter I

came over to the Crow reservation at Christmastime to visit and to see the Indian dances." These are just powwows, social dances that the Crow have every year, at that time for four straight nights.

John went on with his story. He said, "On the second night of the dances, the people were starting to come, so I sat back there, by myself, where the men sit. I was alone, and a whisper came, 'John, now that door is closed. The person who comes in is going to be a Sun Dancer; this person coming in is the man who is selected to follow you, to be your successor.' I did not know yet for sure who my successor would be. I knew the little people were selecting my successor, and I was eager to see who would walk in that door next. After a while, that door opened and in walked a man and wife. The woman walked over and sat down among the women, and this man, who had his dancing costume on with feathers and bells, walked right straight over to me and shook hands with me. He sat with me and visited with me. I did not tell you that you were the man, that you were going to be my successor. I went home; then the next summer, I came back again."

John came to the Crow reservation quite often. He is part Crow, so he comes a lot. He speaks the Crow language fairly well. He came to stay with me. Grandma had gone back east to Washington. We were bachelors together for a month.

In the meantime, John came over to visit. One morning, after we had sent the children to school, John said, "I want to get hold of a tape recorder. There are some songs I want to sing for you so you can learn them."

That day we borrowed a tape recorder and went to town to buy a blank tape. After supper, John said, "These songs that I am going to sing for you are for your prayer meetings. It is a requirement of the Sun Dance to have a special prayer ceremony every month, and these will be used at that time. You sing these songs when you don't have any singers to help you. These three songs replace their singing."[6] He sang them: The first one is the "Opening Song" in the prayer meeting, and the next one is called the "Midnight Song" or the "Song of All the Birds in the Universe." Then the last song is the

"Closing Song." The grandchildren were sitting down, and they were listening and looking on at what we were doing. After singing the three songs, he said, "Let's stand up and you face the east and I will get in back of you. I want to say a prayer for you, and I am going to blow on your back, between your shoulders." So he had me stand in front of him, and he got behind me. He took a smoke. John does not smoke at any other time, only in order to offer a prayer. When we got through with his prayers, he said, "I am going to blow on your back." All this time the kids were watching him with wide-open eyes. He put his hand against my back, between my shoulders here. "Shuhhhh!" He blew hard like that, and when he did that, the spikehorn elk was right here, in the room, bugling loudly. The spikehorn elk has the loudest call of any animal in all Nature. When *koshkisah* bugled inside the house, you can imagine the fright that the grandchildren had. They all jumped behind chairs for cover. They were so frightened that they just peeked out from behind the furniture.

When he blew on my back, I could feel something like a streak of hot energy penetrating into my body through my back. "Now, Tom, the elk is in your body. The spikehorn elk is your main medicine, and the spirit of the elk is in you. He will stay with you all of the time. Your other Medicine Fathers are Seven Arrows, the chief of the little people; the buffalo; the eagle (he calls him Poor Eagle); and up from the far north, way up where the cold comes from, you have two Medicine Fathers you call on when you have your meetings: the white goose and the otter. All six of them. You can call on any or all of your Medicine Fathers." Then he told me what this was all about: "You are the selected man to replace me, and my things are going to go to you now. That is why I am doing this. You have these three songs that we put on your tape. Now the elk is in you. That is what they want me to do, and you are going to be their selected man to be the Sun Dance Chief. This is good. You are selected among five tribes here in Montana, Idaho, Wyoming, and Utah, among all the people who are following the Sun Dance religion. Among all of these people, they have looked for a man: among the Ute; the Bannock; my own people, the Shoshone; the Arapaho; and the Crow. There are a lot of men, and among all these they have selected you to replace me. Now I will retire and you can carry on. But I will stay with you, help you along, until you know it yourself and can conduct the Sun Dance and all the other things that are required. I will give you everything that needs to be used in all these ceremonies. I will show you how to use it all, and I will help you along until you finally have it. Then I will stay away, but I will be with you if you call me." So John didn't quit dancing. He went into dances with me yet; he liked to be there. I would be the one to take care of things, but he would be there to give me instructions if I missed a little something.

He stayed with me every summer for about four years or so. I think the first summer you lived with us, in 1971, was the last summer that John stayed with us. The next summer was his last Sun Dance. You remember that he helped in the Sun Dance that summer and said the morning prayer on the third day during the Sunrise Ceremony.[7] It was after that when he said, "You have got everything pretty well; you are understanding everything now. I will retire." And that is what he did. By that time he could hardly get around anymore, for he was almost ninety. He could dance, he could go forward all right, but he couldn't dance backwards. The year after that, at Lodge Grass, he fasted inside the lodge but did not dance or officiate. The next three or four years after that he would stay outside, at the camp.

One year he said, "I have turned over everything except one thing that I can't take out, like the elk I put into you." He said he had a snake inside of him, a rattlesnake. He told that to Grandma. "I have got only one thing now, Grandma. I will give it to you, if you want it!" Grandma said, "I am afraid of rattlesnakes, I won't have anything to do with them. Keep it." That was pretty good. John was always quite the one to make a joke. Everyone had a good laugh.

At the last dance he was in, at Pryor, he called the announcer, Allen Old Horn, at the entrance and told him to come into the sacred part of the lodge. He told Allen what to say, so Allen said to everyone, "Listen, Absaroke people. The old man has something to tell us. He wants to announce that time has passed. You have all seen him over here with the Crow, to lead Sun Dances for you. Now he is getting old, he can't run the Sun Dance anymore, so he is being retired, and after this he may not dance anymore. But hear this . . . Tom, come up here, Tom Yellowtail. . . . Here is your new man now to replace the old man. He is your man among you to lead your dance as Sun Dance chief. Nobody else has the authority, so call on him. He is your man."[8] People heard on that day. After that, the next year, whoever wanted to sponsor a dance got in contact with me, and I went along with them, wherever it was. It has been that way since about 1971. Every year since, we have had one or two, most times two, dances a year.

In officiating the Sun Dance, I use the pipe and feathers that Seven Arrows gave to John when John had his great vision. The old man has been leading Sun Dances over at the Shoshone reservation since well before 1941, when the Crow first started them on our reservation. Late in the '30s, a Crow man, William Big Day, went over there to Shoshone reservation and danced. There wasn't anybody interested in the Sun Dance at Crow at all. William Big Day went over there and danced a couple of times, and then he brought the dance back to the Crow.

John directed Sun Dances when he was quite a young man, leading dances among the Shoshone and others at the time. He would dance over among the Ute, and so forth. They were dancing already before 1941 over at the Ute reservation. It wasn't until this man among the Crow went over there and finally brought the dance over here. He asked John to come and conduct it for him. So Rainbow did; he came and ran it. It was in 1941 that the Crow started up again. And ever since, every year, the Crow have had a Sun Dance. The last time that the Crow had a Sun Dance before that was in the late 1800s. The white man stopped the Indians from any further Sun Dances because of their piercing and torturing of themselves. They figured it was too severe. Actually, the white men wanted to stamp out all of the religion of the Indians so

that they could make white men out of them, but of course
they didn't say that. So it must have been during the 1890s
when they stopped any further dances. There weren't any
more dances for a long time at Crow—till 1941.

It was really Seven Arrows who preserved the Sun Dance
and instructed John on the correct way of the traditional
Shoshone-style Sun Dance, and that it why we refer to him
as the owner of the Sun Dance. The Sun Dance that I run now,
that John ran, is the same Sun Dance that the Shoshone had
in the olden days. It is a traditional dance that is similar to the
old Crow Sun Dance in many ways, but the present form
originally belonged to the Shoshone tribe. The Arapaho have
a different way from the Shoshone. The Shoshone and Arapaho are next-door neighbors from each other. The Arapaho
dance three days, and the songs are the same, but the way
they perform their dances is different. It is a stationary dancing; they do not dance forward toward the center tree, like
you have seen in our style of dancing. They dance in one place
on the perimeter of the lodge. It is the same kind of lodge, but
they dance just up and down, that's all. The Crow and the
Shoshone owe Seven Arrows thanks for having preserved the
dance. He explained things to John and taught him all the
rules over a period of years just like John did for me. Of
course, no one else could see Seven Arrows when he gave
instructions to John. I do not think that we should describe
Seven Arrows or any of his people. They represent, and pass
on, the power of God, the Maker of All Things, and this is
something we should not say more about.

I will soon be eighty, and I don't think I can keep up my
responsibility of leading the Sun Dance for many more years—
perhaps five or six more. After my heart attack it is more
difficult for me to do certain things. When I have to doctor all
those people on the second day of the Sun Dance, it is almost
as much as I can do. Standing up there in the hot sun all day
and working with my feathers takes a lot out of me. I am
starting to consider a successor now—someone younger who
can take over my duties and run the Sun Dance for many
years to come. I have been praying to the Medicine Fathers to

select a man for me, someone who is sincere and who will be able to carry on. "You have selected me to be your man—to carry on the ways that You have shown to us. I didn't ask to have this responsibility, but after You selected me, I have tried my best to do everything You asked. I have always prayed and tried to live my life in the straight path. You need someone to work among my people so that they will know what is expected of them. If You are willing to have me live longer to serve like I am doing now, then I am going to serve as long as I am able; but as time goes on and I get older, it gets harder for me, and You may want someone to take over my duties. It will take me several years to train a man to take over all of my duties. Help me to select a man who can be strong to carry on for You. I am looking now to see who might be the one, and I am asking You to help me in selecting the right man."

I believe that all indications are clear that a good man is available soon. I will approach him and begin to instruct him in the same way that John taught me; it will take four or five years before everything is complete, and in this way the Sun Dance will be carried on for our Absaroke people.

Rainbow is known by just about all the Indians who follow our Sun Dance way. He not only led the Sun Dance for many of the tribes; he also was responsible for many great healings through his medicine powers. For these reasons many people knew about him and told stories about his most famous healings. Of course John himself never talked about his healings, but others always did. I asked John once about a famous healing story I had heard, and he gave me the account.

I wasn't there to see this, but over at Fort Washakie, a young man, a neighbor to John Trehero, was shot with a good-sized rifle. This happened in the 1950s, when John was a much younger man. This young man was shot in the chest, and the two shots were close together, right by his heart. He was rushed to the hospital at Fort Washakie. The local hospital doctors didn't want to tackle the case because it required difficult surgery to cut into the man's chest to get the bullets out. They suggested that he should be taken to a bigger hospital, for the necessary instruments to work with were not at Fort

Washakie, and no doctors there could perform the surgery to take the bullets out. They put him to bed, and the nurses were looking after him. So the father of the boy thought he should do something. He decided to go to John, for he knew about John's Indian medicine. He hurried and went back up to find his neighbor John. John agreed to help and got his little eagle feather fan, the one he later gave to me. He also took some lightning root. The father took him down there to the hospital and they walked in. The doctors knew that the father of the wounded man had gone to John. Everybody knew that John was the tribe's medicine man. They welcomed him to go ahead and work on the wounded man. John looked at the boy and the places where he had been shot. The nurses had put some patches over the bullet holes. John used his little feather fan, prayed for him, touched him with it. He also put a little of this medicine root into each bullet hole, into the man's chest. When he was through, they took John home.

The next day John was sitting outside his house again and saw a rider coming up. This time the man was leading a horse, and he approached and finally came right straight to John. It was the same man who had come to him the day before.

"Well, how is the boy coming along?" John asked.

The father said, "Well, John, he's home already. He is not sick anymore, just a little sore from the wound. A miracle happened last night. This morning when the nurses came in, expecting to see his bed soiled with blood, there wasn't too much blood. He was not sick; he was able to get around, just sore from the wounds in his chest. They found on his bed the two bullets that entered his body. The bullets came out that night. They were brought out by the medicine that you gave him. Nothing else was given to him by the doctors of that hospital. What you did for him brought those bullets out the way they went in. The surgery is not necessary. They put some disinfectant on the wounds and put patches over them and sent him home. The bullets came out from the front of his chest, the way they went in, even though my son was lying on his back all during the night. All this is thanks to you and your prayers."

The father felt indebted to John about what he had done for him. It was a big thing, saving his son's life. The father picked out a good saddle horse for John and that was what he led up to John as a gift. He also gave him fifty dollars in money.

About two months later, John came over to Wyola, to my district. That year I sponsored the Sun Dance. When I put up the dance that year, this young man came over, feeling indebted to the powers of the Sun Dance that made him get well. His life was saved by the medicine man of the Sun Dance. It was really Seven Arrows who took the bullets out and saved his life. John called upon his Medicine Fathers when he said his prayers for the wounded man. Now the young man came over as a way of giving thanks in the Indian way. He danced with us during that dance that I sponsored. This is how the power of Sun Dance can work.

Some people who hear these stories may not believe them; many people don't believe in our Indian powers. In my time as a medicine man, many people do not believe our sacred ways, and especially they do not believe that our feathers have power. In Rainbow's time there were even more people who did not believe in his power, and many people would criticize both John and our sacred ways. We are always sad for persons when they do not possess a sense of the sacred, but most times the criticisms are not damaging to other people, so we let them go and just pray that these people will be given wisdom.

One instance occurred at the Sun Dance at Fort Washakie when John was the medicine man. He was working with his feathers, the little feather fan that I am using now. As he was doctoring with this little feather fan, a non-Indian woman came out to see the dance. She stood in the audience at the doorway, and as John was doctoring during the second day, the woman kept making criticisms. She said, "I don't think he has any power in his feathers or whatever; he doesn't possess any power to do these patients any good." She kept making all kinds of remarks, and the people around her heard her say these things and didn't like it. So someone told John. They pointed the woman out to John and he saw her. John heard her loud criticism, and she kept talking loudly for all to hear, and this made John mad. He took the little feather fan and went up to the center and made medicine where there is great power, on the center tree. He put more power into the little feather fan by putting it against the center tree, at the base of it. That woman sat there and watched and kept criticizing. She was some thirty feet away from where John was, at the doorway among the people. Finally, in the direction of where she was standing, he pointed right at her, like that. He didn't toss it, he just held the feather fan. He didn't want to really hurt her, so he didn't let it go. His power from that far away struck that woman as if she was shot by a gun. She dropped down like a shot deer among the crowd. She finally came to herself after being out for a while. Someone told her, "Well, you have been criticizing this medicine man, and he didn't like it, and he did this to show you that he had powers that you can feel, like when they struck you." She said, "Oh, well, tell that old man that I can see now that he has great power. Tell him that I'll never do this again."

A lot of people among the Crow know that Rainbow has power and have seen what he has done. He has done great things before a large crowd of people in the Sun Dance, and people know of some of his other miracles. None of our people criticizes him. He never would hurt anyone or use his power except to help others and to point the direction towards the Sun Dance. He didn't hurt the woman spectator at all; he just stopped her criticisms, and she and everyone else was grateful to be shown the truth in such a direct way.

I am the owner of that little eagle feather fan now, and I use it still in the Sun Dances. Whenever I use the feathers, I am careful as to how I toss the power and see that no one is in my sight. It is like the power of lightning striking someone— it is the same thing. In fact, that is where the power comes from, from lightning that was given to John. You remember that on the second day of the Sun Dance, when I paint myself, I use lightning marks. This represents the power that is now within me and is always used for the good of all people.

There are many other stories that could be told concerning

Rainbow, because he has lived a great life.[9] I imagine that he will go on living for some time yet. If I am still living on the day that he passes on to the next world, he will probably send his greeting to me with a rainbow in the sky. I have seen rainbows before at the Sun Dance, and I know he is with us in spirit when we see his greeting. *Aho*, Rainbow, *aho!*

Our religion is the traditions of our ancestors—the dreams of our old men, given them in the solemn hours of night by the Great Spirit; and the visions of our sacred medicine men, and is written in the hearts of our people.[10]

—Seattle, Suquamish

INDIAN MEDICINE

WE have spoken about the power of Indian medicine and some of the great cures that have been made. In olden days, the power of each man's medicine could be seen outwardly not only in the curing of sick patients but also in his success in war. Each great warrior had to have the protection of one or more powerful Medicine Fathers in order to achieve something in battle. Today, much of the sacred power that was present in the tribe is gone, and what remains of it has its most visible form in the cures made by our Indian medicine. The power of the tribe is also great and can be felt at the Sun Dance, but many people who do not believe in our Indian religion look for proof of our religion by asking to see miracles performed by Indian medicine men.[1]

We have all heard accounts of great miracles performed by many medicine men in the olden days and by medicine men who are still living; Fools Crow from the Sioux is certainly a great medicine man, to mention only one. I myself have seen many great things in my time, and I will relate some of them for you, but it is difficult for me to speak about these things, and it troubles my heart to think that people may judge a man only by some outward sign of power and not by his spiritual character. Some men have power even though they may not be worthy of it.[2] Bad medicine is also present among the Indians, and this is very, very bad. We must be careful not to judge a man too quickly by what we see on the outside, and we should know that every religion may have members who are bad people, but this does not mean the religion is bad. In our times it is very difficult to know how to judge things, and it is best to do it on the basis of the traditional ideas that have been handed down to us and not by what others around us think.

When we speak of Indian medicine we should remember that there are many different ways in which Acbadadea works through our Medicine Fathers. I have seen some great medicine men exercise their own skills in my time. Many have powers and ways of healing that are different from the Crow way, and some are very interesting. Take for example the *yuwipi* ceremonies that come from the Sioux. Little Warrior was a great medicine man from the Pine Ridge Sioux reservation and a close friend of Black Elk. He came over to Wyola regularly because he had relatives in the area. About 1945, Grandma and I agreed to raise a little baby boy before he was even born. His father had already passed away while his mother was carrying him, and the mother, who was my niece, asked us to take him. We accepted him and raised him through childhood until he became able to support himself.

When our son, T.R., was just a little boy about three or four years old, he had a bad case of whooping cough that would not leave, and we couldn't give him any relief. So in the evening we drove a few miles to the house where Little Warrior was staying for his *yuwipi* healing ceremony. When we came into the room all of the furniture was cleared away and the floor was completely bare. It was dark out, but they had shut the blinds and hung blankets over the windows. Cushions were laid around the edge of the room so that the witnesses could sit on the floor. The medicine man announced that there should be no furniture of any kind in the room because it was against his medicine ways. In one area there was a singer with a drum ready to sing some of our Crow Sun Dance songs. The only other things in the room were four rattles that were placed one at each of the four directions.

My son and I were told to come into the center of the room. Little Warrior told me that there were many medicine doctors that we could choose from to perform the healing, and he mentioned several. Then he gave us his suggestion: "I would recommend that you ask for the White Owl. He is very good, and I am certain he will cure the boy's sickness." We agreed and requested the White Owl.

Now some men came forward and tied up Little Warrior's hands behind him and then tied up his whole body. Then he was wrapped in a sheet and again tied. He was laid down on the ground a few feet from where I sat with my son asleep on my lap. Then he said, "Turn out the lights and begin the singing." At that moment it became totally black, and you could not see anything. We could hear Little Warrior call upon the Medicine Fathers to come forward, and then we heard wings flapping and we knew that birds of some type were in the room even though no door or window had been opened. All four of the rattles were also flying around the room, and sparks were jumping from the rattles. Then I heard the "clip, clip, clip" sound that an owl makes by opening and closing its beak. I knew that sound, and I knew an owl was very near me. Then I felt the sleeping boy move all around and shake his head. Something was disturbing my little son, and I could hear him breathe heavily. I also heard the sound of a beak touching the bowl that Little Warrior had placed next to us on the ground. All this was spooky, but I knew it was part of the ceremony, and I was not afraid.

Suddenly, Little Warrior ordered the singing to stop and the lights to be turned on. There stood Little Warrior! He was untied and the room was just as we had seen it last, except his bindings were folded up. The medicine man came over and looked into the bowl he had placed beside us. In it were all of the things that had been drawn out of the child's throat— my son was healed! Little Warrior announced that our little boy would cough no more after his sleep that night. We were very happy and showed our appreciation by giving him many presents. True enough, our son was well the next day.

Another time I was present when some Crow men challenged Little Warrior because they thought he was a fake and that the *yuwipi* ceremony was a trick. Well, these people were doubtful. So Little Warrior was tied up with his hands in back. His fingers were tied up in every way a person could think of. They put knots at intervals on him, head to foot, with his hands tied behind him. The men who were tying him up did it any way that they wanted. Not only that, but they put a rope over him outside of the sheet, so it looked as if he wouldn't be able to breathe. After they did that, but before they laid him down—while he was standing all tied up in the sheet—they put a wide rope all around him and bound him everywhere and even on his neck, clear on down to his feet. We watched closely and those knots were tied hard. He would have had an impossible time untying himself even in the light. "Now," he ordered, "Now, lay me down." They laid him down. "Turn the lights off." He meant to sing a song. They turned the lights off.

The windows were all covered. The blinds were put up, and they hung some blankets over the blinds so there would be no light at all. It was pitch dark when they put the lights out. No light anywhere. They laid him down and put the rattles on the floor for the spirits. Then his helper started to sing one of Little Warrior's special songs while beating the small drum. They didn't have to sing many songs, one or two, and short—they don't sing long. About that time, they turned the lights on. When the lights were turned on, there sat Little Warrior in the middle of the room. He was completely free. All his ropes were neatly coiled and in a pile, and the sheets in which he had been wrapped were all neatly folded. He couldn't have done this by himself. No human helper could have done all this so quickly, even in the light. That alone would be hard, and it would take a long time for anyone to help Little Warrior untie the knots. It didn't take the spirits long. They made quick work. That is the power of Indian medicine.

That ceremony is one way in which Indian medicine works, but my Crow way is different, although we have the same results. As you hear of some of my cures, we should remember again that all healings are given to us from Above through our Medicine Fathers, and our prayers allow us to receive these blessings.

In my time as a medicine man I have helped many people.

As you know, I do not like to speak of this, but I will mention just a few so that everyone can understand the greatness of Indian medicine. On one occasion when I was in Wisconsin with the Winnebago Indians, a boy came to me on crutches with a foot that the doctors said needed to be amputated in order to prevent the gangrene from spreading. They were to operate the next day, but I prayed for him and wrapped his foot in bandages after first applying an ointment of different medicines, some of which I have already spoken about. The next day it was better, and I reapplied the medicine. In one more day he could walk, and he was completely healed. The doctors could not believe it and said it was a miracle. He writes me almost every year to thank me again.

On another occasion a woman came to me and asked my help for her niece who was in California. Her niece's kidneys had stopped for some time, and they expected her to die at any moment. I asked the aunt to give me a smoke and told her I would pray for her niece. I went outside and built a fire and had a prayer ceremony immediately. With my incense and then smoke and prayer, I called upon my Medicine Fathers and sent them to California with a wave of my eagle feathers. I was certain the girl would recover.

The next day when I was in town, a cousin of the sick girl saw me and told me about the miracle that had happened: her cousin's kidneys began to work, and the girl was to come home tomorrow because she was well. I hadn't had time to see the girl in person to perform the cure, so I sent my Medicine Fathers. The Medicine Fathers can travel anywhere; no place is too far. They travel on lightning, and lightning is quick. I was very happy to hear the report, though I was certain that my prayer would be answered.

There are many, many other healings that could be related, but they are just not important to hear. I will relate one example of how Indian medicine can work in warfare. I never had the opportunity to make medicine for a warrior until about 1969. I was asked by one of my adopted grandsons, a Winnebago boy, to make something for his protection before he went off to Vietnam to fight in the war there.[3] I made him the protection he needed with the little eagle feathers that had been given to Rainbow and then were passed on to me. They represent the power of the Sun Dance, and they can do great things. I selected a little eagle plume for him to carry. So out of my bunch of feathers, I pulled out a small plume from the eagle. At home I took my little feathers out, took a smoke and took incense out to pray. I didn't build a fire; I used sweet grass. Sweet grass is one of my other incenses. I generally use the sweet cedar for prayer meetings when we have a fire and hot coals. When there is no fire, I use sweet grass. Grandma lit the sweet grass for me, and I used my little feathers and blessed the little plume that was going with the young man. I told him how to carry it with him and to keep it on him at all times and wherever he went. The purpose of that medicine feather was to protect him from getting hurt badly or even perhaps from getting killed. It was just like the medicine that warriors carried into battle in the olden days.

When our grandson returned to us after his period in Vietnam, we found out how well the medicine had worked. He started carrying the plume, and they would go out against the enemy hidden in the brush. When his platoon was in sight where they could shoot at him, the enemy would mow down the whole platoon with machine guns. As a leader he would come back home although many of his men were killed or wounded. It happened that way three or four times, and it was making him feel mad and he wanted to do something. So one day while they were resting in his camp, where they were safe, he wanted to go out. He decided that he was going to do some praying. He took along with him some of the tobacco that was given to him by his Winnebago people. I have had quite a bit of that tobacco given to me, and I have it at home. They raise the tobacco themselves, and this is what they use when they pray. He took some of that with him, and he decided he would go out there a ways and pray. When the Winnebagos pray, they put some of the tobacco into the ground. He did that as he was wandering out there away from his base.

All of a sudden, out from the timber post close by jumped

a Vietnamese. My grandson saw him jump out just a few feet in front of him, and immediately the Vietnamese shot his rifle and down went my grandson, shot right above the heart. He tells that the bullet hit him there, and after he went down, lying on his back, the Vietnamese put the butt of the rifle down on the ground, relaxed, and stood there looking at him. The Vietnamese thought he was dead for sure. After a moment, my grandson realized that he wasn't really hurt. As he got up, the Vietnamese began to cry and then beat it back into the brush. My Winnebago grandson got the rifle the man had left and brought that back with him. After he got up and the enemy had run, he felt over his heart where the enemy bullet had hit him. He wanted to see if there was blood over his heart. When he put his hands up under his shirt to see if there was blood, there was nothing at all. That bullet had ricocheted and didn't hurt him; it didn't penetrate his body even though it left a bullet hole through his shirt. He brought the shirt back.

He showed the shirt to me. We were the first persons he saw when he came back from Vietnam after his term of service, before going on to Wisconsin to visit his homefolk. He brought home the shirt that he wore on the day he was shot by this Vietnamese. The powder was black around the bullet hole, but the bullet went somewhere after hitting him; it didn't penetrate. He figured that this was because of the plume I fixed for him, because he was carrying it in his breast pocket when he was shot. He said that if I hadn't fixed this little plume for him, he wouldn't have returned. He showed the shirt to all of us. Sure enough, there was a bullet hole over the heart. So that is an example of the powers that come from the little feathers that I used that night, as well as the prayers and the incense.

Our grandson really appreciated what we did. So ever since, he writes us, lets us know where he is, and tries to visit us. He is quite a dancer, and he dances and travels all over the country, Indian dancing; he has a beautiful costume. He told us that he would be going to Mexico this last winter and possibly to Japan—a trip to Japan with a little dancing troupe.

He said, "How about you folks going along with me?" We said, "No, no it's too far. It is too tiresome, for we're not able to be active that way anymore." We appreciated his offer but our great traveling days are over.

These stories can show something about the power of Indian medicine, and I can only dream of how wonderful it must have been in the olden days when many, many men had great power. Today, what is important for us is to realize that the old sacred ways are correct, and that if we do not follow them we will be lost and without a guide. We must remember that the heart of our religion is alive and that each person has the ability within to awaken and walk in a sacred manner. The manner with which we walk through life is each man's most important responsibility, and we should remember this with every new sunrise.

Every part of this soil is sacred in the estimation of my people. Every hillside, every valley, every plain and grove, has been hallowed by some sad or happy event in days long vanished. Even the rocks, which seem to be dumb and dead as they swelter in the sun along the silent shore, thrill with memories of stirring events connected with the lives of my people, and the very dust upon which you now stand responds more lovingly to their footsteps than to yours, because it is rich with the blood of our ancestors and our bare feet are conscious of the sympathetic touch.[4]

—Seattle, Suquamish

Thomas and Susie Yellowtail outside the Sun Dance lodge after the Sunrise Ceremony, 1979, Pryor, Montana.

Thomas Yellowtail in 1920.

Mrs. Susie Yellowtail and grandson, Sheridan, Wyoming, 1963.

Chief Plenty-Coups, Crow. (Courtesy Museum of the American Indian, Heye Foundation)

Thomas Yellowtail's mother (seated) and his aunt at Fort Custer, Montana, 1887.

Hawk with the Yellow Tail Feathers, Thomas Yellowtail's father.

Chief Medicine Crow, great war chief and holy man of the Crow, 1871.

Chief Medicine Crow, about 1904–1906.

Crow delegates to Washington, D.C., 1868.

Chief Two Leggings, 1888. (Courtesy Museum of the American Indian, Heye Foundation)

Sweat lodge. (Courtesy Montana Historical Society)

Sun Dance lodge, 1979, Pryor, Montana.

Inside the Sun Dance lodge, facing east toward the Center Pole and the buffalo (1979, Pryor, Montana).

Greeting the sun at the beginning of the Sunrise Ceremony on the first day of the Sun Dance (1979, Pryor, Montana).

Singing the sacred songs during the Sunrise Ceremony on the second morning of the Sun Dance (1972, Lodge Grass, Montana).

Thomas Yellowtail and John Trehero at the Center Pole on the second day of the Sun Dance (1972, Lodge Grass, Montana).

Thomas Yellowtail giving the sunrise prayer on the fourth day of the four-day Sun Dance in 1979 at Lodge Grass, Montana.

John Pretty on Top, Yellowtail's successor as medicine man and Sun Dance chief, saying the sunrise prayer on the third day of the four-day Sun Dance in 1979 at Lodge Grass, Montana.

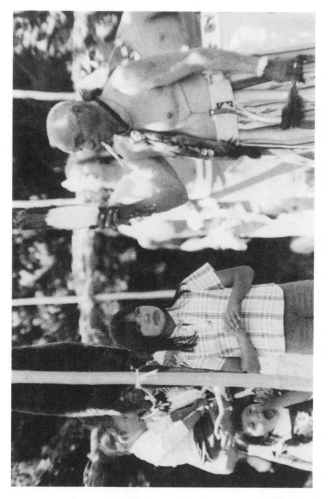

Thomas Yellowtail preparing to doctor patients with a bald eagle tail fan in his right hand and the golden eagle fan presented by one of his Medicine Fathers in his left hand. The tip of the antler of the spikehorn elk is hanging by his belt. He is doctoring near a pole with an otter skin attached (1979, Pryor, Montana).

Thomas Yellowtail doctoring a sun dancer on the second day of the Sun Dance (1979, Pryor, Montana).

Sun dancers on the second day of the Sun Dance (1981, Pryor, Montana).

Sun dancers on the second day of the Sun Dance, with the singers in the foreground (in hats). Two dancers are praying at the Center Pole (1972, Lodge Grass, Montana).

Thomas Yellowtail praying at the Center Pole on the third day of the Sun Dance. Singers are in the foreground (1972, Lodge Grass, Montana).

PART TWO

THE SUN DANCE RELIGION

ACBADADEA, THE MAKER OF
ALL THINGS ABOVE

YOU have asked me to explain the meaning or translation of Acbadadea. This is not easy to do. The two languages are very different, and it is impossible to give an exact definition in English for many Crow words. You would need to speak Crow, or some other Indian language, to understand what I mean. This is mainly the problem with words that relate to Nature and to sacred things. The Indians of olden days lived in the traditional way, in a sacred manner, and were close to Nature, to sacred things, to God. So it is natural that there are many words explaining different aspects of the world in which we lived. You can only understand the entire meaning of a word if you know all of the other words that explain all of the other ideas or events or features that are related to each other. The white man tries to take one word and define it without understanding anything about the way that the language was used or what it meant to the Indians. People may not understand what I am trying to say. I advise them to learn Crow; then they will understand.

Acbadadea is the Maker of All Things. It is the name given to God, the Maker of All Things Above. It is the way the Crow express God as being the Creator, the Maker of All Things, Who is above and beyond this world but Who has created and continues to give life to this world. This is what Acbadadea means. When we pray, we always say our prayers in Crow. We always say, "Acbadadea, Maker and Creator of All Things, we pray to you. You are beyond all things that are in this world, and You are also present through all things." We say that and then we continue on with our prayers. So, when we pray for help to the Medicine Rock or to Seven Arrows or to any of the different Medicine Fathers, we are praying to them as representatives of Acbadadea, because they are closer to Him than we are, and they represent Him in this world that we live in. So when we pray to the Medicine Fathers, we pray to Acbadadea also. That is why the first thing I do in all my prayers is to hold my smoke up high above me and offer my smoke and my prayer to Acbadadea with words like I just said. Then I will come down with the pipe, and I will offer a prayer to Grandmother Earth and the Medicine Fathers, who are represented by the four directions of space.

Grandmother Earth is a way of expressing that part of Acbadadea which is created in this world, because all that we have in this world is created by and from Acbadadea, but Acbadadea is also above all things. It is the same for the Medicine Fathers. When I move the pipe in a circle to all of the four directions, it also has a similar meaning, because all the winds, the powers, and Nature, wherever you look or wherever you go, come from Acbadadea. By recognizing this and by thinking about this, you can understand a great deal about who you are. So when you hear me pray to any of my Medicine Fathers or to Grandmother Earth or to one of the directions of the Four Winds, you will know the meaning of what I am saying. You might say that each of these things represents, in one way or another, part of Acbadadea, but always remember that Acbadadea is much more than all of these things.

The Crow believe that Acbadadea created the world and all the animals, including man, a long time ago. At that time, man lived close to Nature and to God and remembered all the things that God expected of man. There were very few problems between men, as everyone always prayed. As time passed, men forgot to pray and trouble began. Finally it was necessary for Acbadadea to send messages to the Indians and to show them how to pray and how to treat each other. These messages were often given to the Indians through the animals and different Medicine Fathers, and many of the great warriors and medicine men received visions that were important to the entire tribe. The form of the Sun Dance that we use today on the Crow reservation was given to the Indians long ago. It is only through the strict observance of this great ceremony that our tribe and the whole world can stay close to Acbadadea. If we fail to follow the traditional ceremonies, then conditions will become worse and worse for the individuals who forget, for the tribe itself, and for the world as a whole. Finally, the prophecies say that when enough people have forgotten to follow the way to their Maker, then the world will end. It is only through prayer and the observance of the sacred rites that the world can continue. It seems that this is a universal feeling among all Indians, because I have met many men from different tribes who feel this way. There may be some small differences, but most of the spiritual men agree on this outlook.[1] Some of the tribes have specific prophecies about this subject, like our Crow prophecy about the Tobacco Society, which I will relate later. The Navajo and Hopi speak clearly on this, and men from all of the Plains tribes have almost the same view.

It is clear that it is important for each person to follow a religion. In the Sun Dance way, the individual benefits from his prayers, but this is not all. The entire tribe benefits from the Sun Dance, because one part of our prayers is especially for the tribe and for all creation. Without these prayers from all of the different Indian tribes, the world might not be able to continue. You can see how important the Sun Dance is. In our morning Sunrise Ceremony, when we sing the four sacred songs after we have greeted the rising sun, we bring forward all of the Medicine Fathers, and all of the sacred beings in the universe hear our prayers. When I say the morning prayer after we finish the songs, I ask that the tribe and the entire creation be blessed for another year until the next Sun Dance. All of the other dancers share in this prayer. This is a very important time, and anyone who is present can sense that we are all at the heart of creation during these prayers.

I am sure that if everyone in the world joined into prayer and followed a religion, then the world would come close to the Creator again, but I don't think this will happen. Each person should know that his prayers help not only himself, but also all creation. We should all pray because we are men, and that is what our Creator expects of us.

Many people think that this world we see around us is the only world that exists. This is not the way it is for the Indians. There is a first world that you might say we are in now. This includes all the things that we can see with our eyes and touch with our hands. This is really the smallest world.

The second world is where the spirit beings are. The Medicine Fathers live in this world. This world is between the physical world and the world of the pure spirit, where Acbadadea alone exists. This intermediary world contains all of the spiritual things that God, the Maker of All Things Above, has given to us, to the Indian people, long before the arrival of the white man.

There are many powerful spiritual things given for the Indian people to use in certain ways. Many of these powers are given to the animal beings. All of the animals in the world have contact with these spiritual powers, even the smallest animal. You could say that these spiritual powers act as intermediaries between the physical world and God Himself, the Maker of All Things Above.

The third world is for Acbadadea alone, where He dwells above all creation, physical or spiritual. The Maker of All Things Above cannot be compared with the spiritual powers that He has sent to us, because He is beyond all of this. He has created all of these spiritual gifts just as He has created this physical world. If you put this physical world and the spirit world together, they are nothing compared to the Maker of All Things Above. You could say that the Maker of All Things Above is really unseen by most men and that we only see a small part of Him. The real world rests with Him, and this physical world that He has created is really a world of forms that pass through this life and return to Him. While we are here in this life, the Maker of All Things Above helps us by giving us guidance and rules through the spiritual representatives that He has appointed as our Medicine Fathers. So when we pray to our Medicine Fathers for guidance, we are also praying to the Maker of All Things Above. Remember also that while Acbadadea alone is in the highest world, He still has created the other lower worlds, and without His presence nothing would exist.

When everyone understands this, it is easier to understand why it is important to treat all things with great respect. All things have been created by Acbadadea, so all things are connected to Him. We can better know Him if we open ourselves up to Nature and to the sacred rules that He has given us through the spirit world. Since the Medicine Fathers work through animals and Nature, we must live with respect for all Nature, or else we will lose our sacred knowledge.

Many people forget to follow what they think are simple rules because they think they are not important. They probably think it doesn't really matter or that something else they do will make up for something they don't want to do. The Indian knows that even the smallest animal has great importance and can teach us great things. So too, all the little things we do every day have great importance. Our life is full of many little things in each day and in every moment. We should not concentrate on some great event that we expect to come in the future, but on the correct performance of all our daily obligations. In this way, we will show respect for all created things and for Acbadadea.

I am blind and do not see the things of this world; but when the Light comes from Above, it enlightens my heart and I can see, for the Eye of my heart sees everything. The heart is a sanctuary at the center of which there is a little space, wherein the Great Spirit dwells, and this is the Eye. This is the Eye of the Great Spirit by which He sees all things and through which we see Him. If the heart is not pure, the Great Spirit cannot be seen, and if you should die in this ignorance, your soul cannot return immediately to the Great Spirit, but it must be purified by wandering about in the world. In order to know the center of the heart where the Great Spirit dwells you must be pure and good, and live in the manner that the Great Spirit has taught us. The man who is thus pure contains the Universe in the pocket of his heart.[2]

—Black Elk, Oglala Sioux

11

SWEAT LODGE

THE sweat lodge ceremony is very important. People should participate in this ceremony quite often. Some of the young ones take a sweat bath for the pleasure of it and do not see any of its real purpose. But some of the people are very earnest in their use of the sweat lodge, and they observe all of the rules and say all of the prayers. When a person has the proper intention and observes all of the rules, the sweat lodge purifies the person not only on the outside but also throughout his inner being.

The sweat lodge is called the little brother of the big lodge. The big lodge is the Sun Dance lodge. Both are round, and if you understand their meaning, you can see how they are related. I will speak later about the meaning of the form of the Sun Dance lodge, and this meaning is also true for the sweat lodge. We participate in the sweat lodge ceremony throughout the year to prepare ourselves for the Sun Dance. The sweat lodge purifies us in view of our prayers and daily obligations. It is a prayer ceremony, too, for we say prayers in the lodge whenever we enter.

First, a small lodge must be built. You cut twelve small poles from tree saplings and bend them over and tie them together. You should say a prayer before cutting each tree, because the tree has allowed us to use it for our prayer ceremony. You put each sapling into the ground in a circle, with the doorway to the east. When the twelve poles are put in the ground in an upright position, they are like the twelve upright poles of the Sun Dance lodge. The sweat lodge can be made almost any size, but it generally holds five or six men, who will be seated around the pit where the hot rocks will be placed. After the small poles are bent over and interwoven, they are laced together, and the frame is covered with canvas tarps. In the olden days, animal skins were used to cover the frame of the lodge. The completed lodge looks like a big ball cut in half and placed with the flat side on the ground, just like an igloo that the Eskimos use. The doorway always faces the east, and a pit is dug just to the north of the doorway. The pit is usually about two feet deep, or maybe a little less, and about two feet wide. The earth from the pit can be taken to the east of the lodge and placed in an area where the fire will later be built to heat the rocks that will be used. The sweat lodge, or sweat tipi, is now complete. Many Indian people put up sweat tipis, and in Indian country you see them almost everywhere, especially by the side of a river.

As I said, the fire is made directly to the east of the lodge, about twenty feet away. Wood is cut and stacked in such a way that the rocks can be placed inside the fire. Before the fire is lit, we say another prayer to insure that the fire will give power to the rocks. The fire will burn for about an hour and a half, and by that time the wood has burned down and the rocks are getting hot. A bucket of water is put near the fire to heat the water up. We can bathe with the water to wet ourselves down before we go into the sweat lodge; also, by using warm water, the rocks keep hotter for a longer time than if we were to use cold water.

Now we are ready to bring the rocks into the lodge. Everyone is quiet and prayers are being said by one and all. A man is selected to bring the rocks from the fire into the lodge. This man makes a vow or request in his heart and does not speak. No one talks during this time, but everyone is making his own vow in his heart. So the rock man carries the first stone to the lodge. The man who will put the water onto the rocks is already seated inside the lodge by the side of the pit. He has two forked sticks with him to place the rocks correctly. The rocks are brought to the lodge one by one. The first four rocks are placed in the bottom of the pit, one for each of the four directions. During the time the first four rocks are being placed, everyone remains silent and praying. After the fourth rock is placed, everyone says, "*Aho, aho*, thank you for hearing our prayers." Now everyone can talk again, and the rest of the rocks are brought in and placed into the pit. Now the red-hot rocks are glowing brightly as they fill the hole to form our altar. Then the water bucket and dipper are brought in and switches are placed for everyone. The switches can be made of sweet grass or other grasses such as beaver grass. The participants will tap themselves with the switches to help bring out the sweat and purify their bodies.

Everyone is now ready to enter. As I said, we all bathe ourselves with water before we enter. This reminds us of our purification but it also helps to prevent burns when the steam from the rocks first hits us. We have nothing on when we go into the lodge. Some men may wear a loincloth, but generally we are naked. The men always go together, and the women can go together after the men are through. Remember, each person faces Acbadadea alone, and our nakedness represents our return to Him in the same manner in which He sent us into this world. We should not be ashamed of our nakedness but rather remember the holiness of our creation and our humility before our Maker.

The first group will now enter the lodge, each person going clockwise until the lodge is full. A helper generally stays outside the lodge and helps with covering the doorway and lifting the covers of the door at the end of each "quarter." We take the purification in four different periods, called "quarters," each of which is ended with a break, as we come forth out of the lodge. All things are done in four in the Indian way. This reminds us of the four directions that complete the circle of life. The door man can also keep the fire going with additional rocks in case the rocks cool down, or if other participants want to continue later.

When everyone is in the sweat lodge and the door is closed, we begin to say our prayers. The prayers are the same as the Sun Dance prayers we have talked about. After I have said my opening prayers, we pour the first little dipper of water on the rocks; we call this dipper the "April showers." It is just to get the sweat started before the full dippers of water are put on. We must count the number of dippers of water that are poured onto the rocks in each quarter, but the April showers don't count. After the April showers, we all start to switch ourselves so that the sweat will break out, and then we are ready to start pouring the regular dippers onto the rocks. Prayers are being said during all this time.

In the first quarter, we pour four dippers of water onto the rocks. They don't have to be full dippers, if it is too hot. After the four dippers are poured onto the rocks, the quarter is ended. Before the door is raised at the end of the quarter, one of the participants will be asked to say a special prayer. After the prayer, everyone says, "Aho," and the door man helps us raise the covers so that we can breathe a little fresh air. Some will even step outside and take a little walk before they come back for the second quarter. When everyone is back inside, the man who gave the prayer before we went out will repeat his prayer. Everyone will say, "Aho," and then the covers are put down and we go into the second quarter.

In the second quarter we add a few more dippers of water onto the rocks so that seven dippers are poured on. All of the participants should be praying right along during the entire ceremony. Everyone may not be praying out loud; that doesn't matter. But one should pray in one's heart during a sacred ceremony; that is the purpose of the ceremony: to purify the participants both inside and outside. It is not just for fun. When the seventh dipper is finished, the next man away from the doorway says a prayer for all to hear. It can be for good things, for someone special, or for all of the people—anything that we pray for in the Sun Dance. Then the door is raised and we take our second break.

We start the third quarter in the same way: the man repeats his prayer, and the door is lowered. The number of dippers to be put on in the third quarter is ten. Each time after a dipper is poured on, we pause before the next dipper. Everyone switches himself while he is praying. We may also sing Indian songs. This can last fifteen to twenty minutes for each quarter. When we are through, the third man says his prayer out loud, and we are ready for our break.

Before the fourth quarter starts, the same procedures are followed. Then, after the covers are lowered, we can stay as long as we want. The fourth quarter is the quarter of a million dippers. That is because we can put on as many or as few dippers as we like. After everyone has completed his prayers, we can end our ordeal, and the covers are raised. Now individuals can bathe according to their wishes; if they want to use hot water or cold, it is up to them. Most participants will want to bathe in the cold river. After we have rinsed ourselves, we are finished with the sweat lodge ordeal. It is Nature's way that was given to the Indians a long time ago and has been carried on and is still strong today.

As I have told you, each of our sacred ceremonies was given to the Indians long before the coming of the white man, either through a great event or through a vision received by a great chief or medicine man. It is unfortunate that we no longer can remember the exact beginning of some of our greatest ceremonies. Different old-timers may remember part of some of the stories that our fathers told us, but all of the details are not always clear. We can see, though, that the ceremonies are sacred, even if we can't remember all of the details about their origins. The Sacred Pipe Society is one example: I am one of three living members of that society and we do not know the exact origin of it among the Crow. Other tribes can recall all of the details of the origin of the pipe, and this is very good. We know that many, many of our great leaders have had sacred visions relating to these rites, and we know too that the blessings we receive from following our sacred ways are very great.

We do remember part of the story of the first sweat lodge, and I will relate this story to you. There may be details that could be added by some of the old-time storytellers, but you will see that the story is true even if we do not remember exactly how it happened.[1]

In olden days there was a young man who had great powers and was a type of sacred person—even greater than a medicine man. He was adopted by both the buffalo and the eagle, and they gave him great, great medicine. He lived on earth with seven buffalo that had the name of "the seven bulls." These seven buffalo bulls stayed together always and roamed over the country. The young man lived with the seven bulls and learned from them and from the eagle. The eagle gave the young man the power of the eagle and the special power of the eagle plume. The eagle plumes are to be found on the breast of the eagles and are sometimes called "breath feathers." We use eagle plumes in all of our ceremonies, and they have great power. To have the power of the eagle plume is a great thing. You remember that Grandma also had the yellow eagle plume as her medicine and carried a yellow eagle plume with her wherever she traveled. The young boy had this same protection, and it proved to be great medicine.

In those days there was a big buffalo bull whose body was solid bones. All of the other animals were afraid of this animal because he was very vicious, and his body was like solid steel armor because of all the bones. His name is hard to translate, but you could say "Bones Together" or "Bones All Over." Some men called him Bones, but he is also known as Bones Together. Bones Together was just vicious, and he would often kill hunters and even other buffalo. No one could stop him, because arrows would not penetrate him. He would attack the men for no reason, and everyone prayed to find a way to stop him.

Finally the seven bulls decided they would try to stop Bones Together. Bones Together accepted the challenge; the encounter was to take place on the open prairie. The seven bulls came together before the fight and made medicine. They used their front hoofs to tear up the ground and create a cloud of dust around them. In this way they put on sacred paint in the form of the white clay that can be found on the prairies. After they made their medicine, each of the seven bulls was ready to take his turn against Bones Together. One by one each of the seven bulls tried to defeat Bones Together. None was successful, and Bones Together broke one or both of the front legs of each of the seven bulls. After the last bull had charged Bones

Together and had been beaten, everyone thought that all was lost. These were the seven strongest fighters, but their strength alone was no match for Bones Together.

The young man watched this all take place, and now he stood ready. He prayed to his Medicine Father, the eagle, and then he was ready to meet Bones Together. The young man was told to tie his medicine eagle plume into the hair on his head so it would wave in the winds. It dangled in the air and was blown by the four winds. The young man picked up his bow and arrow, and as he approached, he sang his medicine song. Bones Together watched the boy approach and charged. The boy just stood there and watched him come. The vicious bull ran to the young man and hooked him with his horns and threw him into the air, but as he hooked him, the boy turned into an eagle plume and simply sailed up into the air. When the eagle plume floated back to the ground, the boy received his human form again. In the meantime, Bones Together was looking all around for the boy. Now Bones Together saw the boy and charged again, but the same thing happened and the eagle plume appeared and floated back down to the ground behind the charging buffalo. This began to make Bones Together angry, because as he charged on past the boy he could not find him. Bones Together charged in all directions, looking for the boy, with his tail straight up in the air. You may have seen a horse or a buffalo run at full speed; they keep their tail up in the air. While Bones Together's tail was up in the air, the only vital spot where he could be hurt was exposed.

Four times the buffalo charged the boy in this manner, and on the fourth pass when the eagle plume came to the ground and the boy regained his body, he took up his bow and arrow and let an arrow fly at Bones Together. The arrow penetrated Bones Together's rectum and went inside his body and hit his heart. Down he fell! The boy had killed Bones Together with the medicine of the eagle plume that was given by the eagle. The manner in which the boy achieved success helps show us that strength alone is not enough for success, and we can learn a great lesson from this part of the story.

Everyone was happy when Bones Together was defeated,

but the seven bulls were badly hurt, and something needed to be done to help them. The medicine of the eagle had achieved success in the encounter with Bones Together, but now the wisdom of the seven bulls was necessary to show the way to heal.

The young man cut twelve willows and made the form of the sweat lodge. He performed the ceremony of the sweat lodge just as we perform it today. Each of the seven bulls participated in the ceremony, and when it was over, all of the seven were healed and could walk. The seven bulls were all healed and they were very grateful. The seven bulls and the young man realized the importance of this sacred ceremony, and they wanted to do something so that all men for the rest of time would realize the importance of it. They wanted all men to participate in this ceremony for a total purification and to remind them that one must receive a purification of spirit and body before undertaking, and upon completing, any important task. The seven bulls knew what to do: "We'll become stars so that men for all time will be reminded of the sweat lodge. We'll take our son along with us." Everyone agreed, and the seven bulls became the seven stars that form the Big Dipper in our sky every night. The young man joined them and became the Little Dipper.

In this way they knew they would help support the sacred ways for the rest of time, and they are still there. Whenever I see the stars at night I always look for the Big and Little Dippers and then I raise my hand to greet them and say, "*Aho! Aho!*" It is a great thing that we have been given, and it is our duty to remember this.

The Crow should follow this same method for the sweat lodge ceremony unless they have been directly instructed by a Medicine Father to make a minor change and thereby acknowledge the help of that special Medicine Father. Some men are owners of medicine that can allow them to build the lodge in a different way. I have seen some lodges with fourteen poles. Other changes can be made depending on the instructions from the Medicine Fathers. Not just anyone can make a change in the construction of the lodge.

Anyone can take a pipe into the sweat lodge. It is one of the best ways to pray, and this is good. We should always offer a smoke and prayer before and after each sweat lodge ceremony. Also, we will bring sweet grass, sweet cedar, or sweet sage into the lodge and purify the whole lodge with the smoke before we start. We can also purify the lodge with the smoke from the *kinnikinnik* tobacco used in the pipe while we pray. It is always necessary to smudge the lodge with some type of incense before we start, but it is up to the participants to choose the type to be used.

When we are in the sweat lodge and all the covers are closed, there is no light in the lodge except the red glow of the hot rocks. The smell of the sacred incense fills the air. We have entered into another world which is beyond our physical world. When the water is thrown onto the rocks, the heat does not merely cleanse us on the outside; it also goes all the way into our hearts. We know that we must suffer the ordeal of the heat in order to purify ourselves. In that way, we can re-emerge from the sweat lodge at the end of the ceremony as new men who have been shown the light of the wisdom of our spiritual heritage for the first time. This allows us to participate in all of our daily tasks with the fresh remembrance of our position on earth and our continuous obligation to walk on this earth in accordance with the sacred ways.

These rites of the *Inipi* [sweat lodge] are very *wakan* and are used before any great undertaking for which we wish to make ourselves pure or for which we wish to gain strength; and in many winters past our men, and often the women, made the *Inipi* even every day, and sometimes several times in a day, and from this we received much of our power. Now that we have neglected these rites we have lost much of this power; it is not good, and I cry when I think of it. I pray often that the Great Spirit will show to our young people the importance of these rites.[2]

—Black Elk, Oglala Sioux

VISION QUEST

ONE of the main rites of the Sun Dance religion is the vision quest. It is a period set aside for solitary prayer at a remote place.

A person will usually spend three or four days of fasting on the vision quest, saying his prayers during all that time. He goes away up in the hills, gets away from people, and goes off by himself, and there he fasts and prays for either the three- or four-day period he selected before he began his quest.

There are many intentions that a person may have when he prepares to make a vision quest. He may want medicine, some kind of power to help him in battle or in all of his life. Strong medicine powers would protect the man so that he would not be wounded and could not be hit by an enemy's arrow. That kind of medicine would make a man successful in battle with the enemy. A lot of men seek those kinds of powers, and that is what they have in mind when they start out on the vision quest.[1]

Some men might seek different kinds of medicine power or understanding. They may want to be able to heal or doctor people. They may seek the answer to a question or a problem that is bothering them or their family or tribe. And above all, a man may want to pray in this way because this is a way to come closer to Acbadadea. In this rite each man may awaken in his heart the knowledge of the Maker of All Things Above. A man may pray for any of those things because they would be helpful to him, his family, and his tribe, but a man also must pray for virtue and the correct understanding with which to face life.

In olden days, all young men had those kinds of feelings, and that was why they would go on the vision quests. Sometimes a few of them would go out together. Maybe four or five of them would take a sweat bath together and start out together. When they got out to the hills, each one would go on his solitary way. Each one had to face the medicine powers alone. One would take that pointed hill over there; another one would take the next hill. They would scatter, each by himself, putting in his days. Some would stay four days, some less. Some of them might have received something by the time they came back; some may have come back without anything. Some of them would have been successful and might have had a vision, have been visited by an animal, or have had a dream or something to bring back, and that is good—that meant something. Another would come back and say that he did not receive anything. It means that he would have to try again later, and usually he would. He would try again later on and try again and again. Many of them ended their days by saying, "I tried not once, but a number of times, and finally I was visited by a bird or animal that gave me medicine, and I finally have some medicine, some kind of power or understanding." And that was the way in those days.

They would have kept trying until they got something. Some of the most sincere ones would probably receive something the first time they went on a vision quest. It depended on the sincerity of the person. If they had a good, strong intention, then they may have been the ones who were successful in their dream or vision right away. They would have been told afterwards what to do to preserve the medicine power given by the bird or the animal, and they would have done what they were told. Perhaps they might have been told to make a medicine bundle or carry part of the animal with them when they went on their raiding party against the enemy or when they needed to make their medicine.

Before a man would go out on a vision quest, he would first consult with a medicine man. It was the duty of the person who asked for instruction to bring a pipe or a smoke to the instructor. If the medicine man accepted the responsibility to

instruct the younger man, then they would first offer the
smoke with a prayer. Then the medicine man would tell the
young man what to do to prepare—how to go through purification before going up and all the other necessary information.
He would explain to the young man how he should pray and
fast. Not all young men wanted to seek war medicine. Some
would have had a different purpose. The instructions for the
prayer depended on the young man's intention.

In those days when people wanted to go fasting, they first
prepared themselves by taking a sweat bath to purify themselves. This is still my practice because it is very important to
undergo a purification before and after every major undertaking. Right after he was through with the sweat bath, the vision
seeker would get up to where he wanted to spend three or
four days upon the hill or high mountains. According to his
own choosing, he would select a place where he wanted to
fast. Many would sacrifice a finger when they got up there.
They would chop off the top of their finger and offer it to the
Great Spirit or to an animal. If a bird came and took that piece
of finger, then the bird would probably come back after a
while and adopt that person, give him medicine, and tell him
to go home. This could happen in one or two days' time,
although the person's intention may have been to spend four
days. If he was visited by an animal of some kind who felt
sorry for him sitting there torturing himself, then the medicine
power would say, "I have come to see you; you are torturing
yourself; you had better stop that and go home, and I will give
you some kind of power and tell you what to do." After the
man would get home, that bird or animal—it might be a hawk,
or a crow, or a meadowlark, or any kind of bird or animal—
would come to visit that person and tell him what to do. The
person would end the fast right then and there and go home;
he would have received something already.

People on the Crow reservation today still use the vision
quest. Young men and women go out on vision quests. Some
come to me, and we pray, and then I take them into a sweat
bath. I have to go to work and cut some wood and build a fire
and heat up some rocks and sweat with them in there and

pray for them; then they purify themselves and set out afterwards. We take the sweat bath during the day so that they
will still have daylight to go up to the place of the fast, right
after they are through with the sweat bath. If they don't have
a place in mind, then I recommend a good place, take them
there, and I say, "Now this is where you should stay for the
fast," and then I go away. The person should then stay in
exactly the same place. We carry wood along with us which
we gather as we go to the spot. They do not have fire all the
time, just in the morning and evening. One in the morning,
just as the sun rises, and one as it sets in the evening. They
build little fires and put some sweet cedar or sweet grass on
the fire to purify themselves and their pipe. They will carry a
pipe or some cigarettes. For such an important rite an Indian
pipe is better than cigarettes. They say their prayers, and they
retire when the dark comes. Even when the vision seeker
sleeps, he or she should face the east.

In the olden days, the man going out to seek his vision
would wear a buffalo robe, moccasins, and sometimes a loincloth. When he reached the area of the retreat, he removed
all of his clothing and almost always was exposed to Nature
unless he covered himself with his robe while he slept. I
instruct those who ask my advice to follow the traditional way
of the old-timers. Plenty-Coups and all the great Absaroke
warriors sometimes went into battle without clothing, and so
it is also in spiritual warfare. We will speak again of different
clothing for each of the rites of the Sun Dance religion, and
you will see that in almost all cases the person participating
in the ceremony must first humble himself before Creation,
both outwardly and inwardly, before he can receive something of value.

I tell them all these things, and many more: "Watch out if
you are visited by an eagle; watch him; he may talk to you
and drop a feather to you. If so, go and get that feather; it was
given to you by the bird; it means something great."

Yes, I have been consulted by certain people who want to
go on vision quests; they come to me, and I take a sweat bath
with them, and then they start out. If they don't know where

to go, I go with them and get them to the right place. I sometimes give them special advice on what they might say in their prayers. All of this keeps me busy, but that is what I am supposed to do if an Indian youth comes wanting to go on a vision quest. I give them some sweet cedar for incense to be put on the fire, and on the way to the place where they will fast, we stop and gather quite a bit of sweet sage for their bedding. When we arrive, we lay sweet sage in a circle over the entire area where they will fast. This includes the place where they will sleep. At the edge of the bed of sweet grass we make the area where they will build the fire in the morning and evening. This is done toward the east. Light and knowledge come from the east, and this is the main orientation of the prayer.

When a person is on a vision quest, he must have certain attitudes and intentions for his prayers to be sincere, and then he must carry these over into his daily life. It is easy to forget what you learned during this trial; unless you remember to carry on your prayer continually during every day of your life, you will not have learned one of the most important purposes of the vision quest. Each time we talk about one of our sacred rites, you will hear me talk about the spiritual attitudes which a person must possess as that person participates in any rite. It is possible to learn the outer steps that must be accomplished in a rite without learning the inner meanings that are the keys to the sacred traditions. Each seeker must therefore open his heart to the Great Mystery as he tries to follow the sacred way, because the perfect accomplishment of the outer steps of a rite will be worth nothing without the knowledge of the inner meanings. If the intention of a person is to achieve outward glory and superiority over other people, then that person will never be given great medicine, because that person's intention and attitudes are not in harmony with the correct spiritual purpose. If the reason you participate in a rite is wrong, then you will receive no reward. If you participate because you know the purpose of the rites and you want to express your gratitude and love of the sacred ways, then you may eventually receive a great reward.

It will not be the extent of the outward achievement that determines spiritual rewards. Those individuals who possess great physical strength may be asked to give much more in order to show their sincerity. All men are not given the same physical gifts, and when you remember that it is the interior values that make the real worth of a man or woman, you can see that some individuals must sacrifice much more in order to express the same degree of sincerity than another person who has less to give. Everyone should keep these thoughts in mind as they try to understand the Sun Dance way and the meaning of the spiritual tradition that it represents.

For those who have been sincere in the solitary invocation, Acbadadea will send a reward in the form of some medicine power. There are many different medicines a person can receive in different ways: different animals, different birds, maybe the little people, or one of the powers of the universe. When a person returns to the world after a vision quest, he does these things: first, when he gets home, he takes care to say prayers; he must take a sweat bath using sage, and so forth, to purify himself again before he gets back among his people. Then the meaning of the vision must be explained by the medicine men at home. After the instructor hears the whole story of the vision, he can help explain things to the young man which may not be clear. The medicine man knows what must be done by the recipient of the medicine in order for the recipient to protect the medicine. So after the young man tells his story, we take a smoke and say prayers; then the medicine man tells the young man what he has been given and what he must do. The recipient of the medicine usually is instructed to make a medicine bundle that will preserve and protect the medicine power. I have spoken of the bundle which protects the medicine rock of Chief Medicine Crow and the great care which is exercised to protect the medicine in a sacred manner. In the same way, many men and women will make medicine bundles for their own medicines in accordance with the instructions of a vision or a medicine man. These bundles serve as a constant reminder of the spiritual gifts we have been given and the corresponding attitudes which must always be present in order to safeguard our spiritual blessings. The medicine man will instruct the young people in both the outward procedures and the inward attitudes to be remembered by the successful vision seeker.

Young people may think they know enough, that they don't need help or instruction, but that is not so. It is necessary to consult a man who has had experience in the sacred ways in order to help a younger man follow the straight path. Some men may need less help than others, and some men are given great gifts without great effort. You never can tell, because some men will work hard for years and years and they may never receive great rewards that we can see. But all men should seek the help of a man who has learned the spiritual ways before they try to do something by themselves. You can better understand spiritual matters after years of following a sacred path. There is always more that can be done, and you cannot keep your power or understanding unless you continue your walk through life in accordance with the rules regarding spiritual matters. A man must be humble before the great mysteries will grant him anything. A humble man will ask for guidance from a spiritual man.

This is the explanation of one of the four major rites of the Sun Dance way. The sweat bath, the Sun Dance, and the use of the pipe or smoke with prayer are the other main rites. There are many other rites which were important in the sacred lifeway of the olden days, and some of these other rites are even carried on to some extent today. While these other rites should not be neglected, it is important to remember that the four main rites make up the center of our spiritual heritage, and without them we would be lost. In our modern world today, we may seem like drowning men because of the loss of much of our spiritual tradition. As drowning men we should cling to these four rites as our lifeline and never let go, because this lifeline can save us.

The representation of the Medicine Man as a nude figure is not a mere fancy, . . . for in many of the religious rites the priest appeared in such manner. This nudity is not without its significance, it typifies the utter helplessness of man, when his strength is contrasted with the power of the Great Spirit. With his best intelligence and greatest skill in the use of his hands, man is powerless to bring into existence even so much as the tiniest flower, while out of the force of the will of the Mysterious One, all things in the heavens and the earth have come into existence with beauty, grandeur and majesty.[2]

—Francis LaFlesche, Omaha

13

THE SACRED PIPE AND
DAILY PRAYER

WHEN the Crow talk about "the sacred pipe," they are referring to one of the sacred pipes that were used by the Sacred
Pipe Society. The use of the sacred pipes is reserved for members of the Sacred Pipe Society. When we talk about praying
with a pipe, you notice that I don't say "sacred pipe." That is
not because other pipes are not sacred; every pipe a person
uses in offering his prayers is sacred and holy. It is just that
when we say "sacred pipe," we refer to the pipes used by the
Sacred Pipe Society.

Some people today use cigarettes as smokes in offering their
prayers. For special prayers and ceremonies, I use only the
pipe. The pipe is the sacred form that was given to us for our
prayers, but it is the smoke that offers the prayer. It is the
tobacco that is changed to smoke, and the smoke that carries
our prayers to the Four Winds and to Acbadadea.[1] It is important to offer prayers correctly with smoke. The sacred pipes
are used only for the ceremonies of the Sacred Pipe Society
and not in everyday use for prayers. A man should attempt
to use his personal pipe in his daily prayers, but cigarettes can
be used if he doesn't have time to use the pipe.

When Grandma and I were just small children, we were
adopted into the Sacred Pipe Society, and we have always
belonged to it. The elders who belonged to that society and
knew all about how to run it are gone. There is almost no one
left, and no one wants to be adopted anymore and come to
any of the ceremonies. It too is a thing of the past. I do not
think there will be a Sacred Pipe Society ceremony anymore
among the Crow. I am a member, but I do not know all of the
special rules about running the ceremony, and all those who

did are gone. The special sacred pipes of the society remain among us yet, but there will be no more ceremonies. No one stepped forward to accept the responsibility to learn all of the ceremonies and to lead and organize the society. The Sacred Pipe Dance, the Adoption Dance, and so forth, will be held no more, and it is a great loss. That is why I say that it is still fortunate that we have the Sun Dance. The Tobacco Dance can still be carried on, but I do not know how long the tobacco plant will be here. There may not be a tobacco planting anymore, and soon the Sun Dance may be the only major dance rite left.[2]

When young people come to me and ask me how to offer prayers with a pipe, I tell them how to use it correctly. Then after they know that, I expect them to use it in accordance with the correct way whenever they can. I show them how to make *kinnikinnik* from the inner bark of the red willow and how to pack it correctly.[3] They should know how to light it and tamp it so all of the *kinnikinnik* will burn. It is also important to know how to take the pipe apart and clean it after each use. Then they must learn how to pray with it.

First, after you light the pipe, you must offer it with the stem pointed upward to Acbadadea, the Maker of All Things Above. Then come down with the stem toward Mother Earth, and then to all the four directions of the wind.[4] Of course you should also call upon all of your individual Medicine Fathers to be present. Then take a few puffs on the pipe and say your prayers. If you say a long enough prayer, your tobacco might go out. You can relight the tobacco if you need to, and then smoke the pipe until all of the tobacco is gone. Then you are through and you empty the pipe, clean it, and put it away.

No one knows just when the Crow were given the use of the pipe. It has always been with us, and it is a very important part of our religion. You should use smoke to offer your prayers every day. It is one of the main duties of every member of the Sun Dance religion: to pray every day through the offering of the smoke.

I have read Black Elk's account of the meaning of the sacred pipe, and it is very good.[5] It is the same way with the Crow and with all of the other Indians who use the pipe. It is good to understand the meaning of the pipe and to consider this when you use it. You have heard me say that a man should pray continuously throughout each day, but it is also important to offer a prayer with a smoke at least twice a day, in the morning and in the evening. In this way you are participating in the best form of ritual prayer that has been given to the Indian. You may find it strange that I can say this is the best ritual prayer, because I speak of the Sun Dance as the heart of our spiritual traditions, of the sweat lodge as our great purification, and of the vision quest as our extended period of solitary prayer. But the importance of the pipe and offering prayer with a smoke can be seen when you consider that this ritual prayer is present every day and follows the circle of the day from morning until night. Of course, prayer with the pipe also precedes all of our other ceremonies and is a very important act that we undertake all through our life. The presence of the pipe is also important. It serves as a constant reminder of our sacred duties. If we use the pipe correctly, we can never for one day forget the blessings that have been given to us, nor our constant need to return our prayers to Acbadadea. You could say that the pipe represents our duty of constant prayer.

Even as you prepare to smoke the pipe, you can offer your prayers. The use of the pipe demanded special proceedings in the olden days. First, you had to make your pipe, and even finding the pipestone was difficult. You know there is only one place in the world where pipestone can be found, and that place in Minnesota is far from Montana. Then the pipe also needs a pipe bag and a tamper and, of course, tobacco. I generally use the inner bark of the red willow tree along with other tobaccos to make it burn more easily. Preparation of the tobacco mix takes time.

The pipe and tobacco are very sacred, so they were always kept in a special place in the tipi, or carried with great care wherever a man went. You can see that the presence of the pipe, the preparation for its use, and the prayers that are offered through its smoke hold a central position in the daily life of a traditional Indian. In olden days, everything the Indians did had a meaning or purpose. Everything you did from morning till night, even the clothes you wore, were part of the sacred heritage, and you could not separate your daily activities from the presence of the sacred in life. Some of our sacred rites, like the Sun Dance, recur once in the cycle of every year (even though the preparation and responsibilities are spread throughout the year), whereas with the prayer of the pipe the rite recurs again and again in the cycle of each day, and this is a great thing.

As we smoke the pipe and offer our prayer with each new day, we should remember the importance of having a sacred center within us and that this sacred presence is represented by the pipe. It is the pipe that connects us with Acbadadea. We can no longer have its continual support as the Indians of olden days had; but in our time the pipe may have an even greater importance because some of our other supports are gone, and it remains with us as one of our key blessings.

While the prayer with the pipe will start and end the day, it is also important to pray during the day. Each day, whatever I am doing, I am always praying and thinking of God. As I work along, whether I am out in the field or wherever, I am always praying right along when I am alone. Even when I am driving down the highway, like today; I am alone nowadays in most of my travels. If I am going to town or somewhere and driving, I say prayers as I drive along. Or in my work, anywhere; all the time I am praying. Acbadadea knows that I pray to Him, and He hears me. I am always praying, no matter what I am doing. I am so used to it that I just can't stop, and I think that it is the best thing a person can do. I say that if you look for them, then you will find many parts of the day that could be spent in praying. I am sure that there are a lot of people who are that way, continually praying to God, remembering the name of God.[6] For a Crow, "Acbadadea" is probably the best short prayer during the day. This does great honor to God. Praying for people is also good. Once you get used to that, why, you just can't get away from it. You can't forget your day-to-day prayers. People think other things are more important than prayer, but they are mistaken. A person may have plenty of money but doesn't take that along with him. It is good to share what little we have and pray. A person should measure his wealth in terms of the knowledge and love of God.

You have asked me what type of prayer I offer with my smoke in the morning and evening. In the morning as I wake up, I say, "*Aho!* Father, thank you for letting me sleep through the night and see another day. This is a start of another day. Today, whatever we do, be with us and guide us, watch us and protect us. Let us live through this day, helping each other." I will offer a longer prayer of this same sort a little bit later, as I offer a smoke in the traditional manner I have described. Things like that are in the prayers that I say. After we go through that day and nightfall comes, when it is time to go to bed, I will say a prayer again as I offer my smoke: "Father, this is the end of the day and time for us to sleep now. Thank you for watching over us and guiding us during this day. Watch us now and give me a good night's rest and good dreams. If I happen to have a dream, let me dream of something good and not anything bad." I say those things and then I eventually get to sleep until the next morning. Each day we must do the same thing over and over again: morning and evening prayers with a smoke and, of course, during the day, when we say prayers without a smoke—right along throughout the day until we retire that night.

When we offer our prayers, it is just a regular routine that we must go through, and never let a day go by without these prayers. In the prayers that open and close the day, we should be praying for everybody and extending our prayers out, covering much more than just praying for certain people. We should pray for the whole world, for all men, so that we will live in peace much longer. Bad things always happen every day, threatening wars, unjust violence, and so forth. We should pray that people will see that the answer to their problems is to follow their religion, to pray. We should also realize that God may not answer all our prayers. God knows best, and His ways are not always easy for us to understand.

God still wants us to pray even if we can't be certain that we will see the answer to our prayers. It may be that something you have prayed for will not come to pass. If this is so, it is because of a greater purpose that we cannot know, and we must resign ourselves to God's judgment. So when I pray, I ask for the understanding of God's purpose so that I may follow His path. Then, each day, in addition to all the other things we pray for, we ask for guidance for ourselves and for all men, for the whole world. We must pray for each other, that all people in the world will remember their Lord and keep things going straight. Prayer is the best answer to all of the trials that face us, because without prayer, even if we succeed in accomplishing some great goal in the eyes of men, we have failed in our sacred responsibilities, and thus we have failed in what is truly important.

With this sacred pipe you will walk upon the Earth; for the Earth is your Grandmother and Mother, and She is sacred. Every step that is taken upon Her should be as a prayer. The bowl of this pipe is of red stone; it is the Earth. . . . The stem of the pipe is of wood, and this represents all that grows upon Earth. . . . all the things of the universe are joined to you who smoke the pipe—all send their voices to *Wakan-Tanka*, the Great Spirit. When you pray with this pipe, you pray for and with every-thing.[7]

—Black Elk, Oglala Sioux

14

MONTHLY PRAYER MEETINGS

WHEN we speak about the Sun Dance religion we include the sweat lodge, the vision quest, and daily prayer with the Indian pipe, but the Sun Dance contains our entire religion, and it is our most important rite.

Many people think that the Sun Dance is only a ceremony for three or four days each summer, but that isn't true; the Sun Dance is with us throughout the year in many different ways. Anyone who participates in the Sun Dance should carry the remembrance of the Sun Dance within him always.

In addition, during the year, between one Sun Dance and the next, we have Sun Dance prayer meetings at least once a month. People who participate in the Sun Dance should make an effort to come to these meetings, because participating in the monthly Sun Dance prayer ceremonies is one of the duties of the Sun Dance. We try to choose a date close to the time of the full moon, and we will arrive at the selected place about the time of the sunset. This is a special time of day, when we should all take a moment's pause to say a prayer in our heart for the blessings of the day just ended.

Someone who would like to sponsor a prayer ceremony will announce it somewhat in advance. The meeting will then be held at the sponsor's home. The sponsor will invite other sun dancers to come and join in the prayers. In addition, the sponsor should try to arrange to have singers attend the ceremony, and he should provide refreshments for everyone for after the ceremony. The only other duty of the sponsor is to build a good fire outside, close by the house, about an hour before the ceremony begins. I will bring everything else that is necessary.

I try to arrive at the sponsor's home a little early to prepare the medicine things for the ceremony. This doesn't take long but it is important. First, we have to clear away the furniture because we need room to put down our medicine things and for people to sit on the floor, around the medicine things, in a prayer circle. We always leave the way to the east open, and the circle is really more in the shape of the crescent moon. The place for the medicine man, or the prayer leader if there is no medicine man, is to the west of the circle.

In the prayer circle is placed the skin of a spikehorn elk, just in front of the place of the prayer leader. I place a container filled with dirt from the middle of the earth on the skin: dirt that has been brought up from the earth by a mole. This dirt is crushed until it is very fine and there are no small rocks or impurities in it. You could say that this is virgin earth to represent our Mother Earth. I mound the dirt up so that it represents the mountains on which our Medicine Fathers dwell. On top of the mountain I place the tip of the antler of the spikehorn elk and the rawhide figure of the elk that I have already spoken about. The elk is now at home, and we are ready to call upon him to be present.

Next, I put down my eagle feathers. I have three different eagle feathers that I use: the wing of a spotted golden eagle, the tail feathers of the white bald eagle, and the little eagle feathers that were given to Rainbow by one of his Medicine Fathers in his great vision. I will only use one at a time, but having all three of them present renews their power by our prayers, and this is good.

I also have the otter skin present to represent the water animal from the far north. I will also put down two mirrors which have been painted with a thin layer of red Indian clay. You can still see a reflection in these mirrors, and we have been told by our Medicine Fathers that any bad spirits that may be in the room will see their reflection in these mirrors, become afraid, and fly away out of the area. This purifies the room of any bad influences.

We also need a bowl full of water into which I mix some lightning root, one of my great medicines. I then put down

Prayer Circle for the Monthly Prayer Ceremony

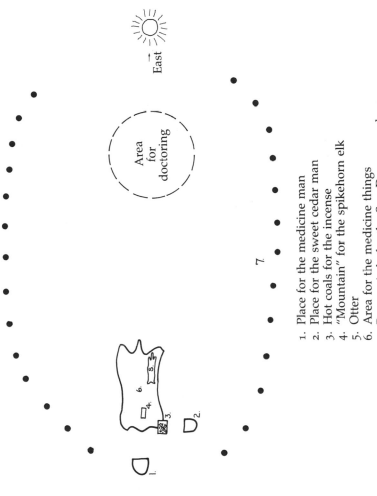

East

Area for doctoring

1. Place for the medicine man
2. Place for the sweet cedar man
3. Hot coals for the incense
4. "Mountain" for the spikehorn elk
5. Otter
6. Area for the medicine things
7. Prayer circle for the Sun Dance members

my eagle bone Sun Dance whistle, my bag of sweet cedar incense, and my tobacco for the smokes with which we will offer our prayers. Everything is now in order, and we can wait for the other people to arrive.

If someone else were leading the prayer meeting, he might have another kind of medicine to be placed on the skin that has become our altar. This would depend on the type of instructions that he might have received from his visions. The shape of the prayer circle would remain the same.

Before all the others are present, I take out my red Indian paint, which is really a powder, and paint my wrists and eyes in a manner similar to the way the sun dancers paint themselves on the second day of the Sun Dance. Now, as the others arrive, the people who follow the Sun Dance religion may sit on the floor in the prayer circle, but others must sit around the outside of the circle, on either side, as spectators.

A person who has never danced in a Sun Dance is not entitled to sit in the prayer circle itself. When the meeting is about to start, I ask those people who have participated in a Sun Dance to sit in the prayer circle around my medicine things, always leaving an opening toward the east. They will receive smokes and pray with their smokes during the cere-mony. Then I say to the others present, "You people may give us smokes so that we may pray for yourselves, your families, your friends, your loved ones, your children. You will be bringing us tobacco to pray for these things, and then you will be sitting back there when we start by offering our smoke and praying. We may be offering many prayers with our smoke. During this time, you should pray along with us. You may pray in your heart, silently, but let everybody in the room pray. You should also pray for the very thing that you are asking us to pray for when you give us smokes. If you pray along with us, it will be better."

Now it is time to begin, and the person appointed to watch over the coals from our fire and to help us offer our prayers with the sweet cedar incense must bring in coals from the fire which the sponsor started earlier. This person is called the "sweet cedar man," although it may be a man or a woman.

The coals are brought in from the outside in a pan and placed by our altar. Then the sweet cedar man puts sweet cedar onto the coals, and the smell of this incense fills the room. The prayer ceremony is now underway. The sweet cedar man may offer a prayer silently or out loud. After the prayer, he will pick up one of the eagle feather fans and bless and purify the feathers by placing them in the smoke rising from the cedar incense on the coals. All during the prayer ceremony, the sweet cedar man will place the incense on the coals every few minutes. If the meeting lasts several hours, new coals will need to be added. After the feathers are purified in the incense, the cedar man may use the feathers on himself, and then he will pass them to me. Next, he will pick up my eagle bone Sun Dance whistle and smudge it by passing it through the smoke. After I put my whistle in my mouth, I dip the tips of the eagle feathers into the water and, while blowing on the whistle, I purify all of the medicine things by sprinkling water over them with the feathers.

Now I am ready to offer my first prayer of the evening and to call upon my Medicine Fathers to come forth and be with us. I will stand and present the smoke in the same manner that I described when we spoke about prayer with the pipe. After offering the smoke to Heaven and Earth and the four directions of the Universe, I say my prayer and then finish the tobacco. Now I sit down and I am ready to sing my first medicine song of the evening. If singers are present, we can use Sun Dance songs, but if there are no singers, then I will use three special sacred songs at these prayer meetings. The first one is the "Opening Song," the second is the "Song of All of the Birds in the Universe," and the third is the "Closing Song." After the first opening smoke and prayer, I sing that first song. These songs are very sacred and they are different from any other songs. The four songs that we sing at the time of the morning Sunrise Ceremony, at the Sun Dance, are similar to these three monthly prayer meeting songs. All of these songs are sung without a drum, and there are no words in the songs. The songs were given to us long ago, and they remain in our hearts until we need to call them forward. These songs connect us directly to all the worlds that are behind this physical world, on up all the way to Acbadadea. The Medicine Fathers hear these songs and are present in a flash, with the speed of lightning.

After the first song, I complete all of the smokes that have been given to us by the spectators, and with each smoke I offer a prayer on behalf of the person who has given me the Indian pipe or the cigarette. If no one else is present, we must smoke at least four times and offer at least four prayers during the ceremony. One prayer is before the "Opening Song," and two prayers after the opening song and before the "Song of All of the Birds in the Universe." After this second song, it is time to doctor any patients who may be present. I will explain all about Indian doctoring when I talk about doctoring at the Sun Dance; it is the same way here. When the patients have all been worked on, I will sing the last song, the "Closing Song," and then offer the last prayer. The power of prayer is very great. If everyone prayed more often and more sincerely, it would be a very different world. Then the ceremony is over. All this can take anywhere from one and a half hours to all night, depending on the number of people who wish to be doctored. Whatever we have prayed for during the prayer ceremony I always pray for in my last prayer of the evening. Sometimes I will announce that I have another special prayer to say, so everyone should be quiet and pray with me. I try to talk loudly so everyone can hear me. I pray for the Crow and other Indian tribes, and the people far away from us, for everyone. In this way the whole world benefits from our prayers.

Sometimes there are special prayer ceremonies regarding some important problem. Just a short time ago we had a special meeting regarding our problem of trying to retain the rights to the rivers that flow through our reservation. Now we have free access to our rivers, to irrigate our crops, to go fishing without buying a license. It is our river, but the white men intend to take away all of those privileges that we have had long before they came. We pray that the judges will be given wisdom to see that the correct solution is to allow us to keep what is naturally ours.

There are other things that a sun dancer should do during the year besides come to the prayer meetings: be sincere, come to meetings, join in continual prayer. When the Sun Dance comes up, some people go in and participate, and when it is over, they don't show up at monthly prayer meetings or pray during the year at all. I don't call that a sincere member. They should remember this is the Sun Dance way of prayer, to take a smoke and say prayers. They should give prayers by themselves, wherever they are, every day, if they want to consider themselves members of the Sun Dance religion.

At these monthly prayer meetings, if many people came to share our prayers, it would be like a prayer for our entire tribe, and it would help to reinforce the circle of our sacred way. The twelve monthly prayer ceremonies complete the circle of the year from one Sun Dance to the next. The Sun Dance religion is the heart of our sacred way, and by continuing our prayers during the year, we can renew the blessings of the Sun Dance lodge and continue to guide our prayers toward the central tree which connects us all directly to Achadadea.

May I send a voice again so that you may hear me and bring my people back into the hoop and at the center there should be the tree that was to blossom and help us and have mercy on us. Hear me, O Great Spirit, that my people will get back into the sacred hoop and that the tree may bloom and that my people will live the ways you have set for them, and if they live, they may see the happy days and the happy land that you have promised.[1]

—Black Elk, Oglala Sioux

15

OUTDOOR CEREMONIES

WHEN the spring comes, after the snow goes away and spring rains start coming, we wait for the first thunder that we will hear. When the thunder returns, then we are ready. The thunder announces that the powers from all of the Four Winds are ready to receive our prayers. After that, we are ready to hold the first outdoor sing at the site of next summer's Sun Dance. Our monthly prayer meetings are held at someone's home, but now it is time to start the preparations at the actual site where our Sun Dance lodge will be constructed in a few months' time. There are four outdoor ceremonies to be held before the main Sun Dance begins, and all of them must be held at the site.

Before the first meeting can be held, the sponsor will have to fix a wooden stake about four feet long at the site where the Center Pole itself will be set up. After we select the site, the stake is driven in right where the center forked tree will be standing. A ceremony takes place before driving that stake. The sponsor and I are present; it could be just the two of us, or anyone who wants to be there. We have a little ceremony. We use either sweet grass or build a little fire, and we use a few hot coals and make the offering of incense. Then we use a pipe to offer a smoke and a prayer. We use an Indian pipe, saying our prayers right where we are going to drive the stake. Both the sponsor and I give prayers to the Maker of All Things Above and announce that this is where we intend to put up the lodge for this summer, for this coming Sun Dance. "This is the site we have selected to put up the lodge and where we are going to drive in the stake which represents where the center forked tree is going to be placed. This is the place where the tree will reach upwards with its branches toward You, the Maker of All Things Above, and where all of the powers of the universe will be present to receive our prayers. The tree that will stand on this spot will directly connect us to You." Then after the prayer is over, the stake is driven in. If the stake did happen to be knocked over by somebody not noticing it there, we would have to set it up so that we would remember where the place is. Set it back in there, but not drive it any- more. We might use some rocks, three or four rocks around it, to keep it from falling. This has never happened to me, but if it did, these are the steps we would take to mark the spot.

When the sponsor actually drives in that stake, we use a sledge hammer or a maul with a big head on it so there won't be any danger of missing it. The sponsor of the Sun Dance takes that big hammer, and if the dance is going to last three days, then he hits that stake three times and no more. It may not be driven very far into the ground by just hitting it three times, but it is enough for it to stand afterwards. If you were driving a nail or something, you would pound on it once and then maybe several times, but this requires the exact number of times indicating how long the dance is going to last. If he forgets and hits it four times, we will have to change and make it a four-day dance. If it is close to home, where I don't have to go so far for the ceremony, we may set a day, maybe a week or two later, to come to that place and have our first outdoor sing.

Before the next outdoor ceremony, we sight a line behind that stake we have driven in to the point where the sun will rise in the east. Then we follow this line back, far enough away from the stake toward the west that we will be standing just outside where the perimeter of the Sun Dance lodge will be made. At this point we will build a fire. The point of this fire lines up with the location of the Center Pole and the sunrise. It is the sponsor's responsibility to bring wood for the bonfire, as he has to provide everything for the Sun Dance.

Now it is time for the first outdoor sing. After the bonfire is prepared, it is time for a warrior, a veteran, to say a prayer. The sponsor will select a young man who has been a soldier.

Sun Dance Ceremonial Area from Above

East
↑
Sunrise

Stake representing
the Center Pole

Spectators

Singers

Sacred fire

Medicine man

Sponsor

There are always plenty of veterans who are around, who have served in some theater during a war. If we do not have anyone, then I can say the required prayer, but there is almost always someone who has been in battle. They should have participated in some battle and successfully gone through it without a scratch. The sponsor should get in contact with the soldier before the time of the outdoor sing. He has to make arrangements with someone before we have the fire. When the sponsor is ready to start the fire, then we are ready to go. He will call this young man to come to tell his story to the people. This veteran should say a prayer something like this: "I have been in a place where I have been in the battle. I have been in action, and I successfully went through that battle without a scratch, not being wounded. I consider that I was fortunate going through a battle like that without anything happening to me. I know that I was helped and I am asking the Man Above, the Maker of All Things Above, to make this coming Sun Dance a success. This man is sponsoring this Sun Dance that is coming up. I want Your help for him also, for the Sun Dance to be successful, for the prayers to be answered. I am wishing everybody the success that I had in my time, when I took part in a battle while the war was going on. You answered my prayers then, so answer his prayers now and help him and my entire tribe. I want whoever will participate in this dance to have his prayers heard. I am asking that for everybody. *Aho.*"

You may wonder why a warrior will be requested to say such a prayer. When you consider that participation in the Sun Dance is a tremendous ordeal for all of the dancers, you can see that the outward warfare of the veteran is similar to the inner warfare of the sun dancer. The warrior has successfully participated in the warfare against enemies of the tribe. It is his prayer that the sun dancer will successfully bring forth blessings for the tribe as a whole. In this way, the sun dancer and the Sun Dance itself will bless all of the tribe and all creation through the inner, spiritual warfare. You could say that the sun dancers will return the blessings of the warrior through their prayer during their ordeal.

There is another way in which the warrior and sun dancer are similar. The warrior fights an enemy who is on the outside; the sun dancer wages a war on an enemy within himself. Each of us must fight a continuing battle to keep to the spiritual values that represent our traditional heritage. If we fail to be continually alert in our prayers and our attitudes and to use good sense in all that we do, then we will fail in our interior war. In olden days, this interior warfare had the support of the whole tribe, and our life itself helped to guide us in our personal struggle. Nowadays, we must follow the Sun Dance way all the more carefully, because it contains the key to our sacred warfare. Now you can see all of the meanings of the veteran's prayer.

After the veteran is through saying good wishes for the coming Sun Dance, the sponsor will light the fire. He lights that pile of wood, and then the sponsor should give the veteran who said the prayer a small gift. The sponsor will have a small giveaway. If the sponsor is a married man, maybe his wife, or his parents, will come and also give the veteran a gift. It won't have to be much, whatever they have to give away. Then the sponsor calls on elders who are there, maybe some of his clan uncles that are there at that gathering, to come receive a little gift. This is a Sun Dance gift, a gift given through the Sun Dance. He will call any elders that are there and give them whatever he can.

I have spoken before about the purpose of a giveaway. In the Indian way, it is a mark of honor to give away much and not to accumulate much. At this time, the sponsor honors those in his family who have given him support in his life. Because many of our people do not have a great deal to give away today, we must always remember the reason why we hold a giveaway, and all who are present should share their prayers with the sponsor.

When everything has been given away and the fire is still burning, the sponsor will hand out smokes. He will probably open up a pack of cigarettes, and he will go and find people that are present who have participated in previous Sun Dances. He can also pass an Indian pipe to the different dancers or bring tobacco for others to use in their pipes. He gives a smoke to all the people who have participated in Sun Dances. We know those who have danced before, we remember them. Then we will ask the singers, who are all there and ready, to sing for us. They will start singing Sun Dance songs. The entire tribe could be said to participate in offering this prayer. The sponsor and I will be the first ones to go up forward, facing the east behind the fire. The prayers are offered in the direction on the horizon where the sun will be coming up. Everything is in line when we get behind the fire facing the east. From where we stand, you can look straight over the fire and the Center Pole onto the place of the rising sun. We are now ready for our prayers, but first I put incense, which is sweet cedar, into that fire, and the smoke comes up from the incense that I put on. This is an offering to the Great Spirit, the owner of the Sun Dance. We call on Him: "We are offering cedar, putting on cedar tonight. We are ready to be offering smoke and prayers. That is what we are going to do, sponsor a Sun Dance here. I am the man who is going to be leading the dance for the sponsor. We offer You the smoke; we want this coming Sun Dance to be like past ones, to have good things, good weather, everything. Nothing should go wrong. We want our prayers to be answered." I say much more; it depends on what we want to pray about. "This is the beginning, this is our first outdoor sing; there are to be four of these."

The ceremony before, when we staked out the site of the Center Pole, doesn't count as one of the four outdoor sings. At this first one we do not dance, we just smoke and offer our prayers. The sponsor and I put on incense, and we light up our smokes with some of the burning wood from the fire and offer our prayer. The sponsor and I pray first. When we are through, we move away from the fire and go back over to the side. The others to whom the smokes were given will come forward, and they do just as we did. They take burning wood, a stick of wood that is down there, light up their smoke, and say a prayer for us. They have to be members of the Sun Dance religion and have danced in the Sun Dance before. They come up four at a time to where we stand, facing the east. They say their prayers for us, and when they are through, they put the ashes of the pipe, whatever is left, into the fire. Then they go back. The singers will sing one song; when they are finished with that song, they will pause, then sing the next one, another song. They must sing four songs, but they usually sing more. There are many Sun Dance songs; they can sing any of them. Then, when everyone is through with the prayers, that is it. It doesn't take very long, maybe an hour's time, then we are through. Then refreshments are brought: coffee, rolls, pudding, and other things for all those who have offered prayers to share.

After this we will probably decide on the date of the next outdoor sing. It may be a week later or two weeks. We designate the time when we will come again to this place. We will use the same place for the fire. That second time we, the sponsor and I, will begin to dance. We dance like we would in a regular Sun Dance, using our eagle bone whistles. We must dance to four songs, but we generally do more than that. The singers think, "We've just started now, we want to sing more," so they'll keep singing and we may dance more than four times.

At this second outdoor sing, we do the same thing again: the sponsor will furnish us with the smokes, and everyone will offer prayers for us. Then we get up and put our incense in the fire and say our prayer. When we are done with our prayers, we back away from the fire and we are ready to dance. Our first dance goes with the first song that is considered one of the required four that we must dance with. They may already have sung several songs, but the song we dance to is the first song. We dance forward toward the stake that represents the Center Pole. So we dance up to the fire which is in line with the Center Pole and the sunrise. A tarp is generally put up as a barrier behind us. We dance to four songs, and then we are through. It is our second outdoor sing. At the first one, we don't dance; we just say our prayers. At the rest of the three outdoor sings, we dance each time we have one. If any announcements are to be made, they can be made after we stop dancing. The singers will stop singing and put their drums away. The sponsor will generally bring tables, set them up, and offer food and coffee. People will line up and come to pick up what is there to be shared. We'll announce when we will have the next ceremony. We will have the third outdoor sing in the same manner.

The first three outdoor sings usually take place before we set up the Sun Dance camp. If we have not had time to complete all three, then we will complete the third sing while we are camped at the site. I generally come and set up my camp one to two weeks before the Sun Dance is scheduled to start. This gives plenty of time to complete all of the preparations.

The fourth outdoor sing is held on the night before we set up the lodge. We gather just after dusk and have our ceremony. The outdoor sing is really a prayer offered by the sponsor, the medicine man, and the tribe as a whole for the benefit of the Sun Dance. The participation of many of the sun dancers in the ceremony represents the tribe. Four is the sacred number for all things in the Indian way and it is only after we have offered four ceremonial prayers at the actual site of the Sun Dance that we are ready to construct the lodge. Four is the number that completes the sacred circle in many ways. The four directions of space complete the circle of the universe from which all the sacred power given to creation by Acbadadea flows to us. The circle of the year from one Sun Dance to the next is also completed by the four seasons. We see that Acbadadea has completed the sacred circle in fours, and we therefore follow His way.[1]

I do not always ask, in my prayers and discussions, for only those things I would like to see happen, because no man can claim to know what is best for mankind. *Wakan-Tanka* and Grandfather alone know what is best, and this is why, even though I am worried, my attitude is not overcome with fear of the future. I submit always to *Wakan-Tanka's* will. This is not easy, and most people find it impossible. But I have seen the power of prayer and I have seen God's desires fulfilled. So I pray always that God will give me the wisdom to accept His ways of doing things.[2]

—Fools Crow, Teton Sioux

16

LODGE PREPARATION

THE preparations for the Sun Dance and the lodge itself take a great deal of time to organize. People will set up their camps in a large circle around the place where the Sun Dance lodge is to be constructed. No tents are set up to the east. The camp of the sponsor and the medicine man are always set up in the same line with the sunrise, the Center Pole, and the fire for the outdoor sings. As others come, they camp to form the circle of all the tents. It makes a sacred circle of everyone who comes to share his prayers at the Sun Dance, even if some of the campers are not to participate in the dance itself. There is the outside circle of all the tribal camps that surrounds the inner circle of the Sun Dance lodge. Prayers flow from the tribal circle to the Sun Dance lodge, and blessings flow from the Center Pole of the lodge to the tribal circle, and then to all of the created world.

Sometime during the week before the lodge is set up, the people are told, "Tomorrow we'll go up to the mountain after the long rafter poles." These are the long rafter poles that will go from the outside of the lodge up to the Center Pole. We will also need some shorter poles, forked posts that are to be set up vertically around the outside of the lodge. These should be from cottonwood trees. They are furnished by different individuals, who will donate them.

After the donated poles are brought forth, we go up to the mountain. That is the hardest chore to do; it takes a whole day. We leave early in the morning, cut all of the necessary poles, and bring them back down. In this way, both the forked, upright posts and the rafter poles used to put up the lodge are there at least one day before the erection of the

lodge. The distance from the outside of the lodge to the Center
Pole is twelve to fourteen paces. We used to have twelve
paces, but now with so many dancers, we try to have fourteen
paces. This means each rafter pole must be at least seventeen
paces long or almost fifty feet in height. It is hard to find good,
straight pine trees of this length, but we try our best.

After the twelve rafter poles are cut, we clean off all the
branches except for the very top. Then we are ready to trans-
port them to the Sun Dance camp. This can be very difficult.
The pine rafter poles are only found way up on the mountain,
so we travel far to find our materials. While we are on the
mountain, we will also cut smaller pines that will connect the
rafter poles on the perimeter of the lodge so that our sacred
lodge circle will be complete.

If not enough upright poles have been donated, we must
go and cut them on another day. They are from cottonwood
trees; they must stand about eight feet long above ground,
underneath the fork that will support the rafter poles. They
should be at least two to two and a half feet in the ground, so
the post will be over ten feet, not including the fork. These
are to be found along the river, and we do not have to travel
so far to accomplish our work.

The center tree is picked by the sponsor early during the
winter. It is always a cottonwood tree. The sponsor will go
into the woods and look for the forked tree and locate one.
On the day before the lodge is to be erected, we go to bring
in the Center Pole. We gather all the men who are going to
help to get the tree. It's heavy; quite a lot of men will go. We
come to it, and we have a ceremony before we cut it. We say
one special prayer before we cut the poles on the mountain,
and now we have another ceremony just for the Center Pole.
I use a pipe and my feathers; I'm the one to do that. After I
smoke my Indian pipe and offer a prayer, I sing the song of
the Center Pole, and when I am through, I use my feathers.
I smudge the feathers with incense and then I pray while I
touch the tree with my eagle feathers. "Now we're going to
use you; at our Sun Dance we are going to use you. You are
going to be the center tree. On you will be the bird; the eagle

will be there and the buffalo will be up there, placed on you. We want you to give us power, transmit the power that is going to be on you when the dance has started and is going on. You will be the staff of this dance that is coming up; it is you who will join us to all of the powers of the universe, to Acbadadea. People will come to you; markings will be put on you indicating our three days that we will spend with you. The power will be placed on you. The Medicine Fathers, Seven Arrows, will be there on the center tree, and the sun dancers will put their hands on you and say their prayers, and we want you to help us. We want you to have moisture that you will provide us, for we are not drinking, we are not eating, we'll be suffering. We'll come to you and put our hands on you and give prayers to all of the Medicine Fathers who are going to be on you watching all of the dancers to see who is sincere. When the sun dancers are through with their smoke and prayer, they will put the ashes of their smoke at your base on the ground where you are to be set up; that is for you. Through you we will send our prayers and from you we will receive all of the blessings from above. Help us." I say all these kinds of words, and the men who are there hear this prayer.

We sometimes have about thirty men or so to participate in cutting the tree and in taking it to the site of the Sun Dance. When I am through with my prayers, the tree is ready for the men who are going to cut it with an axe. When it's down, we all go to the stump where it has been cut. Generally, sap will come up, and everybody wants to bless himself with the sap that is from the tree wherever it is cut. There will usually be plenty of sap there, so people can put their hands on the stump and bless themselves with the sap. "Aho, we are going to have our dance and it is not going to be too dry for the dancers. It will be a good Sun Dance." You can tell by the sap on that tree what the dance is going to be like. If it is a dry one with no sap, we know it is going to be a dry dance with a lot of suffering. So when it's full of sap, they all say, "Aho, aho." All the men that are there will listen and pray.

When we are through with our prayers, they will trim the tree while it is lying there. They will trim off the branches that we don't want so it is clean up to the fork. If there are any big limbs above the fork, we may cut some of those off, but we leave the fork and the tiny limbs at the top of each side of the fork. Now here is the tree, and it is ready to be taken out of the woods. It is brought out by all of these men who will bring it to where the lodge is going to be. We try to bring in the Center Pole on the day before we will set it up and erect the lodge. Sometimes we will cut it on the morning of the day the lodge is to be built, but this is not so good.

Finally it is time to erect the lodge. The Sun Dance itself will start that night at dusk, and we have work to do. When we're ready, the butt, the end of the tree, is placed right next to the hole that has been dug for it. It is a big hole in the ground, about two feet across and four feet deep. We need about thirty-five or forty men; the more the better, for the tree is a good size and heavy. It is put up by manpower, so it requires a good number of men to lift it.

Before we set it up, there is another ceremony. While the tree is still on the ground, a man is selected again—also a veteran who has been in a war—to tell his story and offer a prayer. This veteran must meet the same qualifications as the man who lit the fire for the first outdoor sing. After his prayer, he ties the flags onto each branch of the fork of the center tree near the top. There are two flags: one is a blue one, the other is a white one. The white one represents the earth; the blue one represents the skies, the heavens. After this prayer and after he ties the flags, he receives a little present from the sponsor. A bundle of tobacco will also be tied next to each flag to represent the prayers that are being raised to the Medicine Fathers when the tree is lifted. The tobacco can be tied just above or below where the flag is tied, but the flag and tobacco should be tied very close together. The flags and the tobacco can be furnished by someone who wants to offer a prayer for the coming Sun Dance. After the tree is raised, the flags will be seen flying about forty feet up from the ground. Probably no one even sees the tobacco bundle after the tree is raised, because it is up so high that something that small is almost invisible. But we know that the offering is there, and all of the

Medicine Fathers know that the offering is there and that we have taken great care to prepare everything correctly.

While the tree is still on the ground, the same man will paint three rings on the tree before it is set up. These three rings are about four or five feet above the ground and are made by using charcoal from the fire where the outdoor sings were held and water. This mixture makes a dark-colored paste, and the veteran uses his hands to paint the rings. The three circles represent the three days the Sun Dance is going to last. If it is to be a four-day Sun Dance, then four dark rings will be made. All the people can see these marks. The number three also has other meanings for the Indians. The first meaning of the three rings is the number of days of the dance, but the three rings also represent the sacred circles of progression from the physical world, to the world where the Medicine Fathers dwell, and then to the pure world of Acbadadea above and beyond all other creation. All three worlds are connected in the Center Pole.

The last thing to do before raising the pole is to sing the "Tree Song." The Center Pole is still lying on the ground. A number of men will get on each side of it, and we are ready to lift it. We face each other and clap our hands without using a drum; we use our hands to take the place of a drum. Now we sing the song, repeating it four times, and then we whoop and holler and reach down and grasp the tree and lift it about four feet off the ground. Then we put it down and sing the same song again, four times. After we repeat the sacred song four times, we lift the tree up a second time, then lay it down again. A third time we repeat the song four times, then lift the tree up again and lay it back down again. The next time, the fourth time, is the last; after we sing the song four times, we reach down, pick the tree up and hold it up. We don't lay it down anymore; we come right along with it, on, on, on, and on up, until it is set up right. The more men to do this, the easier it is. There are long ropes that have been placed running around the fork of the tree. The ropes will be pulled from the east side when the top of the tree gets beyond our reach. The men with the ropes will start pulling, keeping the tree from swaying to one side and trying to keep it going straight. Besides that, some large poles about twenty feet long are being used to help. A rope is tied between each set of two poles, and these sets are used to push the tree up from the west, while others pull on the ropes from the east.

Up and up the tree goes, until the butt of the tree drops into the hole that has been dug for it, and now it stands there. We then put dirt around the base and tamp it in tight so that the pole is straight and the opening of the fork faces east. I will be at the outside edge of the circle and direct the raising of the tree. If it is too much one way or the other, the fork will be straightened. I tell them which way to turn, until the fork is just right from the sponsor's position towards the rising sun. As I stand in the position of the sunrise, I can sight a line from the doorway of the lodge to the Center Pole, the chief's pole where the medicine man and sponsor will sit inside the lodge, the sacred fire for the outdoor sings, and on to the camp of the sponsor and the medicine man in the larger camp circle. We know where the sun is going to be coming up in the morning, on the horizon in the east, so we orient the lodge and the camp circle in harmony with the sun. It is the responsibility of the Sun Dance chief to line everything up and run everything properly. Green willows are brought and tied crosswise with the fork of the tree; one bundle goes on the east side, the other on the west side. Then the twelve upright poles that mark the outside of the lodge are set up. The outside ring of the Sun Dance is made by the upright cottonwood trees, each of which has a forked top facing the Center Pole. Each of the twelve pine rafter poles that meet at the Center Pole is placed into one of the upright cottonwood forks. The chief's pole is the first rafter pole that is placed from the upright cottonwood where the sponsor and medicine man are located to the Center Pole. The chief's pole goes up first; the next rafter poles to be placed into the crotch of the Center Pole are opposite the chief's pole from each side of the doorway. Then comes one from the south side and then one from the north side, and then the others can be placed according to where they fit best.

People always ask, "What is the significance of the twelve poles; what do they mean?" Well, I tell them this makes the sacred circle of the lodge. The upright poles form the sacred circle representing the spiritual reality of our tribe. The rafter poles link the sacred circle to the Center Pole, which is the sacred point where all three worlds are connected: the physical world of the tribe, the spiritual world of our Medicine Fathers, and the pure world of Acbadadea. There are other meanings also; the lodge is round, and that represents the earth, which is round. The twelve poles, leading from each forked pole to the center, represent the twelve months of the year. The twelve months represent another circle, because in it we are brought back to a new beginning. Each of the twelve poles represents a month of the year when we must have our monthly prayer meeting, when the moon is full and up in the air, and we should continue prayers each day between the twelve appointed monthly Sun Dance prayer meetings. The drum which we use to help carry our songs to Acbadadea is also round. All things in Nature's way are round.

So you see that the Sun Dance lodge itself contains and represents the world and the time from one Sun Dance to the next. It brings man into direct contact with all of the powers of the universe, with the Maker of All Things Above. The Sun Dance lodge contains all of the dancers and all of the spectators who share their prayers there. Everyone who has been to the Sun Dance should remember all this and carry it with him always.

So, after the center tree is set up, we'll keep on working until everything is done. We start this in the morning, and we may be through by about three or four in the afternoon. Sometimes we are through about one or two o'clock, and that is fortunate because some of the dancers will want to have a sweat bath that afternoon to purify themselves before going into the Sun Dance. When they come back from the sweat ceremony, the sun may be setting, and it will soon be time to go into the lodge. They will have what dinner they want before going in.

After all of the rafter poles are set up and each of the upright

Sun Dance Camp from Above

Direction of sunrise →

Sun Dance lodge

Sacred fire for preliminary ceremonies

Sponsor's camp

Sun Dance chief's camp

(Note the straight line between sunrise, Center Pole, sacred fire for preliminary sings, and the camps of the sponsor and the Sun Dance chief.)

forked poles into which the rafter poles sit are connected to each other to form a complete circle, then brush is placed around the outside of the lodge to enclose it. Many of our helpers have retired to their camps because the heavy work is done, but this final work must be completed. Pine or cotton-woods can be used for the purpose. Only the doorway to the east is left open. The sacred circle is complete.

Now it is for me to place the buffalo and eagle at the center. Before I fix the buffalo head to the Center Pole, its face is painted with a special white clay that we mix with a little water so that the paint will not blow off with the wind. When the buffalo is roaming out in the prairies, he decorates himself with dirt. It is a medicine the buffalo creates by rolling in the dust and whipping it up. He always does this before a battle. You will see him breathe strongly and snort through his nos-trils as he breaks the ground with his front feet, sending up a cloud of dust to paint himself with this medicine before his charge into battle. He is going to war, and he prepares himself by making medicine and painting. He concentrates completely on the task before him.

In the same way, we prepare for our sacred warfare by painting and making special prayers and medicine on the second day of the Sun Dance and by painting the buffalo head before we place it on the tree. You can see now that everything in the Sun Dance has a meaning; if you think about it, you will understand.

After the buffalo is painted, we place him on the west side of the Center Pole, right under the chief's rafter pole. The buffalo will face the sponsor and the Sun Dance chief during the dance. We place a bundle of sweet sage in each nostril of the buffalo and tie the sage so it will stay there for the three days. We use sweet sage to offer a prayer to Acbadadea in many of our ceremonies, and we use the sweet sage in each nostril of the buffalo to represent the buffalo's breath. In the same manner a sincere person's breath can carry a prayer. When we blow our eagle bone whistles during the Sun Dance, our breath does carry a continual prayer. While the singers are beating on the drum and singing, the dancers are blowing on the eagle bone whistles. The drumming is the heartbeat of the Sun Dance, and the heartbeat and the breath of the eagle bone whistles send a prayer to all of the Medicine Powers in the universe and to Acbadadea.

The eagle and the buffalo that we use in the Sun Dance are no longer living but are stuffed. The sponsor may have one or the other that he would like to use, but I have both: I have a buffalo head and an eagle that we generally use. One year when the dance was very, very hot, the buffalo started to cry. All the dancers could see the real tears that the buffalo shed. Then in the heat of the afternoon of the second day, water came forth from the neck of the buffalo. It was a miracle, and all of the dancers came to touch the sacred water and then rubbed their hands on their heart. Everyone got up and danced in thanksgiving for the great blessing that the buffalo was giving to the entire tribe through the Sun Dance. Everyone felt that his suffering was recognized, and all of the dancers knew that their prayers were being heard.

I have had my own eagle for only about five years now. The eagle wanted to give himself to me for the Sun Dance, I imagine, because this great bird came down from the sky into a coyote trap on my brother's ranch. He was found in perfect condition. I had quite a time getting him stuffed, though, because no one wanted to have anything to do with it. It is unlawful for anyone to possess eagles except for those Indians who use them in their sacred ceremonies. Sun dancers need the eagle feathers and the stuffed eagle as part of their religion, and this is allowed. Government men have come to watch our ceremonies to see how we use the eagles. They have asked me many questions, and they were well satisfied that we use them in a sacred manner; therefore they allow us to use them and don't bother us. I was told we could even ask the Forest Service for the feathers from eagles that have been killed in Nature and found by the government. I know they have many birds, but I have never had success in any of my requests when I write or go to their office.

For this reason, no one would help me preserve my bird, but a friend offered to try his hand. He bought a book and

read it and then said, "I'll try and we can see how it works."
It did work out well, and today I have a fine bird thanks to
this young man who stuffed the bird. It is good that I have
both the buffalo and the eagle to use at the Sun Dance. They
are very important and bring blessings to us all.

The last thing to do before the lodge is complete is to put
the eagle on the rafter poles. Of course we purify the eagle
with incense before he is tied onto the poles. When the eagle
is in place, the lodge is complete. Now I have fulfilled my
responsibilities in preparing the lodge, and I may retire for
purification with either a sweat bath that has already been
prepared nearby or at least with a plunge into the river. Then
I have my dinner, and after I take my last drink, I put on my
Sun Dance skirt and prepare for the Sun Dance to begin.

The Sun Dance lodge is like the white man's church; it is
our place to pray to Acbadadea. The Indians do not need a
church to capture the presence of God, because He is all
around us in Nature. We carry out all of our sacred ceremonies
in Nature, without the aid of any permanent building. When
the dance is over, we leave the lodge standing, and over
the years it naturally returns to the earth. In the same way,
everything returns to the earth in its own time.

As each sun dancer approaches the lodge, ready to begin
the ordeal, he should be aware of the sacred character of the
lodge. It represents the earth and all creation as well as the
circle of seasons that travel through time. The center tree
is the staff of life, and on it are these medicines and the
representatives of the Maker of All Things. It is through the
Center Pole that we meet God, so we must go to the center of
the circle and understand the responsibility of being placed at
the center of creation. Spiritual realities are more than you can
imagine, but if you follow the Sun Dance religion correctly,
then you can begin to understand this, and the responsibility
of participation in the Sun Dance will become clear.

You can see that it takes a great deal of preparation to
construct the Sun Dance lodge, but after we have completed
the lodge, all of the medicine powers of the universe are
present on the Center Pole. Seven Arrows and all the rest are

there representing Acbadadea, even though we do not see them. Throughout the Sun Dance, the Medicine Fathers will be carefully watching the dancers. They will see who is sincere. They listen to all the prayers; they see who is continually dancing and who is concentrating on his prayers.

The dancers will have their gaze fixed on the eagle or on the buffalo or on some spot on the tree. All the time they are dancing, they will concentrate on that spot. Oftentimes dancers will see the buffalo or the eagle just as if he were alive. If the dancer has concentrated on the buffalo and has been sincere in his prayers, then the buffalo will know. For those sincere dancers, the buffalo will be alive. To everyone else the buffalo will just be up there mounted, but to that dancer, he will be alive. It is the same for those dancers who watch the eagle. They see him alive up there. The bird or the buffalo may dance with the sacred songs, and it will be a great comfort to the dancers.

The most sincere dancers will dance almost continually for the three days, even though they have no food or water for this entire time. They will always be up, going forward to the center tree and dancing back to their place while always facing the tree and concentrating on their spot. These dancers will be given something by the Medicine Fathers, especially by the buffalo. A wild buffalo will charge a person, hook him with his horns, and throw him in the air and let him fall. The same thing will happen to the dancer in the lodge. It generally does not happen early in the dance, but on the second day. Each dancer is beginning to get dry and to suffer, and those who keep going continually, even after they start suffering, will be rewarded by the buffalo. The buffalo will charge and catch the dancer, hook him up and throw him up in the air, and the dancer will "take a fall," as we say. Before the dancer takes a fall, the spectators see the dancer staggering around as he comes forward to the tree, and he may weave out of his own trail on the way back to his place. Each dancer has his own trail to the Center Pole from his position on the outside of the lodge. The dancers on either side of the man who is ready to take a fall will notice that the staggering dancer can't come back to his post on his own trail and that he may weave into another dancer's trail. So the other dancers will stand stationary at their posts on the periphery of the lodge and blow their eagle bone whistles to give support. The singers also will notice that the man is almost ready to fall, and they'll say, "Don't quit singing. A man is about ready to receive something; he's going to fall, so don't quit." Until the man falls, the singers will keep singing; sing, sing, sing while this man is dancing, wobbling all over the ground. Finally he will take a hard fall. When that happens, it is the buffalo that throws him up in the air; the man hits the ground and he lies there, unconscious.

When that happens, we hurriedly go and cover him up with cattails and sweet sage. Then we pray for him. He is gone into a vision, so nobody bothers him. We will keep the dance going; he lies there. That reward is medicine coming from the Sun Dance, given to him by the buffalo. He will give the dancer something, probably tell him what to do, what kind of feathers, colors, or medicine to make. Different persons will receive different things. The person who has gone into a deep sleep will probably lie there for twenty minutes. After he has received his reward, he will wake up, he will probably hear the singing, and then he is ready to get up and dance again.

A person should not be afraid when this thing happens. It is good for a person to continue dancing until he falls. It could be that some of the other animals that are not visible, but present in spirit, will knock the dancer down and then they will give him something. He may receive some power or message of some kind, and so he may be of some service to his people afterwards, all year round.

That person, by attending later prayer meetings, will be advancing a little toward the understanding of the Sun Dance religion, toward the nature of God. The more a person partici-pates in all of our monthly and daily prayers, the more under-standing he will have of all of the things that are to be learned in the Sun Dance religion. It is the way that was given to us long ago, and has always been, and is still continuing today.

I should explain to you here that in setting up the Sun Dance
lodge, we are really making the universe in a likeness; for,
you see, each of the posts around the lodge represents some
particular object of creation, so that the whole circle is the entire
creation, and the one tree at the center, upon which the twenty-
eight poles rest, is *Wakan-Tanka,* who is the center of everything.
Everything comes from Him, and sooner or later everything
returns to Him.[1]

—Black Elk, Oglala Sioux

17

THE THREE-DAY RITE BEGINS

AFTER the lodge has been finished, each dancer must prepare for the three-day ordeal.[1] Friday is almost always chosen as the day to build the lodge and then start the Sun Dance at the time of sunset. Many people come on that day to set up their camps for the duration of the dance, so there is activity all over the camp as final preparations are made and more and more people come to share in prayers. Everyone in the camp circle can feel the power that is being generated through the Sun Dance lodge. For the next three days, the Sun Dance is the center of the reservation, and many spectators will camp and attend to show their support for the dancers. Even if people have not fulfilled their religious duties during the rest of the year, the Sun Dance brings everyone together in prayer for three days each summer.

Just before dusk, each dancer must be dressed in his Sun Dance clothes and be ready to proceed to the lodge. The clothing that the dancers wear expresses their humility as they prepare to stand at the center of the universe. Each man will wear, wrapped around his waist, a skirt that goes to his ankles. A belt or sash of some kind will hold the skirt. The men will be bare-chested, but all of the dancers, men and women alike, usually wrap themselves in a blanket as they march into the lodge. The women will have on simple cotton dresses that they have made. All dancers will be barefooted, for no one may wear shoes inside the sacred circle, and every dancer will have an eagle bone whistle hanging around his neck. The whistles are made from the longest bone in an eagle's wing, and each whistle has an eagle plume attached to the end which flies as the whistle is blown. Each dancer also holds an eagle plume in each hand. When the plumes are not held, they dangle from leather strips, about eighteen inches long, that are attached to the little finger of each hand. The dancers are dressed in this simple manner, with their main attire from the eagle, the whistle, and the plumes being the most visible adornments on each dancer.

At dusk all of the dancers gather behind the lodge, not in front. Everything is facing east, and they all gather behind the lodge where the fire is, as during our outdoor dances. They line up in two lines, the men toward the front and the women in the rear.[2] When the sponsor and I arrive, we each take the lead of one line. After the two lines are formed, and we are all ready, the sponsor and I start whistling, and then everybody starts whistling. Each line follows us, and they will keep the same position once they are inside the lodge. Both lines start walking around the lodge in opposite directions, and the spectators are all around, further back, watching us. We whistle right along while we walk, and we meet at the doorway in front of the lodge, pass each other, and circle the lodge again before we go in. I go to the right side, and the sponsor goes to the left side, with the ones next to us following behind. And we meet at the chief's place, the chief pole. That is right at the middle, in the back of the lodge. Everyone goes to his place, and then when everybody is in the lodge, the spectators close in behind us. When all are gathered inside the lodge, we stop blowing our whistles.

Before we sit down, the announcer calls on the spectators. He makes all his announcements in the Crow language. Some of those present may not understand, but most people speak Crow and know what he is saying. "All right, people, bring the bedroll for your dancer." The bedrolls are brought to the announcer, and he will start calling the dancers, telling them to come up and get their bedrolls. The dancers go up to the doorway, take the bedroll, and put it down where they are going to be for the duration of the dance. Now the drummers come and seat themselves, ready to sing. But before they start singing, we dancers sit down and sing four songs, the same ones that we sing after we have greeted the rising sun. The four songs come in order, and we sing them with no help from any drum; only the sun dancers sing. Very few know those songs. I always ask them, "Sing with me," but they don't know those songs very well, so just a few will sing with me. Each song is repeated four times; then we blow our whistles four times, and we are ready to sing the next song four times. Then when we are through with all four songs, the sponsor goes up to the Center Pole, smokes, and offers a prayer. When he is through, we ask the singers to start singing. It will be dark already, and a man is appointed to build a fire for us. Just like at the first outdoor sing, we get a veteran to come forward and tell his war stories, where and how he had been given blessings. He will tell his story, and then he will light up the fire for us; then the man in charge of the fire takes over.

The sponsor will give a few gifts to the man who built the fire. He will also call on clan uncles and a few elders and give them presents brought in by his relatives. He asks the recipients to pray for a good, successful year, for a good Sun Dance.

After that, the fire man who has been appointed will keep up the fire all night; it is his duty to stay and keep the fire going. He is chosen by the sponsor of the dance. He takes his sleep during the day, and when nightfall comes again, we call on him, "Fireman, build your fire now, it's getting dark." He brings in the kindling wood, starts up the fire, and keeps it going all night long. When the sun is coming up, he is there; he waits until after the Sunrise Ceremony is over and we are all through. Then he removes all the coals.

During the Sun Dance, it is not compulsory for a dancer to be dancing all the time. He can dance according to his own feelings. If he wants to, if he is sincere and wants to attain something, he will stay up and dance continually. Those are the kind that receive something. If one only wants to dance a few times and then lie down, it is up to him. Of course the singers have to have some sleep, too. They will sing as long as there are some dancers; till past midnight they will sing. As soon as all the dancers have lain down to get some sleep, the singers come to the end of their singing and leave. They also have to get some sleep, for they have to get up early in the morning, before sunrise, and come back to sing again.

The dancers are up before the sun rises. They wake each other up, and the announcer will call, "Get up, all you dancers; the sun will soon rise and we've got to have the ceremony, dancing to the rising sun." So they will get up and make ready. It will probably be about fifteen minutes before the sun rises. All the dancers, including the women, will gather in the center of the lodge and line up facing the east towards the entrance of the lodge. The spectators will have to clear the way for the dancers to see the sunrise, clear on out to the east. Nobody is to stand in the way. We want to dance to the blessing of the rising sun, for the day and for all time.

Now the singers start the "Sunrise Song." They sing that song before the sun peeps over the hill, and they will sing maybe for five, ten minutes while the dancers face the direction of the morning sun and blow on their eagle bone whistles. The moment the first streak of light comes up over the hill, all the dancers stretch out their hands towards the sun and then pass them over their body to bless themselves. After the whole sun has risen over the horizon, the song ends. This is a very sacred time. While this is going on, the spectators out there will line up on each side of the doorway, still looking on to the dancers, but nobody is supposed to cross in front of the dancers. Policemen are appointed to keep people from crossing the path from the dancers to the sun.

After the sun is up and the song ends, the male dancers gather around the fireplace that has been burning all night. Plenty of hot coals are there. We sit by the sacred fire, in horseshoe shape around it. We don't surround it, don't close the passageway to the east. The singers will pause; everything is to be quiet, for we dancers have four songs to sing in order. We sing the first song four times, then we blow our whistles four times. The next song in order is sung the same way, four times. And then the third one, and then the fourth one. All of them have to be sung four times over, followed by blowing the whistles four times.

After all the songs are completed, the sponsor or I will get up and put sweet cedar on the fire. Sweet cedar is the incense that belongs to the owner of the Sun Dance, Seven Arrows, who is one of my Medicine Fathers. We put the cedar onto the hot coals, and the smoke rises and goes all over the lodge, giving blessings. Our first prayer is to Seven Arrows for helping us to preserve the sacred ways that were given to us Indian people through the Medicine Fathers by Acbadadea during the period the Sun Dance was stopped by the white man. Then the rest of the prayer is said. I usually say it the first morning: I pray for the dancers, for all the Indians in the country, all of the governments, everything in the universe. In doing that, my prayers probably last twenty minutes or so. It is a good enough prayer covering everything that is going on in our created world.

People always say I pray too long, but in order to cover practically everything, it has to take some time like that. Our Medicine Fathers have told us that we are to pray for all of creation, and so we do this. Without these prayers the world would quickly come to an end.[3] I always take time to pray for what the Crow own, and all that is on our reservation, like our coal and our river, everything. The government and the white men are always after those resources, trying to take these things away from us. I pray that this will not happen; we want to own our land, our good reservation. We have good land, good country, in which we live. Our reservation is one of the best in the whole country. We have prayed for it throughout the year until we are there at the Sun Dance.

When the prayer is over, the ceremony is finished for that morning. We adjourn for the morning, probably for two and a half hours or so. The people go to their camps, and the dancers will return to their beds and probably take a nap, for they are tired. Before the dancers retire, the sacred fire attendant brings the coals from the fire out of the lodge and places three or four piles of burning coals outside the lodge to the east. Sweet cedar is put on the coals to make sacred incense so that all the dancers can bathe in it. We say the dancers are "smudging" themselves. This smoke gives them renewed

Sun Dance Lodge from Above

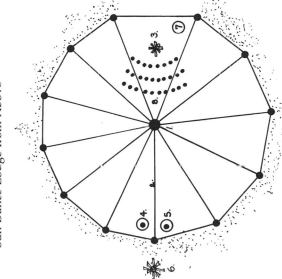

SUNRISE

1. Center Pole
2. "Chief's" rafter pole
3. Sacred Sun Dance fire
4. Chief's place in the lodge
5. Sponsor's place
6. Sacred fire for preliminary
   sings
7. Drum
8. Position of dancers as they
   sing the morning songs
9. Evergreen screen

strength as it floats in the air, taking all our prayers to the Medicine Fathers above.

Some dancers will visit their families outside the lodge. They get around behind it and sit in the shade. We are not drinking any water or eating anything all those days, and we are burning up. The hot sun burns, and your body is burning up because you are dry. Some tribes allow their dancers to drink after sundown during each day of the Sun Dance, but we don't. No drinks or food for the entire duration of the dance. So all the dancers just about torture themselves. One of the few times the dancers may relax during this ordeal is after the Sunrise Ceremony and before the dancing starts for the day.

On the second morning, after the dancing to the rising sun and the songs, it will probably be the sponsor who says the morning prayer. He may appoint another dancer to say the prayer for him and to put on the incense if he cannot do it himself. If he is able to, he can get up and say a prayer; it is up to him.

On the third day, the prayer may be said by a different person, but if there isn't anyone, I sometimes take the responsibility. It is my duty to fulfill whatever cannot be done by anyone else.

The morning prayer and morning Sunrise Ceremony are two of the most important parts of the Sun Dance. In accomplishing them, we help our tribe, our country, and the whole world. People have to realize all that this means, for without our prayers, the world that we see could be very different, even worse than it is now. All our different kinds of prayer during the day and during the year are important. But the prayer at the Sun Dance during the sunrise greeting is one of the most important. The benefits from the Sun Dance extend to the whole world.

About 10:30 the singers will come back to the lodge, and the dancing for the day will commence. The singers will have a position just to the south of the entrance to the lodge. There need to be at least three or four different groups of singers who will rotate during the day, for it is difficult to continue singing and drumming for long periods during the heat of the afternoon. The temperature will be over one hundred degrees, and it is almost impossible to continue singing at the top of your lungs for more than two hours at a time. When the singers start beating on the drum, many of the dancers will arise and begin to dance. At this moment everyone present at the Sun Dance knows in his heart that he is at the center of the universe. The songs from the Sun Dance were given to our people before history began, and these songs link us to our Medicine Fathers and to Acbadadea. As the drum beats, it establishes the heartbeat for the dancers, our tribe, and all of mankind. We feel this link in our hearts, and when the drum gives its call and the dancers respond by blowing their eagle bone whistles, we reach into our innermost center, and blessings penetrate all those present at the same time that our prayers rise up to all the universe. The Sun Dance lodge calls the entire universe to be present, and our prayers are answered.

At this moment most of the dancers will participate in the dancing. Each one will stand in his place and face the Center Pole. The Center Pole contains all of the sacred power of the universe, and as the dancers concentrate on the center tree, so also do they concentrate their prayers on Acbadadea. The dancers know the songs being sung, and at a certain moment in the song, each dancer knows it is time to run toward the Center Pole. Many of the dancers will run in a straight line toward the pole, then stop and dance back towards their position in the circle of the lodge, while always concentrating on the center tree. The dancer may fix his eyes on a certain spot on the tree or on the buffalo or the eagle. The dancer's gaze will remain fixed on that place for the entire time he or she is dancing.

The most sincere dancers will be up almost continually, and their path to the Center Pole will become worn into the dirt. All of the grass that was in the path at the start of the dance will be worn away by the constant wear of the bare feet of the dancer. These dancers are connected to the Center Pole by an invisible cord coming from the tree and penetrating into their heart. The path that the dancer makes to the Center Pole represents this attachment. At the end of the Sun Dance, you can see these trails as reminders of the invisible attachment, that we all possess, to the spiritual domains which are both inside us and yet also beyond us.

In olden days, the Crow people used leather thongs to physically attach themselves to the Center Pole. The dancers pierced their chests and danced toward the Center Pole before breaking their flesh by pulling on the eagle claw or stick which was put through the dancers' skin. With this sacrifice each dancer could physically see the outer form of the inner attachment from our heart to the Center Pole. The Crow no longer practice this part of the sacrifice because our Medicine Fathers have told us in our visions not to continue this part of the Sun Dance. We still understand the meaning of our connection to the universe through our participation in the Sun Dance, and the strength of the inner certainty which each sincere dancer has in his heart can continue without ceasing if the dancer completely follows the Sun Dance way.

While the singers continue, all of the dancers are given strength, and many will go on dancing right along. The first group of singers may not be able to continue for too long, and soon another group will relieve them. Sometime during the afternoon all of the singers may be exhausted, and they will have to return to their camps for rest. They will have to continue later that evening and then on for the next two days. The singing will probably stop for about an hour at this time, and the dancers will lie down in their places. It has been almost a full day without food or water, and people are becoming weak in the sun and from the continuous dancing. Blowing the eagle bone whistles in rhythm with the drum also takes liquid from our bodies and requires great sacrifice. When the singing and whistling stop, the dancers will notice even more of the pain from their sacrifice, because the blessings from the heartbeat of the universe have stopped while the drum is silent.

When the singing starts again, the dancers will get up and continue. Many dancers will be too tired to go on, but the most sincere ones know that they must give up everything in order to show their sincerity. The singing will now last late into the night until there are no more dancers moving. It may be midnight before it is over for the day. Each dancer will then sleep right there in his place, and the singers and spectators will retire to their camps for a short night's sleep before the Sunrise Ceremony of the second day.

The Sioux are raised with the Sun Dance, and it is the highest expression of our religion. All share in the fasting, in the prayer, and in the benefits. Some in the audience pray along silently with the dancers, . . . Everyone is profoundly involved, and because of this the Sioux nation and all of the peoples of the world are blessed by *Wakan-Tanka*.[4]

—Fools Crow, Teton Sioux

CONCLUSION OF THE SUN DANCE

AS we begin our second day, we start to get dry and weak. Our friends, our folks on the outside who are not dancing, will go out to get little trees. They will cut small cottonwood trees, probably about two or three inches thick, and set them up for each individual dancer to make what we call "stalls." To make the stalls, one cottonwood is set up on each side of every dancer's place so that when the dancer is standing, waiting to advance toward the Center Pole, he can grasp them to keep from falling, for we are getting weak. Willows are placed from one upright cottonwood to the next so that all of the stalls are connected and make a circle inside the circle of the lodge. It is beautiful to see. This all happens on the second day, right after the Sunrise Ceremony is over. Our friends take off their shoes and come right in and start putting the stalls up.

In the same way that the buffalo is painted to make his medicine stronger, the dancers are painted on the second day to give them strength for their spiritual warfare, and so also is the lodge itself decorated in its own way with the introduction of an inner sacred circle for the dancers.

The second day, especially from noon to dark, is the hardest time of the dance; that is when anything can happen, when a person might fall and receive a vision. After the stalls have been placed for us at the beginning of the second day, the dancers will start getting ready; they will put on their paints and dress in handsome Sun Dance clothes. Just as the warriors of olden days put on their finest headdresses and feathers, painted themselves, and made medicine in preparation for battle, so too do the sun dancers prepare for their most difficult sacred ordeal on the second day of the Sun Dance. Each person will paint according to his medicine to prepare himself for this most difficult period of the dance that is approaching. A person paints himself in a certain way on his face or on his body, according to what has been shown to him in his dreams or in his visions. Those who don't have any medicine will rely on their clan aunt or uncle to come in and paint them. Whoever paints the younger ones that have no medicine of their own will be given something by them as a gift for his service. The painter will paint that young dancer according to his medicine.

During the first day of the Sun Dance, none of the dancers is painted or wears any medicine feathers. Their simple outward dress reflects the inner spiritual attitudes that each dancer needs to realize during the first day. The inner strength of each dancer is tested during this first day, and the sincere dancers will reach into their hearts and find the courage to give up all their strength to Acbadadea. Some dancers will hold back and not dance continually. They are afraid that they might not have the will to finish the dance; they rely only on their own power to give them strength. Those who are able to give up everything also show humility because they realize that it is not their individual strength that will support them, but rather the source of all power and strength, Acbadadea.

As the dancing for the second day starts, most of the dancers will put on a special skirt made by a member of their family or the dancer himself. Their outward dress clearly reflects a radiation of sacred power. These skirts are more beautiful than the plainer skirts worn on the first day. The dancers have all suffered the first day, and their prayers have been heard by the Medicine Fathers. Now the power in the lodge and on the center tree is great, and all those present can feel the radiation of this spiritual presence. The dancers have changed their dress in honor of this spiritual presence. They are preparing to give up all of their remaining individual strength through more suffering, in order to place themselves at the mercy of the Medicine Fathers. Now the sun dancers prepare for their spiritual warfare.[1]

During this period of preparation, before the dancing commences for the day, each of the dancers should consider the purpose of his participation and the necessary attitudes that he must possess. Soon the dancing and doctoring will start, and it will continue almost without stopping for the remainder of the day. I will be doctoring people who are sick and seek to receive direct blessings from the Sun Dance power. All this time, the dancing will continue. Even before the dancing starts, all of the dancers are exhausted from their ordeal. They have not had anything to eat or drink for almost two days, and many of the dancers have been dancing and blowing on their eagle bone whistles almost constantly. Soon it will be time to resume the dancing, and each dancer will have the opportunity to give even more of himself. For the Sun Dance allows an outward physical reflection of inner attitudes, and so we must consider what Acbadadea and our Medicine Fathers expect of us. Most of the Indians know that sincere prayer is required, and everyone should also realize that there can be no sincere prayer without proper virtue. Humility is probably the most difficult virtue to realize. No person is ever worthy of great rewards on his own account, but only as a receptacle of power from above. If a person expects to receive a special reward for his efforts, then the Medicine Fathers will almost certainly not reward him. The sincere dancer will express his humility by continued dancing so that he cannot continue without aid from above.

Finally, the Medicine Fathers will take pity on a dancer and give him a vision. They are present on the center tree, and they see into the hearts of everyone. This is a great moment for the dancer who receives the vision and also for the entire tribe. The blessings of the visions almost never come on the first day of the Sun Dance but only on the second or third day. As we all prepare for the ceremonies of the day to begin, we should understand all of these things well.

Before we start, we put up the American flag over the entrance, and there is a little ceremony. We sing the "Flag Song," everybody stands up, and we dance in place while a couple of veterans who have successfully returned from war put it up in the military way.[2] Then it's there for the day. By evening, around five, we take the flag down just like they do according to the regular way wherever a flag is displayed.

Then the pipe is filled by the sponsor, and he takes it to the leader of the singers and gives it to him to smoke. The singers will pause, and everything will quiet down as they take a smoke and pray. When they are through, they bring the pipe back. The leader will come forward with that pipe and say a prayer for the dancers and for the Indian people. He says a good prayer and then returns the pipe to the sponsor. After that, it is declared that the doctoring and dancing will commence. The singers start, and all of the dancers will begin. During the remainder of the day the dancing will continue. It is also at that time that I start in, and throughout that day I will be doctoring even until midnight. If there are more sick people to come, then the next day, before the dance is ended, we will do some more doctoring.

Now I am ready to use my feathers to doctor. I aim the feathers high enough above everybody's heads so that I don't hurt anybody out there among the audience. People are always standing at the door, watching what goes on in the lodge, when I work with the eagle feather fans. Most of the time I use those little eagle feathers that John Trehero used for almost fifty years or so before he turned them over to me. I will work on a few patients with the little feathers, and then I will change to another fan, a whole eagle wing. I have three fans that I use. I use one awhile, then change to the other one for a time so that they are not idle and don't become run down in power. I put power into them by placing them against the center tree. Then I use them in working on people. I also carry them wherever I go, for I may be asked to work on somebody. So if I go on a trip, those fans go with me.

Many people who are outside the lodge looking on will want to come in to be healed. These people will have ailments of all kinds. When they come into the lodge, they take their shoes off outside and come in barefoot. They are coming onto holy ground. They come in and stand before the center tree, which means they want me to get up there and help. I generally ask them their ailments and they tell me, and I pray

accordingly with my feather and medicines. Whatever medicine I use, I pray for the person and pray for a cure to his
ailment. I pray to one or all of the Medicine Fathers. "Help
me, Seven Arrows; you are right here on the tree. The tree
has the power; the power is placed on that center tree, and it
is great." We will have them put their hands against the center
tree and then get behind them and touch them from head to
feet. A lot of times, wherever their ailments are, they are
pulled out of the top of the head. It can also be on the body,
whether it is on the chest, on the back, on the shoulder, on
the legs or knees, anywhere. I touch that spot with the feather,
pull out the ailments, and toss them in the direction of the
east, to be gone with the wind. I want the people to get well,
but I don't give them any medicine to eat or drink in there,
just prayers. Then they go out of the sacred lodge, and if any
medicines are to be given, to eat or drink, they will get them
later, outside the lodge. Nothing is to be taken in the lodge,
any water or any kind of medicine, for it is not the place.
Patients inside the Sun Dance lodge don't receive anything
but the blessing and power of the feather, our prayers and the
power of the Sun Dance.

All those kinds of services are of course free; there are no
charges by the medicine men. When we have prayer meetings,
I don't ask anything from the patients I'm working on. If
they feel that they want to give something in return for the
doctoring they have received from the medicine man, they
can offer something. By making an offering to the man who
has worked on him, the patient says thank you not only to
the medicine man, but also to the Medicine Fathers and to
Acbadadea, from whom all blessings flow. I don't care about
receiving any gift, but the attitude that the patient has in
giving the gift is important to the Medicine Fathers.

Before I work on a patient, I touch the center tree to get
more power from my feathers that I'm going to work with. I
also need a little blue tree where I have my otter skin attached.
I have been instructed to find a small pine tree, to remove all
of the bark and branches except for those on the top three
feet, then take blue paint and paint the part of the pole that

has been stripped of bark. The blue represents the water in which the otter lives. I put up this little tree on the second day of the Sun Dance, before I start to doctor patients. A lot of times, I will have the patient hold the blue tree where my otter skin is attached. The otter is one of my Medicine Fathers and he is there with his powers; while I touch the blue tree, I can feel the power that is there come into me like a shock. I feel the power coming in from the points of my fingers down into my arms, my hands. When I touch the tree and the otter with the feathers that I will work with, then the power is put onto my feathers, and then I touch the patients with them. Wherever their ailments are, I touch that spot and put the feathers there and then I draw the sickness out of the patient and toss it to the east. I say go on and on to the ocean where you'll drift away and not return to this person.

In doctoring a patient, some of my strength, of my own body, goes out. I use a considerable amount of my own strength, giving some of it to the patient that I'm working on. So, after working on many people all day long, probably fifty people or more, I feel exhausted. I feel like I don't want to get up, just lie there and rest. I might be able to stand the suffering better if I were a younger man, but I am eighty now, and to work like this takes a lot out of me.

Sometimes I appoint a helper, for there will be many patients; if I were alone, I wouldn't be able to handle all of those who are wanting to be doctored. I ask someone to help me even before the dance starts, so when the time comes, someone will be ready to help. Sometimes there will be about ten patients who will come at once and stand at the center tree, and if I were alone, it would be hard for the dancers and for the singers, for they never quit singing as long as I am doctoring. In between doctoring there may be a short break, and then the next song starts, some more patients come in and I am back at work again.

So, that is how the doctoring takes place. Each song may last almost an hour, and then the singers will rest for a moment. During this pause the announcer will come forward and make any announcement that must be made to the spectators.

Then people will come forward with gifts for the dancers to show their respect and support for the ordeal and to share prayers. Family members, friends, and people from all over the reservation bring in cattails from the creeks and sweet sage and mint from the fields. They also bring tobacco as an offering to the dancers. The name of each dancer will be called by the announcer, and the dancer will come forward to receive his gifts. When the dancer returns to his stall, he will place the cattails on the ground and make a bed of cattails to lie upon. The cattails are cool, and they comfort the dancers. The sage and mint will be placed around the stall so that their scent will fill the entire lodge. This gives great relief from the ordeal, and these gifts are appreciated by all the dancers. The dancers will also receive tobacco with a prayer request. The dancer will then smoke a little from each tobacco offering and in this way offer a prayer on behalf of the person who presented it. When the smoking is finished, the ashes are placed at the foot of the center tree. You can see how the support of the entire tribe flows into the lodge and in turn how the prayers from the Sun Dance are returned to the tribe. It is a participation by the entire tribe in the sacred ceremony, and because of this our tribe receives new strength with which to face the new year.[3]

At the end of the afternoon, the lodge is filled with blessings. Many people have been doctored, some dancers have taken a fall and received a vision, and the entire tribe has had an opportunity to share in their prayers. Now there will probably be a little break while spectators and singers retire to their camps.

The singers must eat to have the strength to continue into the evening. During this pause I lie down until they return and start us up dancing again. Some more patients will come in that evening. I may have to doctor on until midnight and still more would come. They are told to come the next day because I will be finished for the evening then. The morning of the third day is a wonderful time, both because of the great blessing of the Sunrise Ceremony but also because of the blessings which are now greater than ever all over the lodge and among the dancers.

After the Sunrise Ceremony is over, the spectators and singers retire to their camps for a short period. The dancing will commence about 9:30 and continue until the Sun Dance is over. The doctoring will continue until before the water is brought in to break the fast.

Around noon or perhaps a little after, it is time to bring in the water to break the fast. The sponsor will select four women to go and bring it. They will take their shoes off and come into the lodge, to the center tree. I pray over them and ask blessings for the work they are about to do. Then they get the water. They bring it into the lodge and place it in front of the center tree. Enough water is brought in so that it can go around several times among the dancers. Before it is served, the sponsor will call someone—it may be one of the dancers or an outsider, an old-timer dancer who has not participated in the dance—to come forward and bless the water. Then the water is passed to all of the dancers as they are seated in their stalls, and the ordeal is over.

Next, the dancers will select somebody, generally a clan aunt or uncle, to pray for them. Many of the people outside will come in to pray for the dancers, and some of the dancers will pray for each other. Then we march out of the lodge in the same way we came in. The dance is over. Now the sponsor will give a feast for everyone. The feast can be that same day unless it is late in the afternoon; then the feast will be the next day. It is the sponsor's choice, and his decision will be announced. Generally a thousand people or so will participate in the feast, and the cooks will have to start cooking before noon. By the time we are out of the lodge, the dancers will generally want to take time to go and bathe. They are eager to go and jump in the river, cool off, and wash before going to the feast. Some will go right away to take a sweat bath that has been prepared. This helps to prepare them to go back into their everyday life. This is a special time when they should remember why they have made their sacrifice.

After the feast, people can start moving from the camp and go home. The dance for that year is over.

The Sun Dance is so sacred to us that we do not talk of it often.
. . . The cutting of the bodies in fulfillment of a Sun Dance vow is different from the cutting of the flesh when people are in sorrow. A man's body is his own, and when he gives his body or his flesh he is giving the only thing which really belongs to him. . . .

A child believes that only the action of someone who is unfriendly can cause pain, but in the Sun Dance we acknowledge first the goodness of Wakan-Tanka, and then we suffer pain because of what He has done for us.[4]
—Mato-Kuwapi (Chased-by-Bears), Santee-Yanktonai Sioux

19

ATTITUDES AND SINCERITY

SOME people may hear about the Sun Dance and think, "That sounds easy and I would like to try to participate." I encourage everyone to find a religion, but I don't think people should want to join the Sun Dance religion just because it sounds interesting or because they think they will receive some reward for their effort.

I participated in the Sun Dance for close to thirty years before I was to take over the duties of Sun Dance chief from Rainbow. I never asked to become a medicine man—I was selected, and Rainbow was told to pass all these things to me. I danced many times before I was selected to receive something great. I knew that the Sun Dance religion was true and that I needed to pray. I thought, "Maybe I'll receive a vision that would help me be a better person." I never approached John Trehero for anything. I never asked him for his medicine; things came to me. So, a young man participating in the Sun Dance should not expect to have tremendous results immediately; he has to prove his sincerity over time. He may have to try and try like I did, many times, before he may have a vision or receive a recognizable reward.

Many sincere young people follow all parts of the Sun Dance religion. They go on a vision quest out in the hills, in solitude, to try to pray. They sometimes have to go several times on vision quests. It is not easy; it requires repeated effort; one has to be worthy to receive a divine gift, and that requires not only sincerity, but also perseverance.

The Sun Dance and the vision quest are what is most important, but there are other obligations that must be fulfilled in order to really pertain to our religion. During the thirty years that I was participating in the Sun Dance, I was also attending and having monthly prayer meetings. Each month, especially at the time of the full moon, I would pray with a smoke at a prayer meeting. It might be at my home with just Grandma or at the home of someone else, but Grandma and I would never forget to do it.

A person might never receive a great vision or any power—it doesn't matter. The Medicine Fathers know what is in our hearts, and they may help us or bless us in ways we do not see. We must be resigned to whatever trials they send us, and we must be content with what we have been given. If a person expects to receive something great, then that person will probably never receive anything. The Medicine Fathers do not owe anything to anyone. We must realize this and dedicate our lives to living in accordance with the directions given to us from Above—not just once a year, but every day and year after year.

A person must also be old enough to realize all of the responsibilities that come from participating in the Sun Dance. Some young ones may want to come in but are only fourteen years old or so, and that is too young. They ask me, "I want to go in, how about it?" I tell them, "You should wait another few years until you are older, until you realize what it means to join the Sun Dance. There are things here that you are too young to understand. You might even run away from us and spoil our medicine." I am afraid they might give up during the middle of the dance. The person who violates the rule shows disrespect to the Medicine Fathers and Acbadadea, and risks Their punishment. Other dancers will worry about the violation, and this can disturb our prayers. If our prayers are disturbed, each of us, and also our tribe, will not receive the full benefit of the Sun Dance. Youngsters don't take this into account. They might say, "Oh, I will stay, I am sincere, I will make it through the ordeal." But I always make sure that they have watched the Sun Dance before and that they know all of the proper procedures and that they will not run away. It is easy to want to participate, but it is different once they come and start to blow the eagle bone whistle for at least three days, with no food or water in temperatures of more than one hundred degrees. You must be prepared and know the reason why you dance.

They have a story they tell about over there at Fort Washakie, on the Shoshone reservation. In one Sun Dance a young boy was participating. It was the second day, and they could see he was going to do something, like running away. Some of the men outside the lodge were watching him. He got up and went outside of the lodge. As he went to the outhouse, he saw his chance, and he started out. They saw him going and took out after him, but he ran fast, and they couldn't catch up with him. He got to an irrigation canal and just walked right in and took a drink. They could not catch him in time. We are fortunate that we have never had any running away like the one at Fort Washakie.

There are other things that a member of the Sun Dance religion should try to learn. For example, it is important for a man who wants to participate in the Sun Dance to understand the Crow language; then he will understand much more. He will also understand what I say in the prayers. This is very important for a sun dancer. It was wrong when our people were taught the English language and not their own tongue. Some Indians would like to know their own language, but they think it may be too late now. Our own children know Crow, but not all of our grandchildren speak it, so I am also at fault. It is never too late to learn Crow; there are even some white men who study it. It has just been about two years that one of our white adopted grandsons has studied it, and he can understand Indian, but he cannot talk it yet. There are others who have learned to speak their own language after they grew up. I encourage Indians to learn their own language even if they think that they cannot. They can study it now like these white men do; it was not their language, but they learned to speak it.

It is the same with the Indian songs. The young people today should learn them. They should try to sing the songs; they must try to grasp them when they hear them. Indian boys can certainly do it, for we have some white boys who sit down and sing with our Indian singers. All our Indian boys should be able to sing the songs. Some never have tried.

The young people should start now to learn their language and their Indian songs. It is the responsibility of the Indians who want to follow the traditional life way to try to learn these things. Our sacred ways may become a thing of the past if they don't. They must be encouraged to try to learn these things while some of the elders are still here. We old-timers have forgotten many of the stories that we heard orally and that were given to us by the great chiefs when we were children. We try to remember them now, but we can't. As children we listened to warriors telling legends of all kinds, and just hearing the old warriors tell their stories helped us learn about the quality of their lives. They would even sing songs to accompany the story that they were telling. It is just through memory that we try to reproduce these, and that is very difficult. So it is important that the young people today do not let that happen with the knowledge that we still have. We must keep the sacred ways that remain with us, for they can allow all our people to follow a spiritual path.

It is especially important for a young man who is going to participate in the Sun Dance to know the Sun Dance songs, to know about the nature of the rite, and to understand the rules of the Sun Dance. Sometimes people come to the Sun Dance at the last minute and want to go in right away, without knowing any of the procedures and without knowing the other obligations that they should accept after the Sun Dance. Some of the people who come and participate imagine that they can learn the procedures during the dance, but this is bad because it creates problems for the other dancers if they have to help someone else. Each dancer should be concentrating on his prayers and not having to worry about someone else who may violate some rule.

Once a person has participated in one dance, he must participate in an even number of Sun Dances. He should participate in at least four, but if he has any problems, he still must participate in at least two.

You can see that anyone about to enter the Sun Dance

religion should take time to understand his actions before he begins. My heart is very, very happy to see new members, but it is not the number of people who participate that is important but their sincerity and attitudes.

In recent years there has been hardly enough room for all the dancers in the Sun Dance lodge, and it has even been necessary to make a special extension of the lodge in order to accommodate all the dancers. It is good to see so many come to participate. It may be that non-Indians will no longer be allowed because there will only be enough room for Indians. The Sun Dance is an Indian religion, and there must be enough room for the Indians to participate.

We Crow believe that all men are equal in the eyes of Acbadadea. Crow legends tell us that after the earth was formed and the animals were created, that the duck dove deep into the waters covering most of the earth and brought up four colors of clay: red, yellow, black, and white. Out of this clay, our Creator formed the image of man. This is why there are four colors of man, and this shows that all men are the same in the eyes of our Creator although each race is different from the others.

You can see from this story that we Indians do not feel that we are better than non-Indians, but we were given our own religion just as all the other races were given theirs. It is possible for everyone to learn from the religion of another, but white people should only participate in our religion if they have learned our songs and some of our language. With non-Indians participating in the Indian Sun Dance there is, moreover, another problem, the room: there must first be room for all the Indians who want to participate.

I would like to recommend to the sponsor that he announce his decision on white participation at the same time the date for the Sun Dance is set, in late winter or early spring. It must be soon enough so that no problems are caused. I recommend that some standard be established so that no non-Indians be allowed to participate unless they can show their sincerity and their understanding of the Sun Dance. The best way is to limit non-Indians to only those who know the four morning songs that we sing at the time of the Sunrise Ceremony. These songs should be known by every dancer, Indian and non-Indian. If someone has taken the trouble to learn these songs, then they will have shown that they have a good intention. It may be that this prevents some non-Indian who has a good intention from participating for one or two years until he has taken the trouble to learn the songs, but this type of rule will encourage everyone to learn about the religion if he really wants to follow it.

We have had "Hollywood" Indians come and try to show off with special feathers or special dance steps. This can hurt the power of the Sun Dance for everyone else. We cannot allow non-Indians to interfere with our religion. I have heard many Indians complain about white participation because of some bad experiences. It troubles me to have this problem, because some non-Indians are sincere. They know the Indian way is good, and they want to come and join. It is hard to say no to someone if he asks me; the only way I know to solve the problem is to set a standard so that all non-Indians will know what is expected of them.

Last year the sponsor of the coming Sun Dance had a vision in which the Medicine Fathers told him there should be only Indians in the Sun Dance. The sponsor followed these rules, and no non-Indians participated. Everyone knew the Sun Dance was successful, and it may be that more and more Sun Dances will be held with no non-Indian participation.

As I said, the sponsor of the Sun Dance can decide on the rules; I only guide the way. His decisions should be announced far in advance, and also at the time of the four nightly ceremonies that we have at the Sun Dance site. In this way everyone will know. Also, if non-Indians are to participate, they should line up at the end of the line and only enter the lodge if there is room after everyone else has marched in. Sometimes people arrive late, after everyone else is in the lodge, and any dancer can enter until midnight on the night the dance starts. So any non-Indians should wait outside and come in after all the Indians have found a place in the lodge.

When all of this is considered, it can be understood that the

Sun Dance way has requirements that are difficult to meet. People nowadays are lazy and soft; they expect everything to be easy, but the Indian way reminds us that life requires hardship, sincerity, and prayer.

Now I am through speaking about the Sun Dance religion, and I have done my best to speak with my heart. The truth of the Sun Dance way is almost too good to believe, but we must believe, and we must act on what we know is true. There is much more that could be said about the Indian way, but enough has been said so that each person who hears these words can know that the Sun Dance religion is a path that can lead us through this life and lead us to Acbadadea.

The one who instructs a candidate to dance the Sun Dance is the *tunkansila*. This means more than a grandfather. The candidate then becomes like a babe. His instructor governs him in everything. He must do nothing but as he is told by his instructor. The instructor thinks for him and speaks for him and tells him how to think and how to speak. The instructor gives rules and the candidate must obey them exactly. The instructor becomes the candidate's other self.[1]

—George Sword, Teton Sioux

PART THREE

CONCLUSIONS

20

LOSS OF OUR
TRADITIONAL VALUES

IN the olden days the Indians had their freedom, and they followed their traditional ways. Then the whites made us settle on reservations. People had to live close together, and we were not free to live in our traditional way. People also lost sight of the true meaning of these ways. It was not long until a lot of the powers and sacred things that had been given to the Indians were taken back. That is what we were told by prophecies before the time of settlement on the reservations. Many medicine men who had had good medicine, good powers, lost them. This all happened gradually over the last one hundred years, until today there are fewer men with less spiritual power and understanding. Those who still have spiritual gifts or medicine—and there are a few left—don't have as strong a power as in the days when the Indians were still free to roam the country and live in the traditional manner. As time went on, the Indians became more "civilized" and learned to live in the white man's ways, and so all of the spiritual powers were diminished. People lost sight of religion and prayer, so it seems that the old prophecies were correct.

Back in the days when we were free, when our people knew more about Nature and important things, almost every man had medicine powers, and the only life people knew was centered on the sacred. The real medicine man could do wonders in those days. It is really the modern world and "civilization" that is causing us to lose all these things. In olden times, the people had their values centered on spiritual concerns. The spiritual powers, the givers of medicines, are taking those sacred things back from us because we do not know how to care for them correctly.

Modern Indians care little for spiritual things and traditional ways, so there are very few traditional people remaining with real medicine or understanding. Modern civilization has no understanding of sacred matters. Everything is backwards. This makes it even more important that young people follow what is left today. Even though many of the sacred ways are no longer with us, what we have left is enough for anyone, and if it is followed it will lead as far as the person can go. The four rites that we have spoken of in this work form the center of the religion: the sweat lodge for purification; the vision quest for the spiritual retreat; the daily prayer with the offering of tobacco smoke; and the Sun Dance itself. With all this, any sincere person can realize his inner spiritual center. I tell them to join, join the Sun Dance. Try to understand about the old sacred ways, the Sun Dance way. Of course there are a lot of young people who do come in, but their sincerity may not be there. They just come in and out of the Sun Dance and then go away. They do not come to our prayer meetings, and we do not see them again, not until the next Sun Dance. Three or four days a year at the time of the Sun Dance is not enough.

It is important that the young people understand the difference between the traditional ways and the modern world we live in today. I have spoken before about the sacred support that was always present for the traditional Indians. With this support everywhere, from the moment you arose and said your first prayer until the moment you went to sleep you could at least see what was necessary in order to lead a proper life. Even the dress that you wore every day had sacred meanings, such as the bead work designs on the clothing, and wherever you went or whatever you did, whether you were hunting, making weapons, or whatever you were doing, you were participating in a sacred life and you knew who you were and carried a sense of the sacred with you. All of the forms had meaning, even the tipi and the sacred circle of the entire camp. Of course the life was hard and difficult, and not all Indians followed the rules. But the support of the traditional life and the presence of Nature everywhere brought great blessings on all the people.[1]

The world we live in is quite different. Young people today can't read the signs of nature, and they do not even know the names of the different animals. When a bird calls or we see the prints left by an animal, most of our people will not know the name of the animal that stands close by. If we walk down a hill, many of our grandchildren will not even know that they have walked over an "Indian turnip" or some other valuable food. What is worse, many young people do not even look, or sometimes even care, where they are walking and do not observe the beautiful things that Acbadadea has created. It almost makes me cry to see how some young people waste precious gifts. They will let food spoil or waste water and electricity. People do not seem to realize the value of the gifts they have been given; they think things will always be there when they need something. These same people will have a big surprise someday, because sooner or later they will be shown their errors.

Look at the way people travel and work nowadays. You always hear people say, "We are in the fast age." Everything has to be fast, according to the way people want to do things nowadays. If we are going a great distance, the destination or place we are going to isn't going to move; it is standing still, so there is no need to be in such a hurry. In addition to not being safe, there are other dangers in this fast way of life. It is a problem with their entire way of living. I think it is wise to take a little more time in whatever you're doing and do it right; then, whatever it is, it will last longer. If you do something too fast, it will deteriorate. People should ask themselves what it is that they are doing and why it is that they are doing it. So many people today don't even think; they just do something.

Many of the modern things that we have now have made everything worse. We didn't have television until a few years ago, and since the television has come into use, people have just fallen crazy for it. It is something that I don't care for myself. It makes people lazy and gives them strange ideas about life. For instance, it seems as if there isn't any modesty anymore. When people see something on television, they think it is right. They don't think for themselves; they let the television think for them. Television is something that is not good for the world. It is too bad that most people don't realize how something like television can ruin all of our true values.

It seems as if everything in today's world is set up so that everyone can keep going so fast that they never have to consider why they were given the miracle of life. It is too bad that people waste their life and their intelligence by becoming part of this fast society. If they just stopped for a moment and considered that they will all die and meet their Lord, I wonder what they would do?

One of the reasons our society is so fast is the machine. Machinery has changed the manner in which we live, and all of our values regarding this world. In olden days, it required manual labor for just about everything. Everyone had a responsibility, and everyone helped each other. There was no money to keep and to possess, so you couldn't acquire more things than your neighbor. The olden-day Indians moved about the countryside, and they couldn't carry more than what they needed. The qualities that a man possessed within himself were important, not what outward possessions he had. We have talked about how the Indians give away things to express their inner beliefs.

In those days, everyone knew what was expected of him, and the Indian way taught him just how to do it. Not all olden-day Indians lived up to the tribal goals, even though the sacred center was present. Today some people still pray as they should, even though the sacred center is almost gone. But the goals of the society in those days and today are different, and this is something that everyone must understand. We have spoken about the manner in which we carry out our Sun Dance religion and how everything has a meaning, a purpose. So it was with everything the olden Indians did, and so it should be today. You would begin to understand the mysteries of this world in which we have been placed, and you would know what you must do to prepare yourself to meet death, to enter the world beyond that we cannot see.

Many of the Sun Dance ceremonies are difficult to endure;

it is an ordeal to complete them. This is good, and it helps us remember that there is a greater responsibility in life. Life is a gift that you are free to use as you see fit, but you also have to understand that your actions, your choices, are being observed by powers that you do not see. If everything is easy for us and if our concerns are only regarding our possessions, then we lose sight of what is important. In difficult times, we are always prepared to face death; it may come today. So it should be every day in everything we do. We must prepare ourselves today to meet our Lord, the Maker of All Things Above. People always think that there is plenty of time left to pray later. People who want to accumulate more wealth are always thinking that "I'll wait until later." The world today, and the way people do things, encourages people to be lazy in their spiritual duties.

Manual labor is not required anymore; it is all done by machinery. One man can now do a big field of hay all by himself. The hay is cut and baled by machines; they have even got machinery now that picks it up and brings it in. Without touching anything, the machine puts the bales there and they are already on the stack. Many men used to be required to work many days, but now it is practically done in one day with these machines. Sugar beet farming used to require several men; quite a few working people are all now eliminated by modern machinery. Men going around looking for farm jobs can hardly get any work now. No one needs them because the machinery they have takes care of all that.

Even in the cattle industry, it is the same way. There used to be some good cowboys who would take care of the work on the cattle ranch. A lot of them cannot find jobs anymore. There are machines now that take their place. So it looks as if we get to the time when many good men cannot find any work at all. That is not like it should be.

Nowadays men want to accumulate money and then they use the money to buy machines so that all the work can be done more quickly; then they can accumulate even more money. That is all the rich man thinks about. What about the men who want to work for a living? They have no jobs and nothing at all to do. People end up working against each other, as the people without money and machines start to hate the others. Many of the wars in the world today result from this problem. Some men will criticize our Indian boys who can't find work and say that they are lazy, that if an Indian really wants to work, he can find work. In some cases this is true, but it can't be true for everyone. Think about it: If everyone on the reservation really wanted to go out and look for a job, could everyone find one? The reason the answer is "no" can be seen when you realize the problems that money and machinery cause.[2]

Now what happens when one good Indian boy does go out and finds a job with good, hard work? Everyone should be proud of him, but they are not. Jealousy is created by the fact that people are competing against one another. On our reservations today, people are jealous of each other. No one cooperates. People blame each other for all of the problems and criticize people who do work hard and who try to help. Many people will criticize me for talking to you. They will find some fault or try to say that I made an error in something that I have told you. "Why does that white man want to write a book about the Indian religion? What does he know?" If they find one small error, they will condemn everything we have done. This is their problem, and it will only hurt them. People should think about what we have tried to accomplish with this work. Maybe people can understand that what we see in this modern world is bad, that most of the values people have today are backwards. To follow the way of the machine world will not prepare you to meet your Maker either in this life or after death.

It is true that we cannot just go back to the olden days, either. What good does it do to wish you were an olden-day Indian? Why criticize your brother and try to find faults in everyone else? Will that make you a better person because you have decided that someone else has faults? Some Indians will face their problems with a bottle. This is very bad–drugs, too. It corrupts all of our youngsters. How can any of this solve problems? It just makes everything worse, because they don't try to make anything out of themselves. These same people expect that they will be given things by the tribe, the government. They think that it is the responsibility of others to take care of them. They think we should sell our coal, our water, our resources, so that they will be provided for. They don't care at all about our children. All that matters is their own welfare today. These men will certainly receive their just reward when they meet their Maker.

We have spoken about the Sun Dance religion and what it means for us today. You can see that everything is very different today and that many of the sacred things and sacred ways that were with our Indian people in the olden days are lost. This was bound to come, for we did not deserve to keep them because we no longer had respect for them. But it does no good to blame any one person or country for our present-day situation. All these events were foreseen in sacred prophecies from all of the great religions.

No one person is to blame for our present state. Everyone who fails to live up to his spiritual duties causes further problems for everyone. Therefore, I tell people, "Don't criticize your neighbor; that will not help anyone. It is not good to fight Indian against Indian; it just makes matters worse. Work on yourself first; prepare yourself to meet your Lord."

We did not ask you white men to come here. The Great Spirit gave us this country as a home. You had yours. We did not interfere with you. The Great Spirit gave us plenty of land to live on, and buffalo, deer, antelope and other game. But you have come here; you are taking my land from me; you are killing off our game, so it is hard for us to live. Now, you tell us to work for a living, but the Great Spirit did not make us to work, but to live by hunting. You white men can work if you want to. We do not interfere with you, and again you say, why do you not become civilized? We do not want your civilization! We would live as our fathers did, and their fathers before them.[3]
—Crazy Horse, Oglala Sioux

MAKE YOUR CHOICE

EVERYONE can see how things have changed from the olden times, when sacred values were at the center of our life, up to the present day, when our society does not seem to have a sense of the sacred. So many young people wonder what may happen to this world that we are in, and what they should do if they want to follow a spiritual path. They may think, "Are there other people who want to follow a sacred way? Do I have an opportunity to lead a life in accordance with the traditional ways?"

If people continue on their present course, with no prayer and no respect for sacred things, then things will get worse and worse for everyone. Many prophecies from great religions all over the world speak of the end of time. The Crow have a prophecy about this time, too.

The Crow prophecy concerns an important Crow rite: the Beaver Dance or Tobacco Dance. It is the same thing but is known by both names. It is a dance participated in by both men and women who are members of the Tobacco Society. The society used to perform their ceremonies every year. We do not know of any other Indian tribe that has this same dance. You could call it a Crow Indian dance. The Tobacco Society has an Adoption Dance to adopt new members into the society so that the ceremonies can always be continued. Recently, very few new members have been adopted, and the ceremonies are not held as often as they were in olden times.

If older members want to adopt new members, they take them into three dances, and then the fourth time, during the summer, the adoption is completed. Grandma and I are not members of this society, so I do not know much about it, but

I have been to see several of their ceremonies as a guest. Grandma and I were asked to become members once, but we declined because of our other obligations. We have visited the ceremonies to share our prayers with the members.

The plant they use in the ceremony is not really a tobacco. The Crow name for it is *itchichea*. It is very holy. In olden days, every year they would plant the tobacco in a special ceremony in the spring, usually in May. They would harvest it in the fall, and they would keep the plant and seeds and start the process over the next spring. Even when I was a young boy, they completed the planting and harvesting every year so that there would always be tobacco for special ceremonies and prayers. Today the Tobacco Society rarely plants and harvests the tobacco. Almost all of the old members are practically gone, and very few new adoptions take place, so fewer people know about the correct way to perform the ceremony and care for the tobacco. I believe the last time they had a special planting ceremony was several years ago at my sister's place, just below where my brother lives now. They set up their tipis there, and they held their ceremonies for a day or two. Then they came out and planted their tobacco plants. The plant grows all summer, and they harvest it in the fall with another ceremony. I was not present at the time of the harvest ceremony of that planting, but I was told that the seed production and crop production were very poor. The plant is not a very strong plant, and so it appears that it may be gone soon. There might not be any more of the plants left anywhere, since this particular plant is only used by the Crow.[1]

The Crow Indian prophecy says that when this plant is gone, when it is not planted and harvested so that there is no reproduction of the seed, then finally it will be the end of time and the world will end. It looks as if that time is near. I was not there that fall when they went to gather it, but they told me they did not get much production of seed that year. What they have on hand will finally get old and will not produce any more; it will not renew, and that will probably be the end.

There are prophecies from the other religions that also talk about the end of time.[2] The Hopi prophecies are very interesting to hear. I have met Thomas Banyacya several times, and he is very good at explaining the Hopi prophecies. He was a school classmate of my nephew, Joseph Medicine Crow. There are many other Indians who know about these things also. There is an organization that held its first meetings about five years ago, near Three Forks, Montana. That is when I first met many of these men from other tribes. I have seen them every year since then. Last year it was held on the Cheyenne reservation at Busby, Montana, at the home of Austin Two Moons. These meetings encourage tribal medicine men and others interested in the sacred ways to come together, and this is good. It is not just the Crow Indians who believe in these matters, but also Indians everywhere.

I think there will come a time when they will purchase the piece of land where the first conference was held in Montana, near the headwaters of the Missouri River. That might be a permanent meeting place if that piece of land can be purchased. It is centrally located, and once it becomes ours, people will come there where we'll gather every year. But as of now we haven't got that place, so the Indians of different tribes who have been attending these meetings have taken turns inviting the rest of the group for the next meeting place in their respective reservations.

The purpose of the meeting is to encourage Indians to follow their traditional ways and educate everyone about our religion. The younger ones who attend get to know important things that they hear from the elders. I think it is very good that this organization was established to encourage those who are interested in sacred things. Many young people don't know where to turn. At this meeting they can learn something. Each year new ones come in, and it will gradually increase by new members from different tribes. Elders come in, but also young men and young ladies have come to attend these meetings, and it is good.

It is important for the young people to understand and follow their traditional religion.[3] We must help to educate our young ones in the proper manner about our traditions.[4] I always try to encourage the young to forget the other things that they have in mind: "Drop those things and try to learn something about your traditional Indian ways." They should join these meetings that Indians are having and try to continue the use of the different ceremonies and of prayer according to the Indian heritage.

Some people might think, "It doesn't do any good to pray; it won't change anything." But there are many reasons to pray, and those people are wrong. Only God knows when the end of this world will come, and when and how it comes will certainly depend on sincere prayers that are offered to Him in the correct way. Each man will pass from this earth in his own time. Some of the prophecies talk only about the end of time; others speak about the break-up of the modern world as we know it and a return to the traditional ways of our ancestors. I can't say what will happen and whether we will find the spiritual ways of our ancestors in this world or another, but I do know that in either case we still have to make a choice; each one of us must choose at this present moment which path to follow. Each person's prayers can help everyone. The person who prays and remembers God will receive the greatest benefit for himself and for others.

Some people will not believe that they really have a choice in following a religion and in turning to prayer. This is a strange idea. Everyone has a free mind, and at any moment each individual can choose to do one thing instead of another. Think about this. Even a child does not have to obey his parents; he can choose the punishment he will receive if he disobeys instead. So too, can each person choose whether to join a religion and way of prayer. There are different reasons why you should do this: of course you can fear punishment just like the child who disobeys, or you can follow a sacred path because you know and love the sacred ways. Whatever your reason, you must choose one direction or another, in the same way that Rainbow was shown two paths in his vision, one leading not very far, and the Sun Dance way leading as far as he wanted to go. There is nothing more I can say except to raise my voice in prayer:

"During these next years, I need Your help to give me the

knowledge and strength to carry our Sun Dance religion to our people. I have been trying to speak out, so that all the young people will know what is expected of them. Help me to carry this message to their hearts. I am working with my grandson so that this message can be written down for many to see. Help us. Our Absaroke people need to see that their own religion is good and that it can help them if only they open their eyes and hearts. Everyone needs to make a choice; each should choose a religion. Help them to understand that they must make that choice before it is too late.

"You have told our people through our Absaroke prophecies that the world will come to an end. The other religions that have been given to the white people also talk about the end of time. According to what we have been told, that time may be here soon. Help people see that they should select the religion of their choice. Then they must pray every day and live straight."

"There was a time when all the different denominations used to stay away from each other or there was a little rivalry between them. It should not be that way. They should unite and pray together. All the people on the reservation should unite regardless of their beliefs. You have given different ways to different people all over the world. As we know, this earth is round like a wagon wheel. In a wagon wheel, all the spokes are set into the center. The circle of the wheel is round, and all spokes come from the center, and the center is You, Acbadadea, the Maker of All Things Above. Each spoke can be considered as a different religion of the world which has been given by You to different people and different races. All of the people of the world are on the rim of the wheel, and they must follow one of the spokes to the center. The different paths have been given to us, but they all lead to the same place. We all pray to the same God, to You. There are different places on the wheel, so each way may look strange to someone following a different path. It is easy for people to say that their way is the best if they know all about their faith and it is good for them. But they should refrain from saying bad things about other ways that they don't know about. There should be no hard feelings about someone else if he is following a way that leads to You. Help us to see this wisdom.

"A person should learn all about a path to You before he joins. It is not good to just enter a faith and then drop it. I tell this to the young people: 'You must choose a religion, but before you enter one, you should know which one is the best for you. Take the time and find out all you can about the method of prayer and about what that religion tells you about the Maker of All Things Above. You should understand the rules and know what is expected of you. Find a path that provides you with the way you need to live a good life every day.' The Sun Dance religion is not an easy path, it is difficult and demands a great deal from each member. But if a person follows it, the Sun Dance religion will lead as far as the person wants to go. Acbadadea, Medicine Fathers, help all young people to know these things.

"Some people don't want to know what religion requires of them. As soon as they don't like something—because it may not be easy or it may require some sacrifice—they leave in a hurry without asking themselves what You expect of them. They can't get anything out of a religion if they leave every time something hard is asked of them. If they ever do find a way that is so easy that they can always perform everything without any trouble, then they should know they have found a bad thing. That is the time they should leave that false religion. Maker of All Things Above, give people the wisdom to see these things and the strength to resist those who will not follow You.

"I have tried to speak my mind and my heart in the best way I know. Thank You for helping guide my words. Now I have completed my responsibility of speaking about the sacred ways of our Absaroke people, and I feel good about this. Thank You for the help that You have given me already so that I could carry out Your wishes until now. Help me to keep working and praying so that this position as Sun Dance chief can be fulfilled and my people will be able to live. I am ready to follow Your wishes in training a man to take my place, and I will try my best to continue my work until You are ready to take me to You. I ask You to give me guidance in choosing my successor as Sun Dance chief so that our sacred ways will continue and my people will live. *Aho, aho!*"

The Great Spirit will not punish us for what we do not know. He will do justice to his red children. These black coats (missionaries) talk to the Great Spirit, and ask for light that we may see as they do, when they are blind themselves and quarrel about the light that guides them. These things we do not understand, and the light which they give us makes the straight and plain path trod by our fathers, dark and dreary.

The red men knew nothing of trouble until it came from the white men; as soon as they crossed the great waters they wanted our country, and in return have always been ready to teach us to quarrel about their religion. Red Jacket can never be the friend of such men. If they (the Indians) were raised among white people, and learned to work and read as they do, it would only make their situation worse. . . . We are few and weak, but may for a long time be happy if we hold fast to our country, and the religion of our fathers.[5]

—Red Jacket, Seneca

APPENDIX

APPENDIX

HISTORICAL OVERVIEW OF THE ABSAROKE

YELLOWTAIL'S spiritual message can be more fully appreciated if the reader proceeds from a general understanding of the Crow tribe. This appendix therefore provides first a brief historical summary and then a review of the tribal events that led to the Crow treaties with the United States in the late 1800s. The historical overview helps to orient the reader regarding the origins of the Crow tribe and how they came to the geographical homeland in which their reservation is now located. The review of the events that led to Crow treaties with the white government is important in order to explain the situation of the Crow in the modern postreservation period in comparison to that of other tribes. Although this book allows the reader insights into the Crow religious beliefs and the values of the spiritual leader of the Crow tribe, Yellowtail does not comment on tribal history or politics. This appendix will then set an overall context for an understanding of Crow history and the beneficial treatment the Crow received in obtaining a very desirable reservation. This is helpful for both uninformed readers who have little knowledge of the Crow and for Indian readers from other tribes who may not have received such desirable reservation lands.

The Crow tribe is most closely related to the Hidatsa, as evidenced by their close linguistic relationship. The ancestral Hidatsa moved out of the eastern woodlands in different migrations and probably reached the Missouri River in the early 1600s. Different calculations have been made of the time of separation of the Crow from the Hidatsa, but the period of the mid-1600's seems to be a reasonable estimate. Later dates do not provide enough time to allow for the greater differentiation of the Crow language from Hidatsa and from the Sioux language from which both emerge.

The River Crow probably moved into the Yellowstone–Big Horn river valleys between 1700 and 1725. They were well established in this area about 1800, when contacts with whites began. From this area the Crow traded with their friendly surrounding neighbors: the Shoshone to the south, the Nez Percé and Flathead to the north and west, and the Hidatsa and Mandan to the north and east. The Crow were positioned in an ideal geographic area, rich with natural resources, and enemies as well as friends surrounded them.

By 1750 the Crow already had established enemies from among surrounding tribes. The Blackfeet to the north were perhaps the most frequent raiders into the Crow territory. Starting in the late 1700s, the Teton Sioux, Cheyenne, and Arapaho came into increasing conflict with the Crow as these tribes were pushed into closer contact by westward pressure from whites. During the period from the mid-1700s to the mid-1800s, the Crow also had both peaceful and hostile contact with the Comanche, Kiowa, Hidatsa, Assiniboin, Pawnee, and Osage. The increasing conflict with their hostile Indian neighbors, particularly the Teton Sioux, forced the Crow to an even greater amount of trade with the whites in order to protect their homeland. This trade both established the Crow as an ally with the whites against the numerically superior Sioux and also provided the Crow with the modern weapons and utensils necessary to provide an advantage against their enemies.

This increasing trade with the whites culminated in the Fort Laramie Treaty of 1851, in which the U.S. government acknowledged Crow ownership of thirty-eight million acres of land in exchange for a fifty-year annuity in goods and the construction of roads and forts on Crow land. The Crow abandoned all claims to their other lands. The fifty-year annuity was cut to five years as the government violated this first treaty almost immediately. The second treaty with the U.S. government came in 1868, with the size of the reservation being reduced to eight million acres. In this treaty the Crow gave up most of their ancestral homeland but succeeded in keeping their beloved Big Horn River valley. Two subsequent treaties, signed in 1882 and 1905, reduced the reservation to its present size of two million acres.

During the period from 1850 to 1884, the Crow were forced to move the center of their reservation three times, from Mission Creek to a site on the Rosebud River near Absaroka (Absarokee) and then to the current agency near Hardin. They had also seen the size of their reservation continually shrink and the promises made by the government continually broken. Yet still they cooperated with the white government rather than fight against it. There were factors other than the white protection against hostile tribes that continued to influence the Crow cooperation.

While the reservation was part of the historic lands of the Crow, the Crow were one of the few Indian tribes able to retain desirable acreage instead of being given the least desirable acreage or being removed from their homeland altogether. This favorable governmental treatment resulted from early and relatively peaceful settlement with the whites, in direct contrast to the hardships and "trails of tears" suffered by other tribes who more strongly resisted white encroachment on their homelands and lifeways.

This combination of early capitulation to the whites and its resulting reward of desirable reservation lands in some cases has promoted hard feelings toward the Crow by other Indian tribes. It would be tragic if these hostile feelings linger and do not allow some Indian readers to fully appreciate the validity of the Crow religion. In my travels to other Indian reservations, I have on several occasions heard members of different tribes criticize the Crow. After probing their feelings, it appears to me that that negative opinion has been created by the preferential treatment given the Crow in the grant of their reservation and by the perceived failure of the Crow to stand up to the whites militarily. I consider these hostile perceptions to be created in part by a misunderstanding why the Absaroke signed a peace treaty with the U.S. government without first engaging in prolonged wars with the whites.

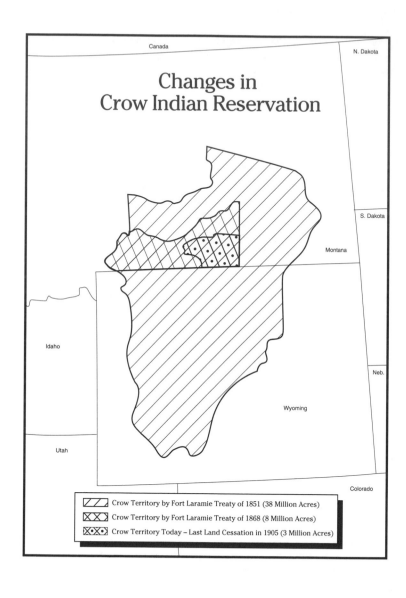

Changes in
Crow Indian Reservation

Canada

N. Dakota

S. Dakota

Montana

Idaho

Neb.

Wyoming

Utah

Colorado

Crow Territory by Fort Laramie Treaty of 1851 (38 Million Acres)
Crow Territory by Fort Laramie Treaty of 1868 (8 Million Acres)
Crow Territory Today – Last Land Cessation in 1905 (3 Million Acres)

However, before considering the specific reasons for the Absaroke response to white civilization, the dilemma that faced all Indians must be understood. In the face of the overwhelming force possessed by a culture that was in every way incompatible with the basic values of the Indians, was it better to fight to the death or to make the best possible terms for peace? There are two important perspectives from which to view this question, one being that of the tribe and the other that of the individual. At the point where it is clear that to resist further is to cause tribal annihilation, each tribe as a collectivity must consider surrender, even though to do so might well mean an end to many of the ways of life that the Indians held sacred. But even in this case, the tribe survives. Had the Crow fought to the death, men like Yellowtail would not exist.

And what is the individual response to the question? The key consideration for each individual warrior was undoubtedly his position of responsibility within the tribe and toward his family. In many ways, the easiest response for a warrior is to die in battle; the much harder response is to submit to a life that is contrary to his very being. Yet this latter response is what is demanded of each man with the responsibility to safeguard the essential values of his heritage for posterity even though he realizes that much that he holds dear will be lost forever. Many Indian leaders, including Chief Crazy Horse and Chief Rolling Thunder (Chief Joseph), came to this decision. If these warriors had lost their lives and families in futile combat, the Indian tradition with its lessons for all men would have been lost forever with them. It takes great courage to die in battle, but in many ways it takes greater courage to choose to live in suffering in order to preserve the tribal heritage, which above all is spiritual.

In order to question whether the Crow decision to make peace with the whites was morally correct, we must ask whether the tribal leaders knew that to resist the whites would mean total annihilation. The history of many tribes shows that typically only complete military defeat brought about this realization. Destiny provided the Crow Chief Plenty-Coups a divine message in a vision that was decisive for all the tribal leaders. His vision is related in complete detail in *Plenty-coups,* recorded by Frank Linderman, (Lincoln, University of Nebraska Press, 1930). In his vision, Plenty-Coups first saw the prairie covered by buffalo, only to see them vanish with not one remaining. Then he saw animals, later identified as cattle, spread over the plains. These were strange to him, as if from another world. Then in his vision he was taken to a place on Pryor Creek (where he later lived) and shown a great forest of tall, strong trees filled with "countless Bird-people." He saw a great storm come and destroy all the beautiful trees and birds like blades of grass. When the storm ended, only one tree was left standing where the great forest had been, and in that tree was the lodge of the Chickadee. Plenty-Coups was told:

> "He [the Chickadee] is least in strength but strongest of mind among his kind. He is willing to work for wisdom. The Chickadee-person is a good listener. Nothing escapes his ears. . . . He never intrudes, never speaks in strange company, and yet never misses a chance to learn from others. He gains success and avoids failure by learning how others succeeded or failed, and without great trouble to himself."[1]

Plenty-Coups was still a young man, and Yellowbear, the wisest of the Crow, interpreted the dream with the complete agreement of the tribal council. It was clear to them that the storm represented the coming of the white man, and all who opposed the whites would be torn from their roots and crushed. The buffalo, representing the Indian life, would be gone, and in their place would be the white man's ways (represented by the cattle). Only by bending in the wind could the tree not be uprooted, and only the apparently weak yet very wise could profit by the lessons of others.

From that moment forward, the Crow knew from the vision that complete resistance was impossible; hence, the whole question of the "morality" of their decision has to be approached with the understanding that the Crow considered themselves under spiritual instruction concerning their conduct towards the whites. There were minor battle victories for the Crow against the whites, but the Crow were among the first Plains Indians to make a treaty because of the certainty of Plenty-Coups's vision. In doing so, they preserved some of the best of their homeland and saved by this means more than they could ever have saved militarily. Those who resisted strongly were ultimately forced to surrender, and their settlements were much worse than those achieved by the Crow.

The final question is whether the Crow were in fact militarily weak. The land originally held by the Crow extended from the Tetons through present-day Yellowstone Park to the Big Horn Mountains and over vast prairies. Only mighty warriors could have held that land against enemies on all sides. The following two quotations from observers of earlier times can best answer the question:

> The country belonging to the Crows was not only beautiful, but it was the very heart of the buffalo range of the Northwest. It embraced endless plains, high mountains, and great rivers, fed by streams clear as crystal. No other section could compare with the Crow country, especially when it was untouched by white men. Its wealth in all kinds of game, grass, roots, and berries made enemies for the Crows, who, often outnumbered, were obliged continually to defend it against surrounding tribes.[1]
>
> They clothed themselves better, dwelt in finer lodges, decked their horses in trappings so gorgeous as to arouse the wonder of early explorers. They excelled all other tribes in the Rocky Mountain region—were brave, devoted to supernatural forces that gave them strength against enemies. Their social laws prevented intermarriage, hardships of life eliminated weaklings, and the women—as strong as men—did not bring forth puny offspring. The Crow repelled constant invasions of Sioux, Cheyenne, Arapaho to the east, Flathead and Nez Percé to the west, Blackfoot to the north.[2]

These statements are provided not to assert that one tribe was better than another, but that all tribes lived as equals. Providence gave the Crow a helping hand that allowed them to foresee the inevitable result of the white conquest. Because of this they avoided the bitter military campaigns that other tribes suffered, and their present situation may be slightly better than that of some other tribes as a result. The heroism with which other tribes met the white invasion is beyond question. While destiny provided different circumstances and guidance to the different tribes in those prereservation days, the basic situation on all reservations is the same today, and Indians must not be divided in their efforts to recognize the validity and strength of their traditional religion.

Regarding the "civilization" that has been thrust upon me since the days of reservation, it has not added one whit to my sense of justice; to my reverence for the rights of life; to my love for truth, honesty, and generosity; nor to my faith in Wakan Tanka—God of the Lakotas. For after all the great religions have been preached and expounded, or have been revealed by brilliant scholars, or have been written in books and embellished in fine language with finer covers, man—all man—is still confronted with the Great Mystery.

So if today I had a young mind to direct, to start on the journey of life, and I was faced with the duty of choosing between the natural way of my forefathers and that of the white man's present way of civilization, I would, for its welfare, unhesitatingly set that child's feet in the path of my forefathers. I would raise him to be an Indian![3]

—Chief Standing Bear, Oglala Sioux

NOTES

PREFACE

1. Joseph G. Jorgensen, *The Sun Dance Religion* (Chicago: The University of Chicago Press, 1972), 1.

CHAPTER 1. YELLOWTAIL BEGINS IN PRAYER

1. Acbadadea is the Absaroke word for "the One Divine Being." This word has been translated in different ways in other texts, including "Great Above Person," "First Maker," and "First Worker," all referring to the Absolute Unity. I have translated Acbadadea as "Maker of All Things Above" throughout this book because this is Yellowtail's preferred literal translation. A more complete explanation is to be found in chapter 10. Acbadadea corresponds to the Sioux Wakan-Tanka and the Cheyenne Maheo, which have also been translated in various ways.

Yellowtail will occasionally use other translations that I have preserved in the text. One such name is "Great Spirit," which will be familiar to many readers. The translation of Indian words can be problematical until the reader obtains a sense of the corresponding concepts. Frithjof Schuon comments on this point as follows:

> Objections are sometimes raised to the name "Great Spirit" as a translation of the Sioux word *Wakan-Tanka*, and of similar terms in other Indian languages; but though *Wakan-Tanka* (and the terms which correspond to it) can also be translated by "Great Mystery" or "Great Mysterious Power" (or even "Great Medicine"), and though "Great Spirit" is no doubt not absolutely adequate, it none the less serves quite well enough and in any case conveys the meaning in question better than any other term; it is true that the word "spirit" is rather indefinite, but it has for that reason the advantage of implying no restriction, and this is exactly what the "polysynthetic" term *Wakan* requires. The expression "Great Mystery" which has been suggested as a translation of *Wakan-Tanka* (or of the analogous terms, such as *Wakonda* or *Manitu,* in other Indian languages) is no better than "Great Spirit" at expressing the idea in question: besides, what matters is not whether the term corresponds

exactly to what we mean by "Spirit", but whether the ideas expressed by the Red Indian term may be translated by "Spirit" or not. (Frithjof Schuon, "The Sacred Pipe of the Red Indians," in *Language of the Self* [Madras: Ganesh Press, 1959], 204–205, reprinted in Schuon, *The Feathered Sun*).

Robert H. Lowie, in *The Crow Indians*, spells the name Akba'tatdi'a, while Frank Linderman, in *Plenty-coups, Chief of the Crows*, uses Ah-badt-dadt-deah, both scientific transcriptions which of course remain unknown to the Crow people. Lowie also mentions Bakukure, "The One Above," as a name of God.

Acbadadea is the highest name for God for the Crow, and they feel that this particular name of God should be used only with the greatest reverence; thus, Linderman reported that the Crow Indian "will scarcely ever speak the name of his God aloud." Rather, other names of God will be used. Yellowtail drew the analogy to Bakukure as the equivalent in usage to "Our Heavenly Father," which does not mean that the Crow have an indistinct view of God or that their conception of God was borrowed from Christianity. In fact, many olden-day Indians would have felt it a sacrilege to repeat the name Acbadadea in front of a white man. This reluctance to indiscriminately speak the highest name of God has parallels in other religions, notably Judaism in reference to the name YHWH.

2. A complete explanation of offering a prayer with the Indian pipe is set forth in chapter 13. Before an Indian makes his prayer, he first offers his pipe and the tobacco smoke in six ritual movements: above to Heaven, below to the earth, and to the east, south, west, and north. These six directions never vary, although the sequence of movements varies slightly among tribes. The four cardinal directions and the six directions of the universe, of which the four cardinal directions are a part, contain the basis for Plains Indian metaphysics. Fools Crow of the Teton Sioux comments:

In these six directions is found everything needed for renewal, physical and intellectual growth, and harmony. There is *Wakan-Tanka* himself, God, the "highest and most holy One"; there is *Tunkashila*, Grandfather, who corresponds to the Son of God; there is Grandmother Earth; and there are the four cardinal directions, moving in order of importance from west to north to east to south. *Wakan-Tanka* is unlimited [infinite], and has given to each of the other directions sacred powers that are their own to impart as they see fit, including such things as purification, joy, good health, growth, endurance, wisdom, inner peace, warmth, and happiness. The directions are holy and mysterious beings. *Wakan-Tanka* remains above them in power, and they are not separated even though they are distinct and identifiable. The powers do the will of God, yet they have a will and intellect of their own. They hear and answer prayers, yet their powers and ways remain mysterious. With them and through them we send our voice to God. (Thomas E. Mails, *Fools Crow*)

3. Raymond J. DeMallie, *The Sixth Grandfather.*

CHAPTER 2. EARLY YEARS AND TRADITIONAL VALUES

1. Throughout, Yellowtail refers to his wife Susie, who died on December 25, 1981, as "Grandma."
Susie Yellowtail was the first Indian registered nurse, and she traveled throughout the country when she served on both the governor's and president's Indian Health Councils. Grandma spoke to both Indian and non-Indian groups everywhere, and she was even interviewed on nationwide television. When she chaperoned the different Misses Indian America, she also traveled near and far. She was cold and quite sore after riding on horseback for six miles in the presidential inauguration parade in January, 1969, and she decided to leave her riding days "well behind" her when she returned.
A book about Grandma's life is now in preparation. Because of that book I have not added a great deal here about her. However, she was an extraordinary women, as reflected in her election to the Montana Hall of Fame. She was always a tireless and outspoken advocate of her tribe and its traditions. At her funeral her son-in-law correctly summarized her relationship with her husband: "If Grandpa is the priest, then Grandma was the general, and we are all really going to miss the general." She was never timid in speaking her mind on any subject and often was the first to explain her husband's feelings on a subject when he would be reluctant to offend someone with a criticism. Readers should understand that in traditional Crow society, the elders were shown the highest respect with the terms "old man," or "old woman." These titles of respect became "grandfather" or "grandmother" within the family and extended clan system—thus the use of "grandma" in reference to Mrs. Yellowtail.
2. In an unpublished letter in the possession of Frithjof Schuon, Joseph Epes Brown wrote:

It is often difficult for those who look on the tradition of the Red Man from the outside or through the "educated" mind, to understand their preoccupation with the animals, and with all things in the Universe. But for these people, as of course for all traditional peoples, every created object is important simply because they know the metaphysical correspondence between this world and the "Real World." No object is for them what it appears to be, but is simply the pale shadow of a Reality. It is for this reason that every created object is *wakan*, holy, and has a power according to the loftiness of the spiritual reality that it reflects; thus many objects possess negative powers as well as those which are positive and good, and every object is treated with respect, for the particular "power" that it possesses can be transferred into man— of course they know that everything in the Universe has its counterpart in the soul of man. The Indian humbles himself before the whole of creation, especially when "lamenting" (that is, when he ritually invokes the "Great Spirit" in solitude), because all visible things were created before him and, being older than him, deserve respect (this priority of created things may also be taken as a symbol of the Priority of the Principle); but although the last of created things, man is also the first, since he alone may know the Great Spirit (*Wakan-Tanka*).

3. On one occasion when I was living with the Yellowtails, an Indian man who had known Yellowtail's father came to their home asking for help. He was passing through Wyola, on his way to some unknown destination, without funds. The Yellowtails gave him a meal, and then Grandpa gave him twenty dollars for gasoline and a pair of boots because the man had poor shoes. This virtually represents the shirt off Yellowtail's back, because the Yellowtails have just barely enough money for their own needs. Yellowtail's generosity is well known, and if Yellowtail has a fault, it is that he is too generous.

4. While the Great Spirit has given a power to all created things, He has also created intermediaries to represent Him in controlling and guarding this medicine from unworthy men. These intermediaries are Medicine Fathers (Wakanpi to the Sioux). Little Wound, an Oglala Sioux, made the following comment concerning these differences:

A *wakan* man is one who is wise. It is one who knows the spirits. It is one who has power with the spirits. It is one who communicates with the spirits. It is one who can do strange things. A *wakan* man knows things that the people do not know. He knows the ceremonies and the songs. He can tell the people what their visions mean. He can tell the people what the spirits wish them to do. He can tell what is to be in the future. He can talk with animals and with trees and with stones. He can talk with everything on earth.

The *Wakan Tanka* are those which made everything. They are *Wakanpi*. *Wakanpi* are all things that are above mankind. There are many kinds of the *Wakanpi*. The *Wakan Tanka* are *Wakanpi*. The spirits are *Wakanpi*. The beings that govern things are *Wakanpi*.

The *Wakanpi* have power over everything on earth. They watch mankind all the time. They control everything that mankind does. . . .

Mankind should think about the *Wakanpi* and do what will please them. They should think of them as they think of their fathers and their mothers. . . .

Animals may be *wakan*. When an animal is *wakan*, then mankind should treat it as if it were one of the *Wakanpi*. Things that do not live may be *wakan*. When anything is food, it is *wakan* because it makes life. When anything is medicine, it is *wakan* for it keeps life in the body. . . .

The songs and the ceremonies of the Oglalas are *wakan* because they belong to the *Wakanpi*. A very old man or a very old woman is *wakan* because they know many things. But an old man is not like a *wakan* man. If he has learned the *wakan* things, then he is a *wakan* man. The spirit of every man is *wakan* and the ghost is *wakan*. (Little Wound, recorded by James R. Walker, *Lakota Belief and Ritual*, 69)

5. In the summer of 1984 at the Sun Dance at Lodge Grass, Montana, Yellowtail announced the choice of John Pretty on Top for his successor as medicine man and Sun Dance chief. A special announcement was made, followed by a ceremony officially transferring the functions to his successor. Pretty on Top was the Sun Dance chief for the Sun Dance at Wyola, Montana, in the summer of 1985; Pryor, Montana, in 1986; and Lodge Grass, Montana, in 1987. In 1986 Pretty on Top was selected to be the spiritual representative of all American Indians at the world prayer meeting sponsored by Pope John Paul II at Assisi, Italy. His prayer with the sacred pipe and meeting with Pope John Paul II and other world religious leaders received wide press coverage.

6. Joseph E. Brown, *The Sacred Pipe*, xx.

CHAPTER 3. MEDICINE ROCK CHIEF

1. Once an Indian is the recipient of a medicine power, he is linked through that medicine power to all creation. The respect which the Indian gives to his own medicine will reflect his attitude toward all creation. He is a brother to all creation, including the stars in the heavens and the plants and rocks of the earth; all these things are living, and each depends in a certain manner on all the others.

2. One of the best outward ways to safeguard the gift of a medicine power is to prepare a leather bundle in which are kept physical objects related to the medicine power. The preparer of the bundle will receive instructions either directly in a vision or dream, or from a holy man. The objects in the bundle represent the Medicine Fathers in the same manner in which all these powers represent the one Divine Reality, of which they are the vehicle:

A thing is not only what it is visibly, but also what it represents. Natural or artificial objects are not for the primitive, as they can be for us, arbitrary "symbols" of some other and higher reality, but actual manifestations of this reality: the eagle or the lion, for example, is not so much a symbol or image *of* the Sun as it *is* the Sun in a likeness (the form being more important than the nature in which it may be manifested); and in the same way every house *is* the world in a likeness, and every altar *is* situated at the centre of the earth; it is only because "we" are more interested in particular facts than in universal ideas, that this is "inconceivable" to us. Descent from a totem animal is not, then, what it appears

to the anthropologist, a literal absurdity, but a descent from the Sun,
the Progenitor and *Prajapati* of all, in that form in which he revealed
himself whether in vision or in dream, to the founder of the clan.
(Ananda K. Coomaraswamy, *Figures of Speech or Figures of Thought* [London: Luzac, 1946])

It is very important to understand the meaning of the medicine
bundle and its relationship to the metaphysical concepts the previous
footnotes have tried to illuminate. The misunderstanding of these
concepts is at the root of most of the misinterpretations that have
been made about Indian life and sacred ways. Because almost every
traditional Indian family had a medicine bundle and treated it in a
sacred manner, the early white men took the Indians to be idolaters.
Without attempting to understand Indian religious beliefs, they created prejudices that in many cases have carried on to the present
time. These prejudices prevented a complete understanding of the
beauty and depth of the sacred rites of the Indians.

3. In May, 1984, I attended the opening of the medicine bundle
of the medicine rock with Yellowtail at Lodge Grass, Montana. The
ceremony was conducted in the manner described by Yellowtail. As
part of the ceremony, the history of the medicine rock was recounted,
verifying Yellowtail's account. The small "children" of the medicine
rock are still stored in the bundle. Also kept in the medicine bundle
is some of the Crow sacred tobacco that Yellowtail discusses later in
this book. The keeper of the medicine rock related that it is believed
that the "children" rocks may be the offspring of both the medicine
rock and the sacred tobacco. The sacred tobacco in the bundle has
not been renewed for many years, and there was discussion of trying
to obtain more recent harvests of the sacred tobacco for introduction
into the medicine rock bundle.

4. The proscription against women in their menstrual period
being near medicine objects carries over to the Sun Dance itself. Any
menstruating women may not even be spectators at the lodge, and
any woman dancer whose period begins during the dance must
immediately leave the lodge, this constituting the only valid reason
for discontinuing the Sun Dance participation early once the entrance
into the lodge takes place.

5. Thomas E. Mails, *Fools Crow*.

CHAPTER 4. EARLY RESERVATION LIFE

1. The Crow tribe had two major subdivisions based roughly on
geographic location: the River and Mountain bands. The thirteen
Crow "clans" were formed without regard to the geographic bands;
rather, membership was matrilineal, because each child became a
member of his mother's clan. The practice of "exogamy" among the

Crow forbade a woman to marry within her own clan, so children were rarely members of their father's clan. Clansfolk recognized mutual obligations similar to family ties which overrode their sense of duty to their geographic bands and in some cases to the tribe itself. An injustice suffered by a different clan member could be avenged against any member of the offending clan. Within the clan, every adult member would be considered a relative to any first-generation member, regardless of any actual blood relationship. At birth each child therefore had at least two sets of relatives: one by blood and one by clan.

Like almost all Indian tribes, the Crow also had societies for many purposes, including various warrior, police, and religious societies. Adoption into these societies was without regard to clan affiliation. As a result, it was possible to have many different sets of "family relationships," both by birth and adoption. Today, many of the society memberships have ceased to exist, but the clan affiliations remain so that an outsider can still become confused in trying to understand an apparent family relationship when the Crow are referring to a clan relationship.

For an excellent in-depth focus on the importance of the clan systems to the Crow, refer to Rodney Frey, *The World of the Crow Indians: As Driftwood Lodges.*

2. It is important to clarify Yellowtail's attitude toward whites because of some of his statements in this book. The Yellowtails have no racial prejudice against whites, as evidenced by their numerous formally adopted white children and grandchildren. They have always opened their hearts and home to anyone in need, regardless of color. The uncomplimentary comments toward whites made in the book are objectively raised with regard to the modernizing elements brought to the reservation by the whites—particularly the discord raised by religion and money in the early reservation periods being discussed here by Yellowtail. These two elements, more than any other, disrupted the traditional authority and focus of the tribe, making it more difficult to face the problems of the early reservation period because of reduced tribal unity. Yellowtail is also a realist with regard to the prereservation period in that he realizes that it was not without its faults because of the failure of tribal members to adhere to the accepted norms. It is this inherent weakness and the tendencies toward individualism and conflict that were increased by the coming of the modernizing elements brought by the whites in the reservation period.

3. Yellowtail has a complete acceptance of all religions and recognizes that most of the prejudice that was initially present in the different denominations toward the traditional Indian ways is now gone. He is against false religions that espouse doctrines that are contrary to the religious truths that he instinctively knows must be

present in every valid spiritual way. He often speaks when called upon at many different churches. He feels that it is impossible to pray in excess, and that one method of prayer does not contradict another on condition that it is part of a valid religion.

4. Frank B. Linderman, *Plenty-coups, Chief of the Crows*.

CHAPTER 5. WORKING DAYS

1. Yellowtail's spiritual strength can be seen by his words. His physical strength is demonstrated by an incident when I was helping to brand cattle at a roundup on the Yellowtail ranch in 1972. After all the cattle and their yearling calves were rounded up into one large fenced enclosure, ropers caught the calves and brought them to a team of "wrestlers," of which I was a member, that held down the yearlings while the branding and other procedures took place. One Charolais yearling bull decided not to participate in this event and headed toward the open gate. I stood in the way and decided to "bulldog" this large calf myself. My next memory was of lying flat on my back with the weight of the yearling's hooves trampling over my chest. As I managed to raise myself off the ground on my elbow, I watched Yellowtail run forward alone to bulldog the yearling and hold him to the ground. I was astonished to see the man's agility and strength. The incident provided an excellent perspective of his health at almost seventy years of age.

2. "Whenever, in the course of the daily hunt, the red hunter comes upon a scene that is strikingly beautiful or sublime—a black thundercloud within the rainbow's glowing arch above the mountain; a white waterfall in the heart of the green gorge; a vast prairie tinged with the blood-red of sunset—he pauses for an instant in the attitude of worship" (Ohiyesa, Santee Sioux, in Charles A. Eastman, *The Soul of the Indian*).

3. Bureau of Indian Affairs. We could add here a few words concerning Robert S. Yellowtail, Thomas Yellowtail's older brother by fifteen years and one of the best known Indians of this century. He was the first Indian appointed a superintendent of an Indian reservation when he was placed in charge of the Crow reservation in 1934. He was selected as the sole spokesman for the Crow Nation when he addressed Congress in April, 1917, to successfully defeat a bill before the Congress to open to Crow tribal lands to white settlement. President Eisenhower offered him the post of commissioner of Indian affairs, but he declined the appointment.

4. A continuing debate among tribal members is in progress regarding the disbursement of the tribal coal revenues. At the time of this writing, the Crow are still in litigation regarding an error in the survey of the eastern boundary of the reservation. The tribe

anticipates a settlement of over sixty million dollars from the government. In an unrelated case, the tribe has prevailed before the U.S. Supreme Court in the coal severance tax case against the state of Montana. Twenty million dollars plus interest is in escrow for the tribe, and the state will have to pay substantial additional damages. The manner in which the tribe uses these funds will effect all future generations of Crow people.

5. Once when I was living with the Yellowtails, I tried to tan a deer hide by hand in the traditional manner. I used the same elk antler scraper that Yellowtail's mother had used to tan hides. After three days' work the hide was so thoroughly destroyed by my efforts that it had to be discarded. The experience gave me added appreciation of the difficulty of traditional Indian life.

6. Eastman, *Soul of the Indian*.

CHAPTER 6. HUNTING STORIES

1. There is no contradiction implied by the Indian recognizing the transcendent qualities of animals while at the same time depending upon animals for subsistence. Each animal can carry a particular divine aspect, but it is man alone who possesses the potential within himself to totally realize the Great Spirit

In the Indian view of creation, Nature and the animals preceded the creation of man; the Great Spirit can therefore manifest itself to man through each aspect of his creation. Everything is a part of the Great Spirit. Each animal therefore possesses an "essential" aspect, while at the same time possessing only a fragmentary or "accidental" aspect that allows man to kill it and use it for clothing, shelter, and nourishment.

2. The "little people" that have provided guidance and assistance to the Crow are not without analogies from other cultures, such as gnomes, fairies, elves, and jinn. Their existence is primarily in the subtle world but they have the ability to bridge the physical and subtle world so that they can appear in physical form in circumstances of their choosing. In a sense they are part of the natural world in which the Indians live, and as such they can assume the function of a Medicine Father in order to protect or, in a more profound sense, preserve elements of the Indians' sacred life. Many different Plains Indian tribes accept the existence of the little men who live in all of the mountains associated with the Rocky Mountain ranges in the United States and Canada.

In considering analogous manifestations of these "little people," it should be pointed out that other great religions acknowledge the existence of subtle beings that can appear in physical form, and in Islam, for example, the Koran even addresses certain chapters to both men and jinn. Just like their human counterparts in the physical world, these "little people" can have both positive and negative aspects, but the little people who have helped the Indians are among the best.

3. The eagle is one of Yellowtail's Medicine Fathers, and "Poor Eagle" is the chief of all the eagles. As "master of the species," Poor Eagle is directly called upon on behalf of all eagles in a time of need.

As one of Yellowtail's primary Medicine Fathers, the eagle follows Yellowtail almost everywhere he goes. When I have traveled with Yellowtail, we frequently are greeted by an eagle when we arrive at our destination. For example, on his first trip to Bloomington, Indiana, we were greeted by a large eagle circling low overhead on the afternoon when he first arrived at my home. Yellowtail greeted the eagle and thanked him for watching over his safe journey.

4. "*Aho*" is the Absaroke word for "thank you." It also implies a blessing.

5. Rainbow is the traditional name of John Trehero, the Shoshone medicine man and Sun Dance chief who passed his medicine power to Yellowtail. He is the subject of a chapter later in the book.

6. Virgin Nature was central to the life of the Indians, and their life in Nature shaped their sacred values. This veneration is not without parallels in other cultures.

7. Luther Standing Bear, *Land of the Spotted Eagle*.

CHAPTER 7. TRAVELS NEAR AND FAR

1. LeComte, *Dictionary of Last Words* (New York: Philosophical Library, 1955).

CHAPTER 8. RAINBOW

1. John Trehero passed away in January, 1985, on the Shoshone reservation in Wyoming. His exact age and even the spelling of his last name are in controversy. The records at the hospital care center where he died show that his name is spelled Trehero and that he was born August 14, 1871. This spelling coincides with Yellowtail's understanding. Fred Voget, in *The Shoshoni-Crow Sun Dance*, spells his name Trujuho. His father was part Mexican, and the family name is probably derived from Trejillo.

Voget states Trehero's year of birth as 1887. According to Trehero's own statement to me in 1972, his age was then 89, so his year of birth would have been 1883, and he was therefore 102 at the time of his death.

2. Rainbow recounted this same vision to me, and his account is identical to Yellowtail's recollection except for one detail. I recall

Rainbow's description of his exit from the cave as follows: "As Seven Arrows was leading me back to the entrance of the cave, I realized that there was a solid stone wall in front of us. As we reached it, we walked right through the wall, and I saw my body lying there on the ground. I realized then that my vision had not been in the physical world. When I reached my body, I felt as though I was lying down on top of myself, and then I was awake."

3. Yellowtail's natural universalism stops when it concerns churches that preach against the Sun Dance religion and situations in which he is asked to subordinate the Sun Dance religion to a less qualified way. Several years ago he was asked to come to hold a traditional house blessing ceremony at a new home on the reservation. A peyote ceremony blessing the house had already been held, so Yellowtail politely declined the offer for what he termed "the traditional Sun Dance blessing." He explained to me that it would be improper for the Sun Dance blessing to follow a peyote blessing, because the Sun Dance must be recognized as coming before the peyote way.

4. The function of Seven Arrows is quite significant, because he has been the Medicine Father primarily responsible for preserving the essence of the Sun Dance during the interruptions when it was repressed by the government. Many of the olden-day Sun Dance chiefs passed away during the early reservation days, and much of the ceremony was forgotten because, depending on the account, it was not held at all or held only intermittently for at least thirty years. It was through Seven Arrows' intercession that many of the details were preserved. Rainbow was the appointed Sun Dance chief who received from Seven Arrows the instructions that have enabled the Sun Dance to maintain its essential form.

5. Other commentators have remarked on the "political process" by which a Sun Dance chief is selected and consolidates power. There have also been references made in other writings about the concern of the Sun Dance chiefs with the accumulation of power. Based on my first-hand observations and the comments I have heard directly from Trehero, Yellowtail, and Pretty on Top, I conclude that there is no political process taking place at the center of the Sun Dance religion. I spent one summer living in the Yellowtail home while Trehero was also there with Yellowtail. Subsequently, I have visited the Yellowtails almost every summer, including some extended visits camping together in the mountains, and they have visited my home for two weeks every year since 1978, accompanied by Pretty on Top and his wife since 1984. My observations therefore come from the central figures in the Sun Dance religion.

Some Indians not directly connected with these men may be said to be engaged in a political process to try to obtain medicine power or to become a Sun Dance chief. Observations of these peripheral figures should not lead to the incorrect conclusion that the central figures in the Sun Dance religion are also involved in a political process. No material consideration passed from any of the successors to the spiritual predecessors other than natural respect and devotion. Yellowtail shared his thought process with me each year during his own search to find a successor, and the thought of choosing someone on any basis other than spiritual qualifications, even to the exclusion of his own blood descendents, never entered his mind. Yellowtail felt as early as 1982 that Pretty on Top might be the successor and began testing him with various requests that represented hardships without telling him any of the reasons. Even before the Sun Dance in 1984, Yellowtail told me that the time had not yet been made clear when to appoint his successor. Then after the morning sunrise ceremony on the second day of the Sun Dance, he told me that he was certain that Seven Arrows had also selected Pretty on Top and that the announcement would be made that afternoon.

6. The three songs used in the monthly prayer ceremonies and the four songs used during the morning Sunrise Ceremony at the Sun Dance have a unique and primordial quality that distinguishes them from other songs. These songs have no words and are sung without drum accompaniment in a solemn and penetrating manner that constitutes a liberating passage from this world directly to the Divine Archetype which the songs represent.

The special ceremonial songs just mentioned are only one example of the many unique possibilities of Indian music, each of which is impossible to describe adequately in words. Most are sung to drum accompaniment, and the majority of Indian songs do not have words but rather connect the Indians to the natural beauty that surrounds them.

7. After the morning Sunrise Ceremony on the third day of the Sun Dance in 1972, when Rainbow was ninety, we sat together with Yellowtail outside the Sun Dance lodge. Rainbow turned to me and said, "I am like a horse that loves to return to his favorite pasture and watering place. Each time I return, I just become stronger and stronger."

8. The distinction must be clear between the function of a medicine man and the function of the Sun Dance chief. By obtaining medicine power through the intercession of a Medicine Father, a person may be able to doctor patients in the Indian manner, thus becoming a medicine man. There must be authorization either directly from a Medicine Father in a vision, or through transferral of a medicine bundle, or from a medicine man who is allowing a helper to use the medicine powers to doctor on his behalf. For example, Trehero and Yellowtail have both authorized men to help them doctor

patients in the Sun Dance because of the large number of people who come to a Sun Dance to receive Sun Dance blessings during the time for healing. This authorization confers the function of "medicine man" to the helper during the period of the assistance. The authorization may be temporary or permanent, depending on the wishes of the person conferring the authorization. The ability to use or keep the authorization assumes moral conformity, without which the medicine power would be forfeit in any case.

The function of Sun Dance chief is a separate and more important function, for while a Sun Dance chief is by definition a medicine man, few medicine men hold the authorization to become a Sun Dance chief. In public announcements and in private conversations, Trehero was precise in stating that only Yellowtail had received his authorization to be Sun Dance chief and that no other person was authorized through Seven Arrows to run a Sun Dance. Both Trehero and Yellowtail have left open the possibility that a chain of authorization to another authentic Sun Dance was possible, as evidenced by other tribes. Trehero went on to say that none of the men he had previously authorized to help him doctor at Sun Dances were authorized to run a Sun Dance. Yellowtail has been equally clear that Pretty on Top is the only authorized Sun Dance chief to his knowledge able to run a Crow—Shoshone Sun Dance. I have heard both Trehero and Yellowtail discuss what they term "unauthorized Sun Dances" and question other purported Sun Dance chiefs' authority to run a Sun Dance. In 1972 I remember a conversation with both Trehero and Yellowtail regarding a Sun Dance that was to take place with a Sun Dance chief whose legitimacy they doubted. Trehero said, "That man is like a child that is playing with things he doesn't understand. He may cause great harm." When that Sun Dance was almost ready to start, a snowstorm came up to prevent the ceremony.

Since Trehero passed the function of Sun Dance chief to Yellowtail, and even more so during the middle and late 1980s, various men among the Crow and Shoshone have announced their ability to officiate a Sun Dance, thus conferring on themselves the function of Sun Dance chief. This is a concern to Yellowtail, who believes that harm can come to those who do not have proper authorization. While the presence of Sun Dance medicines from ancestors is important to the function of medicine man, it does not alone confer the function of Sun Dance chief. He is equally concerned with the introduction of any changes into the Sun Dance, which he feels must come only from a direct intervention by a primary Medicine Father and not from any human choice, and which in any case may only be superficial changes that would not alter the central rite materially.

It is clear that Trehero was universally recognized as the Sun Dance chief of the Crow—Shoshone Sun Dance, with all other helpers, except Yellowtail, receiving temporary authorization from him. During Yellowtail's tenure as Sun Dance chief, he was also accorded virtually universal acceptance as Trehero's successor. There can be no question that only Pretty on Top has received Yellowtail's authorization, an authorization that was confirmed by Trehero when he was still alive and met with both Yellowtail and Pretty on Top in Fort Washakie, Wyoming, in late 1984. However, during the revival of interest in the Sun Dance in the 1970s and '80s, other members of these tribes have sought to be recognized as Sun Dance chiefs. While it is possible that a valid authorization exists to some source unknown to any of these Sun Dance chiefs, it is of concern to them that there are almost certainly unauthorized individuals who are attempting to achieve the status of Sun Dance chief illegitimately. The concern of Yellowtail is that the living strength of the Sun Dance continue unbroken, providing support for the tribe and the individual members. He has insured that continuity with the appointment of his successor. Yellowtail holds no ill will toward other purported Sun Dance chiefs, as evidenced by his prayers for their guidance, which I have heard on different occasions, but he has withheld active support of other men with unknown credentials and in so doing has received animosity from some of them, even though he bears no bad will toward them and has even provided advice to some. Yellowtail is careful in his responsibility to safeguard the traditions for which he is responsible and continues to work closely with John Pretty on Top in all matters pertaining to the complete training and support of the new Sun Dance chief from the Trehero line.

9. On the plains of the western United States it is possible to watch a storm come from the distance, pass overhead in a fury, and proceed toward the horizon. The dark storm clouds, with their thunder, rain, and lightning, manifest tremendous power and provide a sharp contrast to the sunny skies that can be seen over different parts of the plains during a storm. The first time I saw one of these storms approach the Sun Dance camp, I watched Rainbow pray to have the rain fall elsewhere. Immediately the clouds split, and the storm passed on both sides of the camp while the sun shown down on the Sun Dance lodge. I have seen Yellowtail accomplish this same feat twice, and he translated his prayer for me after one such occasion: "Thank You for bringing the rain. It is needed and the earth is very dry, so all living things rejoice with the rain. But today we are about to start our Sun Dance, and this is our most sacred ceremony of prayer. We therefore ask that You allow the rain to fall on other areas where it is also needed and that we be given fair weather. After we are finished, it will be a better time for the rain to fall here and bless this land. *Aho!*"

10. Seattle, address to Governor Stevens, 1855 (*Washington Historical Quarterly* 22 [no. 4, October 1931]).

CHAPTER 9. INDIAN MEDICINE

1. See Frithjof Schuon, "The Shamanism of the Red Indians," in *Light on the Ancient Worlds* (Bloomington: World Wisdom Books, 1984), 81–82, reprinted in Schuon, *The Feathered Sun:*

As regards the magical practices of the shamans, one has to distinguish ordinary from what might be termed cosmic magic: the latter operates in virtue of the analogies between symbols and their prototypes. Everywhere in Nature, including man himself, one can discover possibilities of this kind, namely substances, forms and movements which correspond to one another qualitatively or typologically. Now the shaman aims at mastering phenomena which by their nature or by accident lie outside his control by using other phenomena of an analogous (and therefore metaphysically "identical") kind which he himself creates and which are therefore situated within his own sphere of activity. The medicine-man may wish to bring rain, to stop a snow-storm, to cause the arrival of a herd of bison or to cure an illness and for this purpose he makes use of forms, colours, rhythms, incantations and wordless songs; all this, however, would be insufficient but for his extraordinary power of concentration, acquired, as it is, through a long training carried out in solitude and silence and in close contact with virgin Nature. Concentration can also be the result of an exceptional gift or may come thanks to the intervention of a celestial influence.

Behind every sensible phenomenon there lies in fact a reality of an animic order that is independent of the limitations of space and time; it is by getting in touch with these realities, or these subtle and supersensorial roots of things, that a shaman is able to influence natural phenomena or foretell the future. All this may sound strange to a modern reader whose imagination is very different from that of mediaeval or archaic man; a whole series of prejudices of a supposedly intellectual or scientific kind blurs his mentality. Without going into details here, let us simply recall, in the words of Shakespeare, that "there are more things in heaven and earth than are dreamt of in your philosophy."

It must be added that the shamans are also, and even especially, expert magicians in the ordinary sense; their science operates with forces of a psychic or animic order, whether individualized or otherwise; it does not introduce, as in the case of cosmic magic, analogies between the microcosm and the macrocosm, or between the various natural reverberations of one and the same "idea." In "white" magic, which is normally that of the shamans, the forces called into play, and likewise the purpose of the operation, are either beneficent or else simply neutral. On the other hand, wherever the spirits are maleficent, as also the purpose in view, one has to do with "black" magic or sorcery; in such cases nothing is done "in God's name", and the link with the higher powers is broken. It goes without saying that practices socially so dangerous, and in themselves unholy, were strictly prohibited among the Red Indians as with most other peoples; this does not mean, however, that these practices did not undergo in the case of certain forest tribes and on the eve of modern times something like an epidemic extension, in conformity with their sinister and contagious nature.

2. A man may be granted a vision or medicine power based on his intention and his potential to fully realize his function and natural gifts. Normally such a recipient will be a model of personal virtue and behavior. Fools Crow commented on this point: "What is important for everyone to know is that holy men and medicine men must be measured by more than curing abilities. They must also be measured by their manner of life" (Thomas E. Mails, *Fools Crow*).

It can be that the recipient never fully realizes his potential, and a spiritual fall may even take place. Such an event could result in behavior which is an apparent contradiction to the power or function of the individual. This explains why some seemingly great medicine men or holy men do not appear to live up to their function in every respect. If his actions are not evil or detrimental to the tribe—which is to say they stem simply from human weakness and not from evil— the Medicine Fathers may even allow the individual to retain his power or function.

3. Boye Ladd is the Winnebago Indian who was the recipient of the medicine. He reviewed and approved this account of his experiences in 1984 when I met with him in Browning, Montana.

4. Seattle, typescript of speech in the Seattle Historical Society, Seattle, Washington.

CHAPTER 10. ACBADADEA, THE MAKER OF ALL THINGS ABOVE

1. Yellowtail is referring not only to the prophecies from the great world religions, including the three major revelations of the Western world, Christianity, Judaism, and Islam, but also to prophecies from other Indian tribes. A Cheyenne friend explained to me that Sweet Medicine, the Cheyenne cultural hero from centuries ago, prophesied that men with pale skin and hair all over their faces would come from the east in later days. With them would come a "white sand" that would hurt the Indians, and the ways of the "hairy faces" would almost completely destroy the sacred ways of the Cheyenne. The Cheyenne prophecy says that only a handful of men will cling to the sacred ways, and at the last moment when it appears that all is lost, a great change will come upon the world and Sweet Medicine will return to lead the Cheyenne back to their sacred ways.

My Cheyenne friend further explained that the "white sand" is sugar, which has hurt the Indians in the form of alcohol and all the bad food that the Indians now eat. He also believes that the time of the great change is close at hand.

2. Black Elk, unpublished statement recorded by Joseph E. Brown and in a letter in the possession of Frithjof Schuon.

CHAPTER 11. SWEAT LODGE

1. Yellowtail is referring to the truth of the essential teaching of the creation myth of the sweat lodge, whether or not minor details of the myth vary from one account to another. Black Elk made a similar comment after he recounted his version of the story of the descent of the Buffalo Cow Woman (Pte San Win) with the sacred pipe of the Sioux: "This they tell, and whether it happened so or not I do not know; but if you think about it, you can see that it is true" (John G. Neihardt, *Black Elk Speaks*).

2. Joseph E. Brown, *The Sacred Pipe*.

CHAPTER 12. VISION QUEST

1. Among all Plains Indians, each member of the tribe may receive his own revelation, creating a collective prophethood which is strictly regulated within the framework of the tradition in general. This widespread prophethood has many different degrees and does not prevent major tribal revelations such as the Sun Dance, sweat lodge, and Indian pipe. The apparent "individualism" of the Indian is partly a product of fidelity to one's own vision, or "medicine," a personal relationship with a particular theophany which is supported by the relationship between the individual and the tribe with a reciprocity of virtues, gifts, and duty.

2. Francis LaFlesche, *Who Was the Medicine Man?* (Hampton: Hampton Institute Press, 1905).

CHAPTER 13. THE SACRED PIPE AND DAILY PRAYER

1. The smoke from the tobacco burned in the pipe and the smoke from the sacred incense placed on the fire preceeding all sacred ceremonies represent the spiritual presence of man in the face of the supernatural presence of God, as affirmed by this Iroquois incantation: "Hail! Hail! Hail! Thou Who hast created all things, hear our voice. We are obeying Thy Commandments. That which Thou hast created returneth back unto Thee. The smoke of the holy plant riseth up unto Thee, whereby it may be seen that our speech is true" (Paul Radin, *Histoire de la Civilisation Indienne* [New York: Dover, 1963]).

2. Thomas and Susie Yellowtail were two of the four living members of the Sacred Pipe Society. With the passing of Susie, only three remain, none of whom know the proper way to hold the traditional rites. Other ceremonies have been lost through neglect during the reservation period, although some of the traditional ceremonies,

such as the tailfeather ceremonies, have been resurrected after a period of disuse. While this reference and other references made by Yellowtail to the loss of traditions or the eschatological prophecies might appear pessimistic, no one who knows Yellowtail well can believe that he is pessimistic about the future of his tribe. His recounting of these facts is set forth in the solemn manner that he uses when discussing concepts and facts of such importance. Such discussions do not lend themselves to the light-hearted references that naturally pervade his speech at most times. Yellowtail's true concern in relating such matters is that the listener or reader realize the urgency to begin to pray that is the consequent reaction to understanding such matters. He is not concerned that any attempt be made to improperly reconstruct a lost rite or that there be any undue regret for what has already happened, only that people use the valid spiritual rites that have been preserved.

3. *Kinnikinnik* is the Indian name for the tobacco that is smoked in the Indian pipe. There are different barks, herbs, or tobaccos that are mixed together, and these elements vary slightly among different tribes. The inner bark of the red willow tree is a universal ingredient.

4 Fools Crow described the ceremony as follows:

> In our pipe ceremony, which is really very simple, the pipe is smoked and pointed stem first and horizontally in a clockwise direction to the west, north, east, and south; then down to Grandmother earth; up to Grandfather; and finally in an almost imperceptible higher movement to *Wakan-Tanka*. So while we speak of six directions, there are actually seven movements of the pipe, and our God is a Trinity, consisting of *Wakan-Tanka, Tunkashila*, and the Spirits. As the Pipe Ceremony is done, the pipe first of all opens the gates to release the powers, and then becomes the very channel through which the powers flow, moving from the six directions to the one who prays, blessing the person, and then through the person and out to bless the rest of creation. Therefore we say that the pipe itself has the power to transport power, and it is sacred. (Fools Crow, Teton Sioux, quoted in Thomas E. Mails, *Fools Crow*)

5. Many different passages have been recorded of Black Elk's description of the sacred pipe. The following is one excerpt:

> I fill this sacred Pipe with the bark of the red willow; but before we smoke it, you must see how it is made and what it means. These four ribbons hanging here on the stem are the four quarters of the universe. The black one is for the west where the thunder beings live to send us rain; the white one for the north, whence comes the great white cleansing wind; the red one for the east, whence springs the light and where the morning star lives to give men wisdom; the yellow for the south, whence come the summer and the power to grow. But these four spirits are only one Spirit after all, and this eagle feather here is for that One, which is like a father, and also it is for the thoughts of men that should

rise high as eagles do. Is not the sky a father and the earth a mother, and are not all livings things with feet or wings or roots their children? And this hide upon the mouthpiece here, which should be bison hide, is for the earth, from whence we came and at whose breast we suck as babies all our lives, along with all the animals and birds and trees and grasses. And because it means all this, and more than any man can understand, the Pipe is holy. (John G. Neihardt, *Black Elk Speaks*)

6. One Sioux prayer used by Black Elk is "*Wakan-Tanka unshima-laye oyate wani wachin cha!*" ("O Great Spirit, be merciful to me that my people may live!")

A Cheyenne Sun Dance instructor once told me, "One of the greatest gifts the Cheyenne have been given is the name 'Maheo.' " He went on to explain methods of invoking this name, one of the best being "*Maheo shiwata mem men!*" ("O Maker of All Things Above, have pity on us!")

The prayers of both the Sioux and the Cheyenne are strikingly similar to the prayer of the Russian pilgrim, "Lord Jesus Christ, have mercy on me" (R. M. French, *The Way of a Pilgrim* [New York: Seabury Press, 1965], 12). One is also reminded of the First Epistle of Saint Paul to the Thessalonians, when he said, "Pray without ceasing."

7. Joseph E. Brown *The Sacred Pipe.*

CHAPTER 14. MONTHLY PRAYER MEETINGS

1. Raymond J. DeMallie, *The Sixth Grandfather.*

CHAPTER 15. OUTDOOR CEREMONIES

1. According to Black Elk:

Everything an Indian does is done in a circle, and that is because the power of the World always works in circles and everything tries to be round. In the old days when we were a strong and happy people, all our power came to us from the sacred hoop of the nation, and so long as the hoop was unbroken, the people flourished. The flowering tree was the living centre of the hoop, and the circle of the four quarters nourished it. The East gave peace and light, the South gave warmth, the West gave rain, and North with its cold and mighty wind gave strength and endurance. This knowledge came to us from the outer (transcendent or universal) World together with our religion. Everything the Power of the World does is done in a circle. The sky is round, and I have heard that the earth is round like a ball, and so are all the stars. The wind, in its greatest power, whirls. Birds make their nests in circles, for theirs is the same religion as ours. . . . Our tepees were round like the nests of birds, and these were always set in a circle, the nation's hoop, a nest of many nests, where the Great Spirit meant us to hatch our children. (John G. Neihardt, *Black Elk Speaks*)

2. Thomas E. Mails, *Fools Crow*.

CHAPTER 16. LODGE PREPARATION

1. Joseph E. Brown, *The Sacred Pipe*.

CHAPTER 17. THE THREE-DAY RITE BEGINS

1. Among the books cited in the Suggested Readings, two stand out to provide additional information about the development of the Crow Sun Dance from its historical form to the present adaptation from the Shoshone: Robert Lowie, *The Crow Indians,* and Fred Voget's *The Shoshoni—Crow Sun Dance*. Each of these books provides substantial additional details that are valuable in an exhaustive study of the Crow—Shoshone Sun Dance. Such comparisons of the historical Crow Sun Dance of prereservation days are beyond the scope of this book; however, for the reader interested in further study of the Sun Dance, the orientation of these authors must be understood. Lowie has drawn the conclusion that vengeance was the key motivation for the original Crow Sun Dance. Based on comments from Yellowtail and other elderly Crow informants, many of whom are now deceased, I question whether this may be too narrow a view of the primary motivation. Even Lowie observed that during the Sun Dance the tribe attempted to bring the entire universe in accord with the prayers of the dance. During the prereservation period, the nomadic and warring tribes were undoubtedly concerned with military prowess as a key element to tribal preservation and renewal. Such concerns certainly manifested themselves in the Sun Dance, accentuating military aspects, including superiority over one's enemies. To limit the motive of such a rite to the exclusion of the prayer for general tribal prosperity, including the general physical and spiritual health of all members, is not to take into account a current accentuation of the Sun Dance on behalf of the entire tribe. While the motivations of certain sun dancers both in olden times and today will vary according to their perspective, the spiritual aspect of the rite should not be ignored in favor of merely material gains.

Voget also concludes that the participants in the modern-day Sun Dance are predominately concerned with the accumulation of power. While this is undoubtedly true for some, to conclude that the motivation of most if not all dancers is based on the material plane to the exclusion of the spiritual motivation, based on prayer for the sake of prayer, is not to understand the more profound and living spiritual tradition that exists within the Indian people.

2. Women are the spiritual equals of men in terms of their capacity to pray and receive visions. Their role in the Sun Dance is also equivalent to that of the men with one exception: they are not able to officiate or hold the role of Sun Dance chief. This is analogous to the exclusion of women from the priesthood in other religions. This subordinate role of women is manifested in two ways in the Sun Dance. First, the women enter the lodge after the men and are therefore located farthest from the chief's pole, and second, the women stand behind the men while greeting the sunrise and then return to their locations on the outside of the lodge while only the men participate in the singing of the four morning songs during the sunrise ceremony. It should be noted that only women are chosen to bring the sacred water that will be used to break the fast at the end of the Sun Dance, thus echoing the traditional concept of the women owning the tipi and preparing the food.

3. In the Crow Sun Dance, the most obvious meaning of the Sun Dance is the inner prayer of each individual toward his Maker. A second meaning is represented by the collective presence of the tribe as a whole, and particularly in the Morning Prayer said as part of the Sunrise Ceremony on each day of the Sun Dance. This more outward meaning is for the prosperity of the tribe as a whole and all of creation. An individual's outward intention can also be to fulfill a personal vow for some benefit he or his family has received or is asking to receive. Whatever the apparent meaning, the inward intention is to be united with the Great Spirit by reestablishing the direct link from the heart to the central tree to the Sun. The Sun is the heart of creation just as the human heart is the sun within each person, so each dancer may attempt to reestablish the preexistent rays between the Divine Sun, the visible sun, and the heart.

Among the Sun Dances of the different Plains Indian tribes one of these two meanings can be accentuated. The Crow Sun Dance accentuates the inner prayer of each individual. The outward motive of tribal and world renewal is present but less prominent. The Cheyenne Sun Dance in some ways is at the opposite extreme. For the Cheyenne, the Sacred Arrows (Mahuts) represent the male aspect of the tribe, and Is'siwun, the Sacred Buffalo Hat, represents the female principle of the tribe. Each of these two sacred symbols has its own special ceremonies for renewal. Both the male and female aspects of the tribe are symbolically brought together and merged in the Sun Dance. In this way the Sun Dance represents the annual procreation and regeneration of the universe. This outward intention is thus accentuated, and detailed procedures are followed to ensure the correct regeneration of creation. The inner meaning is of course present in the heart of each of the participants.

The Sioux Sun Dance also has both meanings, and the clear symbolical role of the tribe as a whole is represented, among other ways, in the exchange of the sacred pipes between the participants and the spectators, with the entire tribe actually offering the ritual prayer with the pipe. The inner vow of prayer is in fact outwardly symbolized by the piercing of the dancers' chests and their attachment to the Center Pole by thongs. Of the two tribal Sun Dances I have observed, the Sioux Sun Dance has a greater accentuation of the outward tribal intention than does the Crow Sun Dance, but each is a perfection in its own way. It is impossible to forget the experience of the Sun Dance because of the overwhelming sacred presence that it confers on any spectator or participant.

4. Thomas E. Mails, *Fools Crow*.

CHAPTER 18. CONCLUSION OF THE SUN DANCE

1. Descriptions of the differences between the dress of the dancers on the two days are somewhat inadequate. Color photographs would best convey the contrast in the dancers' paint and costumes. Each dancer will wear the costume for the first day into the lodge and will bring the costume for the second day into the lodge with his or her bedroll. The patterns and colors of the second costume will be more detailed and vibrant. Many dancers will also adorn themselves with medicine feathers or objects. Most dancers will also wear a Sun Dance necklace which is only worn for sacred ceremonies. An excellent essay on Indian clothing, entitled "Symbolism of a Vestimentary Art," is contained in Frithjof Schuon's *The Feathered Sun*.

2. The Indians are patriotic to a degree that is in some ways astonishing, given the manner in which they have been treated by the government of the United States. A special Indian song honoring the American flag is sung in the traditional Indian way before many Indian events, the Sun Dance included. This is explained, in part, by their respect for authority, for the latter always comes, in essence, from God.

3. The holding of a Sun Dance would be impossible without the support of the tribe, and many people play a vital role in addition to the dancers. At least thirty to forty men are necessary to construct the lodge, which involves concentrated effort for many days before the dance to obtain all the necessary items. The singers play an essential role which requires at least two and in most cases up to five groups, each of six singers who sing for periods of over two hours at a time. Such an effort is completely draining, and the singers must be fed after each rotation. The "spectators" also cut the poles for the construction of the individual stalls on the second day, finish

construction of the stalls, and cut the sweet sage and cattails. The announcer and the keeper of the sacred fire also donate large amounts of time. Many members of the family and clan of the sponsor will participate in the giveaway and the feast. A significant amount of money is necessary to provide all the support for the dance to be successful. The Sun Dance is therefore truly a tribal event.

4. Frances Densmore, *Teton Sioux Music*, Bulletin 61, Bureau of American Ethnology (Washington, D.C.: Government Printing Office, 1918).

CHAPTER 19. ATTITUDES AND SINCERITY

1. James R. Walker, *Lakota Belief and Ritual.*

CHAPTER 20. LOSS OF OUR TRADITIONAL VALUES

1. In the vast expanses of Nature in which the traditional Indian roamed, he was in one sense without limits on his freedom; in another sense he was always confined to the strict role placed upon him by his religious universe. In every moment and in every place, everything reinforced the sacred obligations of his heritage.

2. United States government estimates place unemployment on the reservation at a minimum of 60 percent, while tribal estimates put the figure at over 80 percent. Most of the economic development on the reservation is based on the tribe's natural resources, notably coal, oil, and gas. Even if the energy base of the Crow could provide sufficient one-time per capita payments to tribal members so that they could live without working, the duration of those resources would be limited. Upon their depletion, the tribe's situation would be dire. The ability of tribal leaders to find long-term solutions for Crow economic development with the energy funds and to overcome pressure for excessive short-term per capita payments will determine the future welfare of the tribe.

3. T. C. McLuhan, *Touch the Earth* (New York: Promontory Press, 1971).

CHAPTER 21. MAKE YOUR CHOICE

1. In May, 1984, Yellowtail and I visited two of the oldest members of the Tobacco Society to inquire about recent ceremonies. Both informants verified Yellowtail's recollection that the last planting took place between 1976 and 1978. A severe frost killed all of the tobacco seed production that year, and the only known seed is from a previous planting. This seed is being kept by two different society

members, but it is not known if the seed will germinate, and no plantings are scheduled at this time.

2. Apocalyptic views are found in every religion, since they have a sense of eternity and of the relative; they indicate the end of the world or cycles, as the case may be. The prophecies which Yellowtail discusses are not even alone among Plains Indians. For example, the Sioux have the symbolism of the buffalo and its four legs. Each year the buffalo loses a hair off one of the legs. The end of this cycle comes when the buffalo has no more hair on its legs. (The Hindu have an almost identical prophesy.) Moreover, the Indians feel that industrial civilization, since it ruptures the balance of Nature, cannot endure. This "world view," which stresses the simple virtues, is in fact incorporated in all religions.

3. Fools Crow commented on this same point:

> I decided to go again to Bear Butte to fast and pray . . . and do you know what happened? *Wakan-Tanka* and *Tunkashila* gave me the same answer I was given on my trip there in 1927. The Sioux should go back and pick up the good things that our grandfathers, grandmothers, aunts, uncles, fathers, and mothers had taught us. Our only hope was to fall back upon our traditional way of life. It was the only foundation we had that would give meaning and purpose to us. I brought this message back to the elders. . . . (Fools Crow, Teton Sioux, in Thomas E. Mails, *Fools Crow*)

4. Each Indian tribe should be given autonomous control of its own schools in order to determine the appropriate curriculum and teaching standards. Guidelines set forth by the North Central Association must be met in order to ensure basic "standards," but latitude would then be given for traditional education, including native language instruction. Both the North Central Association and the Navajo tribe are to be congratulated for their cooperative efforts in achieving independent accreditation for the Navajo tribe. The Navajo now have primary responsibility for education on their reservation.

Another proposal of great benefit to the Indians would be the creation of several very substantial wilderness area parks in different geographic regions, such as the Black Hills, the Big Horn Mountains, and the Rocky Mountains. These parks would be limited to the use of Plains Indians. Similar parks could be established throughout the United States for the use of tribes in the respective environs. This would encourage the renewal of traditional ceremonies in these remote areas, which are so sacred to the Indians. This could never replace what has been taken from the Indians, but it would represent a first step.

5. Frederick W. Hodge, ed., *Handbook of American Indians North of Mexico,* Bulletin 30 of the Bureau of American Ethnology (Washington, D.C.: Government Printing Office, 1907).

APPENDIX. HISTORICAL OVERVIEW
OF THE ABSAROKE

1. Frank Linderman, *Plenty-Coups, Chief of the Crows.*
2. Edward S. Curtis, "The Apsaroke, or Crows," in *The North American Indian*, vol. 4.
3. Luther Standing Bear, *Land of the Spotted Eagle.*

SUGGESTED READINGS

GENERAL-INTEREST MATERIAL
ON INDIAN TRADITIONS

Alexander, Hartley Burr. *The World's Rim: Great Mysteries of the North American Indians.* Lincoln: University of Nebraska Press, 1953. Reprint, 1967.

Brown, Joseph Epes. *The Sacred Pipe: Black Elk's Account of the Seven Rites of the Oglala Sioux.* Norman: University of Oklahoma Press, 1975.

———. *The Spiritual Legacy of the American Indian.* New York: Crossroad, 1982.

Buffalo Child Long Lance. *Long Lance.* New York: Rinehart, 1928.

DeMallie, Raymond J., ed. *The Sixth Grandfather: Black Elk's Teachings Given to John G. Neihardt.* Lincoln: University of Nebraska Press, 1984.

Eastman, Charles A. *Indian Boyhood.* New York: McClure, Phillips & Co., 1902. Reprint, New York: Dover, 1971.

———. *The Soul of the Indian: An Interpretation.* Boston: Houghton Mifflin, 1911. Reprint, Lincoln: University of Nebraska Press, 1980.

Hamilton, Charles, ed. *Cry of the Thunderbird: The American Indian's Own Story.* New York: Macmillan, 1957. Reprint, Norman: University of Oklahoma Press, 1972.

Hilger, Inez. *Chippewa Child Life and Its Cultural Background.* Bureau of American Ethnology Bulletin 146. Washington, D.C.: Government Printing Office, 1951.

Hungry Wolf, Beverly. *The Ways of My Grandmothers.* New York: William Morrow, 1981.

McClintock, Walter. *The Old North Trail; or, Life, Legends and Religion of the Blackfeet Indians.* Lincoln: University of Nebraska Press, 1968.

Mails, Thomas E. *Fools Crow.* Garden City: Doubleday, 1979.

Neihardt, John G. *Black Elk Speaks: Being the Life Story of a Holy*

Man of the Oglala Sioux: New York: William Morrow, 1932. Reprint, Lincoln: University of Nebraska Press, 1961.

Schuon, Frithjof. *The Feathered Sun.* Bloomington: World Wisdom Books, 1990.

Standing Bear, Luther. *Land of the Spotted Eagle.* Lincoln: University of Nebraska Press, 1978.

Walker, James R. *Lakota Belief and Ritual.* Ed. Raymond J. DeMallie and Elaine A. Jahner. Lincoln: University of Nebraska Press, 1980.

SPECIFIC INFORMATION ABOUT THE CROW

Curtis, Edward S. "The Apsaroke, or Crows." In *The North American Indian,* vol. 4. Norwood, Massachusetts, 1909. Reprint, New York: Johnson Reprint, 1970.

Denig, Edwin Thomson. *On the Crow Nation.* Ed. John C. Ewers. Smithsonian Institution, Bureau of American Ethnology Bulletin 151. *Anthropological Papers* 33 (1953): 1–74.

Frey, Rodney. "Re-Telling One's Own: Storytelling Among the Apsaalooke (Crow Indians)." *Plains Anthropologist* 28 (1983): 129–35.

———. *The World of the Crow Indians: As Driftwood Lodges.* Norman: University of Oklahoma Press, 1987.

Linderman, Frank B. *Plenty-coups, Chief of the Crows.* Lincoln: University of Nebraska Press, 1962. Reprint, New York: John Day, 1972.

———. *Pretty Shield, Medicine Woman of the Crows.* Lincoln: University of Nebraska Press, 1932. Reprint, New York: John Day, 1972.

Lowie, Robert. "Social Life of the Crow Indians." *American Museum of Natural History, Anthropological Papers* 9 (1912): 181–247.

———. "Societies of the Crow, Hidatsa and Mandan Indians." *American Museum of Natural History, Anthropological Papers* 11 (1913): 45–358.

———. "The Sun Dance of the Crow Indians." *American Museum of Natural History, Anthropological Papers* 16 (1915): 1–50.

———. "Notes on the Social Organization and Customs of the Mandan, Hidatsa and Crow Indians." *American Museum of Natural History, Anthropological Papers* 21, part 1 (1917): 3–99.

———. "Myths and Traditions of the Crow Indians." *American Museum of Natural History, Anthropological Papers* 25, part 1 (1918): 1–308.

———. "The Tobacco Society of the Crow Indians." *American*

Museum of Natural History, Anthropological Papers 21, part 2 (1919): 101–200.

———. "The Material Culture of the Crow Indians." *American Museum of Natural History, Anthropological Papers* 21, part 3 (1922): 201–70.

———. "Crow Indian Art." *American Museum of Natural History, Anthropological Papers* 21, part 4 (1922): 271–322.

———. "The Religion of the Crow Indians." *American Museum of Natural History, Anthropological Papers* 25, part 2 (1923) 311–444.

———. *The Crow Indians.* New York: Holt, Rinehart and Winston, 1935. Reprint, 1956.

Marquis, Thomas B. *Memoirs of a White Crow Indian (Thomas H. Leforge).* New York: Century Company, 1928.

Medicine Crow, Joe, and Charles Bradley, Jr. *The Crow Indians: 100 Years of Acculturation.* Wyola: Wyola Bilingual Project, 1976.

Nabokov, Peter. *Two Leggings: The Making of a Crow Warrior (Manuscript of William Wildschut).* New York: Crowell, 1967.

Old Coyote, Henry. *Crow Indian Child Raising.* Crow Agency: Crow Agency Bilingual Education, 1974.

Old Coyote, Mickey. *The Tribal Emblem and Flag of the Crows.* Lexington: In the Flag Bulletin, 1967.

Vogt, Fred W. *The Shoshoni-Crow Sun Dance.* Norman: University of Oklahoma Press, 1984.

Wildschut, William, and John Ewers. *Crow Indian Beadwork: A Descriptive and Historical Study.* New York: Heye Foundation, Museum of the American Indian, 1959.

Yellowtail, Robert, Sr. *At Crow Fair.* Albuquerque: Wowapi, 1973.

Index